Medieval Futurity

New Queer Medievalisms

Series Editors
Christopher Michael Roman, Kent State University
Will Rogers, University of Louisiana at Monroe

Editorial Board
Michelle M. Sauer, University of North Dakota
Anna Klosowska, Miami University
Gabrielle Bychowski, Case Western Reserve University
Bill Burgwinkle, King's College, Cambridge

Volume 1

Medieval Futurity

Essays for the Future of a Queer Medieval Studies

Edited by
Will Rogers and Christopher Michael Roman

DE GRUYTER

ISBN 978-1-5015-2733-3
e-ISBN (PDF) 978-1-5015-1370-1
e-ISBN (EPUB) 978-1-5015-1397-8
ISSN 2701-1143

Library of Congress Control Number: 2020947340

Bibliographic information published by the Deutsche Nationalbibliothek
The Deutsche Nationalbibliothek lists this publication in the Deutsche Nationalbibliografie; detailed bibliographic data are available on the Internet at http://dnb.dnb.de.

© 2022 Walter de Gruyter GmbH, Berlin/Boston
This volume is text- and page-identical with the hardback published in 2021.
Cover image: © Bibliothèque nationale de France (Detail from: Latin 919 Fol.82. Horae ad usum Parisiensem [Grandes Heures de Jean de Berry]. Jacquemart de Hesdin) Typesetting: Integra Software Services Pvt. Ltd.
Printing and binding: CPI books GmbH, Leck

www.degruyter.com

Acknowledgements

The idea for this collection was born at the Sewanee Medieval Colloquium in 2016 from a series of panels on the "Queer Middle Ages" organized by Will Rogers and me. I must first thank Matthew Irvin for organizing the Sewanee Medieval Colloquium and encouraging us to develop this into a series of panels because of the near-flood of abstracts we received. As well, thank you to Stephanie Batkie for creating such an enlivening, welcome, and inspirational space at Sewanee and the University of the South. My co-editor, Will Rogers, has gone on to be my partner in a number of medieval endeavors since we hatched the plan for those panels and this collection; as well, he has become one of my very best of friends. This collection could not have been executed in any way without him and his brilliance, generosity, and thoughtfulness. As always, this work was inspired by my ever-growing queer medieval family who have become way too numerous to count, but please know your fingerprints are all over this collection. As well, thank you to my medieval colleagues at Kent State University, Susanna Fein and David Raybin, whom I affectionately call my medieval parents, for your support, as well as mentorship in all things. Other members of the Kent State medieval studies family – Ann Martinez, Susan Sainato, Elizabeth Howard, Heidi Frame, Greg Rabbit, Elizabeth Pafford, Rosann Gage, Charmae Cottom, Annie Brust, Katie Simko, and David Kohl – have been influential in my thinking on the future of medieval studies. Finally, all my work has its inspiration in the love of my life, Nicole Willey, who is always with me in every queer thing that I do; as well, thank you to our ever-enlivening and adventuresome family: Jacob, Isaac, and The Groot, y'all always show me the ways in which love is boundless, horizonless, and ever present.

—CMR

Of course, it is only fitting that my acknowledgements follow Christopher's, and that we have double acknowledgements – this work and the book series which it inaugurates and which we founded depended on lots of folks and their faith in us. Dr. Ilse Schweitzer VanDonkelaar was our guide and champion for the series and this collection. Her patience and knowledge are without peer. I would be remiss in not thanking Christopher directly, who sees in me a scholar I often wish I saw. He has helped me accomplish goals in my life I would have struggled to see through without him. Find a writing and research collaborator who looks at your work like Christopher looks at mine. I have been lucky to have had such support from graduate school on. My dissertation co-advisors, Dr. Andrew Galloway and Dr. Masha Raskolnikov, convinced me that my ideas were worth pursuing and helped to revise my writing to make those ideas clear. Their example is one I try to follow for my own students at University of Louisiana Monroe, where students in my Chaucer seminar and my Middle English graduate courses help to test out my newer ideas, and their questions and challenges have made me a stronger writer, teacher, and researcher. Along with these students, my colleagues Mary Adams, Janet Haedicke, Jack Heflin, and Elizabeth Oldfather give me all the encouragement one could ask for in a department, and their collegiality and kindness know no bounds. In addition, I would like to thank Tommy and Mary Barham – their financial support, given through the Tommy and Mary Barham Endowed Professorship in English, made possible the time and travel such collections and ideas require. Finally, I need to thank my family: my partner Joseph who will always be part of my future; and my parents Billy and Paulette Rogers whose love showed me what a future might look like, even as I had to say goodbye to my mother this year who died just as this collection was finished.

—WAR

Contents

Acknowledgements —— V

Will Rogers and Christopher Michael Roman
Introduction: Clearly, Queerly: Toward a Medieval Queer Futurity —— 1

Part I: Queer Latinities: Authorizing Same-Sex Desire

Michael Johnson
Chapter 1
Sexual Ethics in the Medieval Grammar Classroom —— 11

Will Rogers
Chapter 2
Failed Orientations: The Spaces of Sexual Histories and Failures —— 39

Part II: French Kisses: Queer Romance

Joseph Derosier
Chapter 3
Guillaume de Lorris's Unmaking of the Self: The Dreamer's Queer Failures —— 61

Lynn Shutters
Chapter 4
Sodom, Bretons, and Ill-Defined Borders: Questing for Queerness with the *Knight of the Tower* —— 83

Maud McInerney
Chapter 5
Queer Time for Heroes in the *Roman d'Enés* and the *Roman de Troie* —— 107

Part III: Insular Queerness: English and the Nonnormative

Margaret Cotter-Lynch
Chapter 6
The Gender Genealogy of St. Mary of Egypt —— 131

Micah Goodrich
Chapter 7
"Ycrammed ful of cloutes and of bones": Chaucer's Queer Cavities —— 153

Haylie Swenson
Chapter 8
Resisting Sex and Species in the *Squire's Tale* —— 181

Epilogue: Opening Up Queerness

Michelle M. Sauer
Chapter 9
Queer Time and Lesbian Temporality in Medieval Women's Encounters with the Side Wound —— 199

Notes on Contributors —— 221

Index —— 225

Will Rogers and Christopher Michael Roman
Introduction: Clearly, Queerly: Toward a Medieval Queer Futurity

During the 1990 Pride Parade, an anonymous pamphlet entitled *Queers Read This* was published (later reprinted in 2009). A manifesto, a call-to-arms, a resistance declaration, this influential pamphlet drew attention in stark terms to the problems of straightness, heteronormativity, and respectability politics. The queers that wrote *Queers Read This* attack the corporatization of gay identity and the assimilationism that had begun to creep into queer politics:

> Being queer means leading a different sort of life. It's not about the mainstream, profit-margins, patriotism, patriarchy or being assimilated. It's not about executive directors, privilege and elitism. It's about being on the margins, defining ourselves; it's about gender-fuck and secrets, what's beneath the belt and deep inside the heart; it's about the night.[1]

It's about the night. One of the thrusts of the intersection of queer theory and medieval studies is to explore the night: the secrets, the desires, and the heart of historical queer people. What did it mean to be queer in the Middle Ages? It is no secret that this is a political move. Queer medievalists, seeing ways in which the queer has been repressed in contemporary academia, as well as historically, reach back, in the memorable words of Carolyn Dinshaw, "for partial, affective connection, for community, for even a touch across time."[2]

Medieval Queer Futurity: Essays for the Future of a Queer Medieval Studies offers a reappraisal and new avenues for exploring the role of queer theory and queer subjects in the Middle Ages. This volume addresses exactly where modern medievalists see these glimpses of the queer; from Latin texts written and read in England and France to chivalric works, the contributors mine these contexts in order to structure a more capacious and historically attuned notion of the medieval queer, a necessary move considering the relative paucity of venues dedicated to publishing works centering both on queer theory and medieval texts and subjects.

In 2016, we advertised a call for papers for a subtheme on "Sexuality and the Law" at the Sewanee Medieval Colloquium. Expecting just one panel, we actually

---

[1] Anonymous, *Queers Read This* (a leaflet distributed at Pride March, New York, June 1990).
[2] Carolyn Dinshaw, *Getting Medieval: Sexualities and Communities, Pre- and Postmodern* (Durham: Duke University Press, 1999), 21.

filled three; we were delighted to see how much exciting work was still happening in medieval studies and queer studies. It was also somewhat surprising: many of the traditional venues which had given space to the explorations of queer theory in medieval studies had ceased to exist – imprints at Chicago and Duke University Presses had shuttered – and we both wondered, before the Sewanee call for papers, if we had seen the eclipse of much of this queer work.

We can boldly say that the answer to that question is no. This collection is part of a long and continuing resurgence of intersections between queer theory and medieval studies. This collection, in particular, explores the contours of queerness in medieval texts, written, copied, or read in England and France in the early, high, and late Middle Ages. Moving from Latin materials to French and finally English materials, these essays all ask, in different ways, what medieval queerness looks like, and who and what is interpolated by the "medieval queer."

The Medieval Queer: What, When, How?

What is queer theory? Defining queer theory might in fact prove impossible. Indeed, the fact that, in spite of its various different formulations, queer theory has managed to elude one master definition is a feature, not a bug of the scholarly practices of the queer theorist. It is precisely the body of theoretical tools that proves to be indefinable, because queer theory doesn't seek one *telos*. Indeed, instead queer theorists have been interested in disparate, even contradictory, foci, including the perils of reprofuturity, temporality, sexuality (queer theory can and does exist without sex), or as a critique of traditional gender, race, or class structures. It has, at points, been all these things. And, in spite of its commonalities with other theoretical tools, among which one might count Marxist, deconstruction, or feminist critiques, queer theory is different. As Elizabeth Freeman makes clear, "what makes queer theory *queer* as opposed to simply deconstructionist is also its insistence on risking a certain vulgar referentiality, its understanding of the sexual encounter as precisely the body and ego's undoing."[3]

When is queer theory? Queer theory, from its inception in the early 1990s till today, has been obsessed with its future, even as the denial of that futurity is a characteristic of much of the work which laid the groundwork for the

---

[3] Elizabeth Freeman, *Time Binds: Queer Temporalities, Queer Histories* (Durham: Duke University Press, 2010), 11.

theory's practice. Inevitably, as it borrowed much from then-contemporary feminisms, and because queer theory was wedded to social movements which saw greater promise in the destruction of then-contemporary oppression, queer theory has always been about the future:

> Queerness is not yet here. Queerness is an ideality. Put another way, we are not yet queer. We may never touch queerness, but we can feel it as the warm illumination of a horizon imbued with potentiality. We have never been queer, yet queerness exists for us as an ideality that can be distilled from the past and used to imagine a future. The future is queerness's domain. Queerness is a structuring and educated mode of desiring that allows us to see and feel beyond the quagmire of the present. The here and now is a prison house. We must strive, in the face of the here and now's totalizing rendering of reality, to think and feel a then and there.[4]

Jose Esteban Muñoz's evocative description – not definition – of queerness is especially helpful. He discusses what belongs to queerness – the future – and what queer is not. But his terms for defining queerness remain, programmatically, elusive. What Muñoz doesn't mention is the past: the future belongs to queerness, the present to the prison, and the past, well, it is erased, unvoiced, unarticulated.

In fact, queer theorists have been largely consumed by the conception of queer's future and the foreclosure of a non-queer present; much work remains to be done, not only on the past of queerness but the queerness of the past and the foundations of queer theory. As Annamarie Jagose writes:

> Queer, then, is an identity category that has no interest in consolidating or even stabilizing itself. It maintains its critique of identity-focused movements by understanding that even the formation of its own coalitional and negotiated constituencies may well result in exclusionary and reifying effects far in excess of those intended.[5]

This volume features essays firmly tied to the specific historical circumstances of the texts they discuss. Nevertheless, the charge against anachronism is an old one. It is, however, odd that this question has to be answered *ad infinitum*, but similar questions about stemma and editorial theory, or uses of scientific terms and concepts coined long after 1550 do not need justification. Queer theorists, and those medievalists using queer theory, ultimately understand that they are working with texts and ideas that trouble a regiment of minutes, hours, days, months, and years which is constructed and partially contrived.

---

4 Jose Muñoz, *Cruising Utopia* (New York: New York University Press, 2009), 1.
5 Annamarie Jagose, *Queer Theory: An Introduction* (New York: New York University Press, 1997), 131.

And our understanding of the medieval past's queerness, even if partial and hazy, also helps to bring into focus the blurriness of our queer present, and to give us tools to anticipate the futurity of queerness.

John Boswell, writing in 1980, indicates this historical slipperiness of desire and sexuality:

> Therefore, "gay" has been contrasted in the study with "nongay," an expression which may startle some readers but which is no less justifiable than "non-Jewish," "non-Catholic," "non German," or "non-" anything else which comprises the focus of attention. This terminology has advantages beyond semantic precision. The word "homosexual" implicitly suggests that the primary distinguishing characteristic of gay people is their sexuality. There does not seem to be any evidence that gay people are any more or less sexual than others, and from the historian's point of view, tacitly suggesting such a thing is unwarranted. "Gay" allows the reader to draw his own conclusions about the relative importance of love, affection, devotion, romance, eroticism, or overt sexuality in the lives of the persons so designated. Sexual interest and expression vary dramatically in the human population, and a person's sexual interest may be slight without precluding the realization that he or she is attracted to persons of the same gender and hence distinct in some way from the majority.[6]

Although almost forty years old, this passage from *Christianity, Social Tolerance, and Homosexuality* outlines some of the energies that prompted this volume (and book series). Writing past and beyond charges of anachronism, Boswell pinpoints what is still so relevant about the search for nonnormative identities in the medieval past. What Boswell and his book suggest is that the contours of this reclamation of a queer past (we have moved personally as scholars from "gay" to "queer") are ongoing – the future of the queer might be the discovery of that identity, and everything associated with it, in the past.

As Eve Sedgwick writes in "Queer and Now," "I think many adults (and I am among them) are trying, in our work, to keep faith with vividly remembered promises made to ourselves in childhood: promises to make invisible possibilities and desires visible; to make the tacit things explicit; to smuggle queer representations in where they must be smuggled, and with the relative freedom of adulthood, to challenge queer-eradicating impulses frontally where they are to be so challenged."[7] Scholars have taken up Boswell and Sedgwick *frontally* in

---

[6] John Boswell, *Christianity, Social Tolerance, and Homosexuality: Gay People in Western Europe from the Beginning of the Christian Era to the Fourteenth Century* (Chicago: University of Chicago Press, 1980), 45.

[7] Eve Sedgwick, "Queer and Now," in *Tendencies* (Durham: Duke University Press, 1993), 1–20 at 3.

extending explorations of the queer in the Middle Ages. Carolyn Dinshaw comments that "queer histories are made of affective relations" and "one thing that makes this history queer is its view that sex is heterogeneous and indeterminate – not the view that we can never know what really happened sexually in past cultures because their immediacy is lost, but the view that sex . . . is at least in part contingent on systems of representation, and, as such, is fissured and contradictory."[8] As was mentioned earlier in this essay, queer theory is resistant to easy definitions; some scholars have imported modern terminology into the past to argue that there have always been queer people. We would agree, though, that those categories are not equally mapped onto historical identities which, in fact, offer up even richer possibilities for the history of queer identities.

Other scholars resist using modern terminology. For example, Karma Lochrie's *Heterosynracies* (2005) dismantles the idea that modern heteronormativity can be found in the medieval past and asks us to consider the ways in which Nature, which often engenders the unnatural, affects the discourse defining (female) sexuality. Lochrie writes, "It is possible, I want to argue, to imagine a pre-heteronormative past that is neither hopelessly utopian nor inveterately heteronormative, and furthermore that such a project calls us ineluctably to our present – to our assumptions about what we know and to the medieval residues that must now be accounted for in the way we will imagine sexualities in the future."[9] As well, Tison Pugh points out that "the Western Medieval world lacked a hermeneutic sense of homosexuality *contra* homosexuality as a defining feature of an individual's identity, yet this predominantly Christian culture faced continuous struggles in defining the proper role of love and eroticism for its people."[10]

Not Quite Gay, Beyond Gay

One of the assertions that these essays make is that the figure of the medieval queer – as person, identity, and affect – both echoes and anticipates a move past traditional binaries of nonnormative sexuality. In the first section, "Queer Latinities: Authorizing Same-Sex Desire," Michael Johnson and Will Rogers

---

8 Dinshaw, *Getting Medieval*, 12.
9 Karma Lochrie, *Heterosyncracies* (Minneapolis: University of Minnesota Press, 2005), 25.
10 Tison Pugh, *Chaucer's (Anti-)Eroticisms and the Queer Middle Ages* (Columbus: Ohio State University Press, 2014), 5.

explore a history of queer figures in Latin texts of the high Middle Ages and treat texts and ideas that find queer renaissances in then-contemporary and subsequent French and English literatures. Introducing the grammatical disagreements about sexuality, queerness, and language in Alan of Lille's *De planctu Naturae*, a text that serves as the focus of Michael Johnson's "Sexual Ethics in the Medieval Grammar Classroom," Johnson asks how grammar education in the medieval classroom might have shaped erotic desire and the framing of queerness and language. In his wide-ranging, yet focused essay, Johnson examines the enlarging role of classroom education, the increasing autonomy of teachers of grammar, and the often-slippery status of grammar, both as moralizing power and subversive force. Johnson's essay begins with a discussion of *Altercatio Ganimedis et Helene*, interrogating the text's use of pagan materials and the lessons those sources impart, before fleshing out a comparison of certain grammatical treatises and treatments, among which Lille's *De planctu* looms large. Will Rogers's handling of Helen and Ganymede and the dream vision that depicts their debate necessarily follows Johnson's handling of the productive spaces where sexuality, grammar, and education collide. In "Failed Orientations: The Spaces of Sexual Histories and Failures," Rogers fleshes out the intersections of space and orientation in the twelfth-century poem *Altercatio Ganimedis et Helene*. In the debate between Ganymede and Helen, he addresses the poem's handling of what Jack Halberstam has termed "queer failure," as the Dreamer positions Ganymede against Helen. While the poem arguably ends in success and marriage, its unraveling of traditional gender structures and concentration on deviant figures (Ganymede, Helen) challenge medieval heteronormativity, orienting its reader to the prehistories of deviation that undergird feminist critique and queer theory, while also fleshing out the queer time and spaces of Ganymede in relation to Helen.

In the second section, "French Kisses: Queer Romance," Joseph Derosier, Lynn Shutters, and Maud McInerney engage with the figure of the queer in medieval French literature, tracing how vernacular treatments of queerness both build upon and move away from the authorizing power of the Latin queer figure. Derosier's "Guillaume de Lorris's Unmaking of the Self: The Dreamer's Queer Failures" concentrates on the figure of Narcissus in the first portion of *Le roman de la Rose*, highlighting again the influence of Alan of Lille's *De planctu* and suggesting that Guillaume's text forecloses any kind of completion or success in interpretation or reading. By tying the reader to the figure of Narcissus, Derosier posits that not only does the reader see themselves in this text, but that that identification is necessarily a queer one. In tracing Guillaume's revision of Narcissus, Derosier asks provocatively, what does it mean for identity and interpretation not to really see Narcissus? This reliance on self-identification with queerness, which is nevertheless not really *seen*, is central to Shutters's "Sodom, Bretons, and Ill-Defined Borders: Questing for Queerness with the *Knight of the Tower*." Her essay seeks to examine an apparently heteronormative conduct manual, one which is invested in regulating the proto-heterosexual household, which nevertheless imagines in the over-determined regulation and promotion of this household the possibility of failure and the specter of Sodom (and sodomy). Thus, while Shutters is clear that the queer might be a ghostly presence for this conduct manual, it is one which is visualized by the male narrator and constructed for and about women, especially in his discussion of the sins of Lot's wife. According to Shutters, this association not only links wayward female desire to nonnormative feelings but also demonstrates the ambivalence of the narrator to discourses of *fin amor*. Shutters's emphases on both queerness and time, in particular Elizabeth Freeman's "chromonormativity," connects her investigation of conduct manuals to the conduct of classical heroes in "Queer Time for Heroes in the *Roman d'Enéas* and the *Roman de Troie*." There, Maud McInerney discusses how characters who live outside the normative frames of courtly love – procreation and land acquisition effected through proto-heterosexual coupling – experience time not as Bakhtin theorizes "romance time" but as a kind of failed temporality. These heroes, who exist outside economies of procreation, find themselves in moments of "stasis, interruption, excess, and death," a temporal frame that McInerney productively links to the AIDS crisis and the wasting of time and bodies in another war-like landscape, as gay men seemed to exist outside a heteronormative timeframe.

In "Insular Queerness: English and the Nonnormative," the third and final section, Meg Cotter-Lynch, Micah Goodrich, and Haylie Swenson examine how the medieval queer is fleshed out in Old and Middle English. Meg Cotter-Lynch's "The Gender Genealogy of St. Mary of Egypt" returns to the focus of the first few essays in the collection, as she ties gender to grammar in order to flesh out the relationship among sanctity, gender, and sexuality. By examining the grammatical and semantic markers that establish the often-obscure or unclear gender and sex of St. Mary of Egypt in both its Old English version and probable Latin source, Cotter-Lynch's essay seeks to see St. Mary as genderqueer, freeing both her and us from seeing sexuality and gender as inextricably tied. Zooming in on bodies which prove hard to characterize, Micah Goodrich's essay, "Ycrammed ful of cloutes and of bones: Chaucer's Queer Cavities," focuses on the bodies and bags, holes and cavities, of the Pardoner and the Summoner. Goodrich's essay not only sees in the various purses, wallets, and bags carried by the Pardoner a series of cavities where queer reproduction can occur, but also sees the bodies of various pilgrims as purses and containers themselves. Tying together these material and corporeal spaces, Goodrich investigates how value and absence are queered by social exchanges, processes which, in Goodrich's words, "uncover how the medieval queer is assembled, reassembled, and interchanged among a social collective." Finally, Haylie Swenson, in "Resisting Sex and Species in the *Squire's Tale*," examines how the *Tale*'s animals – both the falcon who complains of her sadness to Canacee and the magical, yet seemingly crafted, horse – push at the boundaries of chivalric spaces. Swenson's essay subverts the order in which the animals appear in the tale, moving from the falcon's description and interactions with Canacee to the promise of the marvelous horse. In their interactions with the humans who surround them, these animals exhibit a slipperiness in the space between human and animal, "in the process creating space for both interspecies and intrasexual relationships of care outside of the gendered human norms of chivalric romance."

Finally, "Epilogue: Opening Up Queerness" is a closing gesture, and an invitation for future paths in queer medievalism. Michelle M. Sauer's "Queer Time and Lesbian Temporality in Medieval Women's Encounters with the Side Wound" builds on contemporary ideas of queer time, showing how a certain lesbian potentiality resides in medieval depictions of Christ's side wound.

These essays are a testament to the capacious qualities of queerness in the Middle Ages. Singularly they point to the local and contingent medieval queer – embodied, open, multivalent, powerful. Together, as a *richness*, these essays point to a queer medieval future, one in which the past is never finished with us, new bonds are formed in surprising ways, and knowledge is shared in the spirit of love, visibility, and affirmation.

Bibliography

Anonymous. *Queers Read This* (a leaflet distributed at Pride March, New York, June 1990).
Boswell, John. *Christianity, Social Tolerance, and Homosexuality: Gay People in Western Europe from the Beginning of the Christian Era to the Fourteenth Century*. Chicago: University of Chicago Press, 1980.
Dinshaw, Carolyn. *Getting Medieval: Sexualities and Communities, Pre- and Postmodern*. Durham: Duke University Press, 1999.
Freeman, Elizabeth. *Time Binds: Queer Temporalities, Queer Histories*. Durham: Duke University Press, 2010.
Jagose, Annamarie. *Queer Theory: An Introduction*. New York: New York University Press, 1997.
Lochrie, Karma. *Heterosyncracies*. Minneapolis: University of Minnesota Press, 2005.
Muñoz, Jose. *Cruising Utopia*. New York: New York University Press, 2009.
Pugh, Tison. *Chaucer's (Anti-)Eroticisms and the Queer Middle Ages*. Columbus: Ohio State University Press, 2014.
Sedgwick, Eve. "Queer and Now." In *Tendencies*, 1–20. Durham: Duke University Press, 1993.

Part I: **Queer Latinities: Authorizing Same-Sex Desire**

Michael Johnson
Chapter 1
Sexual Ethics in the Medieval Grammar Classroom

In trying to contextualize the famously extravagant grammatical metaphors in Alan of Lille's *De planctu Naturae*, Jan Ziolkowski has argued that Alan and his peers were inheritors of an earlier medieval textual and pedagogical tradition that associated linguistic rectitude with moral rectitude, orthography with orthopraxy.[1] This association stemmed, among other things, from the physical dimension of cathedral school grammar instruction where boys would have learned technologies of writing through an assiduous disciplining of body and mind. Indeed, in the iconography of Lady Grammar she is typically represented as a teacher, with whip or scourge in one hand and balm or ointment in the other, emphasizing grammar's disciplinary and redemptive dimensions, respectively.[2]

However, if we jump roughly sixty years later into the early decades of the thirteenth century, we see that grammar becomes increasingly associated with sexual perversion. In Gautier de Coinci's *Miracles de Nostre Dame* (ca. 1218), for example, the corrupt sodomites imagined to have overrun the Roman clergy are described as favoring the laws of grammar over those of Nature ("Il metent *hic* en toutes parz;/ La gramaire *hic* a *hic* acouple,/ Mais nature maudit la couple" [They are putting *hic* all over the place. Grammar might couple *hic* with *hic* but Nature curses that coupling]).[3] Nearly a century later, Dante places Priscian into the circle of the sodomites in his *Commedia*, a decision Boccaccio claims was motivated by the widely acknowledged proclivity of grammarians toward sodomy.[4] This apparent shift in the perceived ethical value of grammar raises a

---

[1] Jan Ziolkowski, *Alan of Lille's Grammar of Sex: The Meaning of Grammar to a Twelfth-Century Intellectual* (Cambridge: Medieval Academy of America, 1985), 1–6 and 95–104.
[2] See Gary P. Cestaro, *Dante and the Grammar of the Nursing Body* (Notre Dame: University of Notre Dame Press, 2003), 9–48; and Laura Cleaver, "Grammar and Her Children: Learning to Read in the Art of the Twelfth Century," *Marginalia* 9.1 (2009): n. p., http://www.marginalia.co.uk/journal/09education/cleaver.php.
[3] Gautier de Coinci, *De Sainte Leocade: Au Tans Que Sainz Hyldefons Estoit Arcevesques De Tholete Cui Nostre Dame Donna L'aube De Prelaz: Miracle Versifié* / Vilamo-Pentti, Eva, Suomalaisen Tiedeakatemian Toimituksia. Annales Academiae Scientiarum Fennicae (Helsinki: Suomalainen Tiedeakatemia, 1950), 172.
[4] Dante Alighieri, *The Divine Comedy: Inferno 2*. Commentary, trans. Charles S. Singleton (Princeton: Princeton University Press, 1989), 270.

number of questions relevant to the history of sexuality in medieval Europe. Broadly, we might ask how the early medieval cultural association of grammar with moral rectitude gives way to an association with sexual perversion and moral turpitude in the later Middle Ages. But also, more narrowly, we might ask what specific role medieval grammatical education played in shaping conceptions of erotic desire. To what extent was the grammar classroom perceived as a desirous space, or a space for the disciplining of desire? I will suggest that twelfth-century developments in the theory and practice of *Grammatica*—from the emergence of speculative grammar to innovations in grammatical pedagogy made necessary by increased enrollments and an increasingly autonomous professoriate—are at the root of this dramatic shift in perceptions of grammar's ethical value in regards to sexuality. By examining this shift, I believe we can gain insight into the role and evolution of sexual ethics in the medieval grammar classroom.

Introduction: Grammar's Ambivalent Status

Alan of Lille's use of grammatical terminology in his theological treatment of natural and unnatural desires is attached to a specific moment in the history of the nascent European university. And although *De planctu Naturae* is uniquely systematic in its deployment of grammatical metaphors, Alan was far from alone in his use of metalinguistic terminology from the trivium as a means of encoding questions of sex and gender. In the high Middle Ages, the language of Latin grammar became imbued with a powerful and deeply conflicted erotic aura to a degree unseen in any other period of European history. Poets and theologians of the period found grammar to be an endlessly rich source of concepts, structures, and metaphors with which to encode, reflect on, regulate, and even take pleasure in writing about sex.[5] Erotic uses of grammar appear in all manner of writings during the period, to a variety of ends, and even, quite often, to opposing ends. On the one hand, grammar was a regulatory art, dedicated in every sense to the straight line (from the Greek γράμμα, "line of writing"), both in the sense

---

[5] Examples abound in Latin poetry from the high Middle Ages from Goliardic poetry (especially the *Carmina Burana*) to debate poems such as the *Altercatio Ganimedis et Helene*. See Thomas C. Moser, *A Cosmos of Desire: The Medieval Latin Erotic Lyric in English Manuscripts* (Ann Arbor: University of Michigan Press, 2004). Vernacular examples are perhaps more well known and can be seen in troubadour *sirventes*, the *Roman de la Rose*, Henri d'Andeli's *Bataille des Sept Arts*, and the *Roman de Silence*, among many others.

that grammar students had to develop the manual mastery necessary to write correctly (orthography) and in the sense that linguistic rectitude was thought necessary to the cultivation of moral rectitude (orthopraxy). On the other hand, the discipline of grammar was also always potentially deviant, threatening to lead its practitioners away from the straight path of linguistic and, by extension, moral rectitude. The reasons behind this association of grammar with linguistic excess and deviance were complex and multiple. For one, the medieval grammar classroom was where young boys first encountered pagan literature in all its exuberant and puzzling alterity. Classical attitudes toward sexuality reflected in the *Sex Auctores*[6] and the works of Ovid and Virgil (somewhat later in the grammar curriculum), combined with the difficulties in using literary, and thus often highly figural, language to teach elementary Latin, we must imagine, would have led *grammatici* to develop a conflicted erotic rapport with the grammar classroom.[7] Beyond the erotic landscapes of pagan literature, however, even the non-literary aspects of grammar were permeated with a sense of eroticism and sin. Given that Latin was understood to be a post-Babelian language, its grammar was correspondingly imagined to mirror the fallenness of nature;[8] that the word *casus* (grammatical case) is derived from the perfect passive participle of *cadō* ("I fall") further cemented the association of grammar with fallen nature, as John Alford observed.[9] Thus, in the imagination of a writer such as Alan of Lille, fallen grammar cannot help but generate sexual monstrosities such as the two-sexed heteroclite

---

6 The elementary Latin curriculum that included, in this order, the *Distichs of Cato*, *Eclogue of Theodulus*, fables of Avian, elegies of Maximian, Statius's *Achilleid*, and Claudian's *Rape of Proserpina*. These would have been taught in conjunction with the standard grammar textbooks: Donatus's *Ars minor* and (beginning in the early thirteenth century) Alexandre de Villedieu's *Doctrinale Puerorum* and/or Evrard de Béthune's *Graecismus*.
7 Although this ambivalence arguably goes back as far as Augustine (see Brian Stock, *Augustine the Reader: Meditation, Self-Knowledge, and the Ethics of Interpretation* [Cambridge: Harvard University Press, 1996]) and is certainly informed by Augustine's thinking, I would argue that it takes on new meaning as soon as the *moderni* begin modifying the grammar curriculum.
8 Cf. John of Salisbury, "While grammar has developed to some extent, and indeed mainly, as an invention of man, still it imitates nature, from which it partly derives its origin. Furthermore, it tends, as far as possible, to conform to nature in all respects" (*Metalogicon*, trans. Daniel D. McGarry, 1.14 [Berkeley: University of California Press, 1962], 39).
9 John Alford writes, "Medieval poets, noting the literal meanings of such terms as *casus* and *declinatio* – both signifying 'fall' – drew elaborate comparisons between grammar and the story of Adam and Eve: original sin is referred to as 'the first declension,' and Adam and Eve are 'oblique' nouns that fell away or 'declined' from God" ("The Grammatical Metaphor: A Survey of Its Use in the Middle Ages," *Speculum* 57.4 [1982]: 728–60 at 728).

and the passive-in-appearance-but-active-in-meaning deponent, and harbors the constant threat of metaleptic, or insufficiently teleological, signification.

Grammar had long been harnessed in the service of regulating sexual ethics and in a way that was tied to the intensely homosocial and, in certain ways, homoerotic, atmosphere of the cathedral schools. However, as the discipline of grammar became imbued with dialectical reasoning and thus became more categorical and compartmentalized, its earlier association with the disciplining of desire in a homosocial environment became suspect. Moreover, speculative grammar's tendency to ontologize grammatical categories informed and propelled the creation of new norms just as the Church began to intensify its regulation of sex and marriage.

Since the publication of John Boswell's *Christianity, Social Tolerance, and Homosexuality: Gay People in Western Europe from the Beginnings of the Christian Era to the Fourteenth Century* and Mark Jordan's *The Invention of Sodomy in Christian Theology*, a number of scholars interested in premodern sexuality have acknowledged the fact that medieval thinkers tended to view matters of sex and gender through a grammatical lens. However, aside from Ziolkowski's (1985) *Alan of Lille's Grammar of Sex* and, to a lesser extent, Cestaro's (2003) *Dante and the Grammar of the Nursing Body* and Curry Woods's (2010) *Classroom Commentaries: Teaching the Poetria Nova across Medieval and Renaissance Europe*, existing scholarship on the subject does not contextualize this phenomenon in relationship to pedagogical practice in the medieval grammar classroom, which would have been almost certainly a crucible for the emergence of this peculiar use of grammatical terminology and reasoning to describe and reflect on erotic desire and gender. Moreover, by focusing on the more concrete register of pedagogical practice instead of high grammatical theory, the historical shift in *Grammatica*'s status, from a discipline of orthopraxy to one associated with disordered desire and sodomy, comes into view with more clarity.

This essay therefore considers medieval grammar instruction from a few different angles and is organized around a series of pairings. I look first at the presence of the *Altercatio Ganimedis et Helene*, an erotic debate poem, in the context of its manuscript tradition, manuscripts that were likely produced and used in conjunction with grammar instruction. By situating it in its manuscript tradition, we are able to view the *Altercatio* as a product of the homosocial environment of the cathedral school where boys learned a certain disciplining of desire through their grammatical studies. However, by placing it into dialogue with Gilles de Corbeil and Gautier de Coinci, both of whom cite the *Altercatio*'s famous grammatical justification of same-sex desire, we also see how quickly the textual legacy of the grammar-as-orthopraxy tradition would become not only indecipherable to readers in the thirteenth century and beyond, but also suspect and perverse. The next section of the essay pairs John of Salisbury and Alan of Lille with Petrus Helias and Alexandre de Villedieu, respectively. John and Alan are both transitional figures, caught between the early medieval pedagogical grammar model and the emergent fields of speculative and modistic grammar, and both advocate for grammar instruction as a mode of disciplining desire. Petrus and Alexandre, on the other hand, represent innovations in grammar instruction that remove or bracket desire, in various ways, from the grammar classroom.

By placing these medieval intellectuals into dialogue with one another, the presence and concern with desire in the grammar classroom come into relief. For example, John of Salisbury and Petrus Helias are rarely, if ever, studied in relationship to the history of sexuality; nor are they examined for their reflections on desire.[10] However, by considering John of Salisbury's lament about the loss of an earlier generation's pedagogical methods against the emergence of the *summa* as both cause and supplement to the loss John describes, the desirous homosociality of the early medieval grammar classroom comes into view with a degree of clarity that would be impossible looking at either of these thinkers alone. By pairing Alexandre de Villedieu with Alan of Lille, the cosmological stakes of setting *De planctu Naturae* in the grammar classroom become more evident. The endeavor undertaken by Alexandre in his *Doctrinale* to excise pagan eroticism and desire from the classroom is undercut by the intrinsic eroticism of grammatical structures themselves, which Alan imagines as a sort of glue binding Nature and language together. Expansive and infinitely transferable, profoundly ambivalent but also necessary and ineluctable, the grammar classroom is where desires find their attachment to objects, whether good or bad, and thus also where these desires must be disciplined according to Alan's reckoning.

Disciplining Desire in the Medieval Grammar Classroom

In this section of the essay, I will consider the shift in grammar's ethical status described above as it is reflected in one particularly evocative manuscript history.

---

[10] With the notable exception of Elena Lombardi's fascinating discussion of Petrus Helias in *The Syntax of Desire: Language and Love in Augustine, the Modistae, Dante* (Toronto: University of Toronto Press, 2007).

In *CSTH*, Boswell notes the existence of a manuscript (the MS Biblioteca Apostolica Vaticana, Lat. 2719) that contains Priscian's *Institutiones grammaticae* bound together with the anonymously written debate poem, the *Altercatio Ganimedis et Helene*.[11] The presence of these two works together in a single manuscript raises important questions about grammatical pedagogy during the high medieval period, including, significantly, whether grammar teachers, in some way, saw the training of desire as one of their pedagogical tasks.

The *Institutiones grammaticae* (ca. 520) together with Donatus's *Ars grammatica* formed the core of the Latin grammar curriculum during the medieval period and into the renaissances. As Sluiter and Copeland note, the *Institutiones* "acquires enormous authority in the Middle Ages," attested by the existence of nearly a thousand manuscripts.[12] It became popular as early as the eighth century, cited by Bede, Alcuin, and, slightly later, Hrabanus Maurus. Then, during the mid-twelfth and thirteenth centuries, the *Institutiones* became particularly important as the common substratum of all speculative and modistic grammatical theories. It is, arguably, the modistic appropriation of the *Institutiones* that influenced Dante's inclusion of Priscian among the sinners against nature.[13] In either case, a manuscript containing the *Institutiones* would likely have been used to pedagogical ends, whether in a cathedral school or a monastic context.

If the MS Vat. Lat. 2719 was indeed used for pedagogical purposes, the anonymously written *Altercatio Ganimedis et Helene* (composed after 1160 and before 1176) might seem a strange addition; the poem, at least according to John Boswell's reading of it, may have been an apologia for same-sex love. It may also have been a condemnation of same-sex desire, judging by the last three stanzas. Or, if we believe Boswell that the Cambridge, MA Houghton MS Lat. 198 was the autograph copy, it may have been written originally as a veiled apologia but was then modified by copyists in such a way as to be interpreted

---

11 John Boswell, *Christianity, Social Tolerance, and Homosexuality: Gay People in Western Europe from the Beginning of the Christian Era to the Fourteenth Century* (Chicago: University of Chicago Press, 1980), 259.

12 *Medieval Grammar and Rhetoric: Language Arts and Literary Theory, AD 300–1475*, ed. Rita Copeland and Ineke Sluiter (Oxford: Oxford University Press, 2009), 167.

13 This might explain why Priscian and not Donatus is included among the sodomites; speculative grammar represents a metaleptic, or tautological, relationship to grammar (as its own end) against the anagogical model of the liberal arts as a bridge articulating God and world through a certain structuring of knowledge. However, the prevailing theory is that Priscian was associated apocryphally with Julian the Apostate (see Eugene Vance, *Mervelous Signals: Poetics and Sign Theory in the Middle Ages* [Lincoln: University of Nebraska Press, 1989], 230–55).

as a condemnation of same-sex desire.[14] Whatever the case, the *Altercatio* is unequivocally concerned with sexual desire, which becomes the primary object of debate between Ganymede and Helen, each of whom defends the virtues of sex with boys and women, respectively. What use would such a debate have in a grammar classroom?

Two further details about the poem might explain its inclusion in MS Vat. Lat. 2719. First, nearly the entirety of the poem derives its metaphors using language from the *trivium*—grammar, dialectic, rhetoric—citing Martianus Capella's widely known characterization of the language arts.[15] Its use of grammatical language seems to have been precisely what brought it some degree of fame. Ganymede's grammatical argument that like should be coupled with like according to the rules of *congruitas* was striking enough to have been cited in a dozen or so antisodomitic works during the late twelfth and thirteenth centuries. Ganymede's argument:

> Impar omne dissidet, recte par cum pari
> eleganti copula mas aptatur mari.
> Si nescis: articulos decet observari,
> hic et hic gramatice debent copulari. (ll. 141–44)
>
> Opposites always disagree; the right way is like with like.
> Man can be fitted to man by elegant conjunction.
> If you don't know this, look at the gender of their articles[16]
> *Hic* and *hic* should be coupled according to the rules of grammar.

Whether the author intended the poem as an apologia or a condemnation, Ganymede's argument seems to have cemented the association of grammarians with sodomy. Only a decade or so later, Gilles de Corbeil cites Ganymede's grammatical argument in his virulently phobic anticlerical treatise, *Hierapigra ad purgandos prelatos*, where he worries that "men have made themselves into grammarians" (volentes grammatici fieri)[17] so that they might have sex according to the rules of grammar rather than the rules of Nature.

---

14 Boswell, *Christianity, Social Tolerance, and Homosexuality*, 260.
15 *Martianus Capella and the Seven Liberal Arts: The Marriage of Philology and Mercury*, trans. William Harris Stahl, Richard Johnson, and E. L. Burge (New York: University of Columbia Press, 1992).
16 Thomas Stehling, *Medieval Latin Poems of Male Love and Friendship* (New York: Garland, 1984), 112. The Latin "Articulos" best translates as "pronouns" in this context.
17 Cited in Bruce Holsinger, *Music, Body, and Desire in Medieval Culture: Hildegard of Bingen to Chaucer* (Palo Alto: Stanford University Press, 2001), 174–75.

The second detail that might explain its inclusion in MS Vat. Lat. 2719 concerns the poem's pagan setting. Although sodomy was a relatively novel concern in Christian theology[18] at the time of the poem's composition, the *Altercatio* contains no references to Christianity, nor does it feature any specifically Christian argument about sexual desire. It is written as though the same classical figures who populated the literature of the medieval grammar classroom were given a retroactive opportunity to debate their sexual mores. In addition to opposing two objects of desire, the *Altercatio* also stages a confrontation with the historical and cultural alterity of the classical past. This speaks directly to the pedagogical concerns of twelfth-century grammar teachers: can students attain literacy in Latin without unmediated exposure to the potentially perverting influence of classical literature? And hasn't the subject of study already been "perverted" by its classical origins? The poem's concern with sexuality is thus difficult, perhaps impossible, to separate from its concern with the value of pagan literature in the medieval grammar classroom. And this was the subject of a highly contentious debate in the twelfth and thirteenth centuries.[19]

What's more, the MS Vat. Lat. 2719 is not alone. Of the eight known manuscripts that contain the *Altercatio*, one—in all likelihood, the autograph—is freestanding and six of them contain works directly connected to grammar and rhetoric, including works by Matthew of Vendôme, Isidore of Seville, John of Garland, Gautier of Châtillon, Alan of Lille, and others. Given what we know about its manuscript tradition, it is difficult to imagine the *Altercatio* was not used in the grammar classroom.

What is fascinating and puzzling about MS Vat. Lat. 2719 and its sister manuscripts is that authors and defenders of grammar who wrote roughly contemporaneously to the composition of the *Altercatio*, such as Alan of Lille (to whom some have attributed the *Altercatio*'s authorship)[20] and John of Salisbury, seemed to believe that the discipline of grammar had some concrete value in the realm of sexual ethics. The author of the *Altercatio* itself most likely believed so as well. But the *Altercatio* elicited such a phobic reception in writers like Gilles de Corbeil and Gautier de Coinci, that less than a century later the *Roman de la Rose* was alone in entertaining the possibility of grammar's ethical value—and even then, Genius's

---

18 See chapter 2, "The Discovery of Sodomy," 29–45 in Mark Jordan's *The Invention of Sodomy in Christian Theology* (Chicago: University of Chicago Press, 1997).

19 See, for example, Marilynn Desmond's discussion of the *Ovides moralisées* in Desmond, *Ovid's Art and the Wife of Bath: The Ethics of Erotic Violence* (Ithaca: Cornell University Press, 2006).

20 See Rolf Lenzen's "'*Altercatio Ganimedis et Helene* Kritische Edition mit Kommentar," *Mittellateinisches Jahrbuch* 7 (1972): 161–86.

grammatically encoded excommunication of the sodomites (vv. 4313–14) suggests that Jean de Meun did not fully endorse this by-then-outdated understanding of grammar. In either case, Gilles de Corbeil's claim that men become grammarians just so they can find a way to justify their sexual sins by drawing upon the laws of grammar rather than the laws of nature was so highly influential that it made its way quickly into the vernacular, as was the case with Gautier de Coinci's wildly popular *Miracles de Nostre-Dame*:

> Plus volentiers les font movoir
> A Perrotin qu'a Perronnelle
> . . .
> Terre, terre, por quoi n'awevres,
> Si les transglouz de toutes parz?
> Il metent *hic* en toutes parz;
> La gramaire *hic* a *hic* acouple,
> Mais nature maudit la couple.
> . . .
> Nature rit, si com moi samble,
> Quant *hic* et *hec* joignent ensamble.
> Mais *hic* et *hic* chose est perdue.[21]

They are more turned on by Pierres than by Pierrettes . . . Oh, Earth, why don't you open up and swallow these men down all the way? They are putting *hic* all over the place. Grammar might couple *hic* with *hic* but Nature curses that coupling.

And roughly a century later, it was this way of thinking about grammar and sex—not Alan of Lille's—that likely influenced Dante and Boccaccio to ascribe a proclivity for sodomy to grammarians. Alan of Lille's profoundly nuanced attempt to show what he saw as continuities and discontinuities between natural law and grammatical law, and the anonymous author of the *Altercatio*'s extremely subtle harnessing of grammar's eroticism to arouse productive anxiety among his students, I believe, were both written to the end of regulating sexual orthodoxy. However, their willingness to walk the student-reader through a gamut of erotic configurations, even if expressed via grammatically euphemistic metaphors, was perhaps too subtle, leading certain readers to reject grammar altogether as dangerous terrain.

---

[21] Gautier de Coinci, *De Sainte Leocade*, 172; translations mine.

Nostalgic Homosociality and the *Summa* as Supplement

The early Middle Ages inherited the late antique model of grammar, which had two primary functions: the first, to teach the Latin language (a facet of grammar characterized as the *ars recte loquendi et scribendi* by Isidore of Seville[22]) and the second, to teach how to make basic judgments about literature, the facet of grammar known as the *enarratio poetarum*. As Martin Irvine notes in his study of early medieval grammar, "*grammatica* was universally understood to supply the discursive means for constructing language and texts as objects of knowledge."[23] Grammar was thus concerned with literacy, in the broadest sense possible, the stakes of which heightened in the early Christian era as the primary objective became that of biblical literacy. And it was the most interpretively oriented of the verbal arts, more so even than rhetoric, which was focused more on mastering forms while grammar focused on recognizing and parsing those forms. The practice of textual glossing, for example, which we still practice a version of today in literature classes, was solidly within the purview of grammar. As far as grammar textbooks were concerned, the *Ars minor* and the *Ars maior* of Aelius Donatus, written in the mid-fourth century, were mainstays of curricula from the late antique period all the way through the early print era. The *Ars minor* was an elementary classroom handbook simply delineating parts of speech while the *Ars maior* was a more advanced and complete handbook of rules that outlined stylistic faults and graces, and parsed the difference between figurative language use and incorrect language use, listing such figures as metaphor, synecdoche, allegory, anaphora, sarcasm, and so on. Both are written plainly and enumeratively (e.g., "Pronomen quid est? Pars orationis, quae pro nomine posita tantundem paene significat personamque interdum recipit"[24]), and the latter drew nearly all of its examples of usage from Virgil's poetry. As Copeland and Sluiter note, "The Middle Ages erected its curricula on a relatively small group of essential texts from Latin antiquity."[25]

---

[22] *The Etymologies of Isidore of Seville*, ed. Stephen A. Barney, W. J. Lewis, J. A. Beach, and Oliver Berghof (Cambridge: Cambridge University Press, 2006).
[23] Martin Irvine, *The Making of Textual Culture: Grammatica and Literary Theory, 350–1100* (Cambridge: Cambridge University Press, 1994), 2.
[24] Aelius Donatus, *The Ars Minor of Donatus: For One Thousand Years the Leading Textbook of Grammar*, trans. Wayland Johnson Chase (Madison: University of Wisconsin Press, 1926), 28.
[25] *Medieval Grammar and Rhetoric*, 62.

But one thing that grammar was *not* during the early Middle Ages, with the possible exception of Duns Scotus, was a speculative discipline. In other words, grammar was rarely, if ever, the object of theoretical debate. It was a *tool* used in theological and legal debates—quite frequently, in fact—but, until the early twelfth century, grammar was almost exclusively concerned with Latin literacy, and a fairly stable understanding of literacy at that. The grammar curriculum remained essentially unchanged and unquestioned for six centuries. What's more, grammar was taught in the institutional context of cathedral schools and monastic schools that served a very small, relatively elite, portion of the population, and generally taught no more than a hundred students at a time.[26] Grammatical pedagogy was painstaking, involved lengthy memorization exercises, and was mostly transmitted through tradition. That is to say, techniques for teaching Latin grammar (beyond the minimal question/answer structure of the *Ars minor* and *Ars maior*) were not incorporated into the grammar texts themselves and were more likely handed down through tradition. Grammar was in this sense a kind of boutique discipline.

At the beginning of the twelfth century, however, two major and interrelated factors led to a serious reworking of both the pedagogy and theory of grammar. To begin with, on the heels of the wide dissemination of Boethian logic in the eleventh century, the discipline of dialectic (also referred to as logic) became ascendant and veered to become a master-discipline, to the point that grammar itself became "logicized," its categories imagined to reflect deeper logical/ontological categories. This fusion of grammar and logic gave birth to speculative grammar, a branch of the discipline interested in finding correspondences between grammatical distinctions in language and ontological distinctions in reality. It was the speculative grammarians who first formulated the notion of a universal grammar. So, whereas early medieval grammarians were for the most part only interested in the preservation of Latin, speculative grammarians examined linguistic categories thought to transcend Latin; in Saussurian terms, it might be said they favored *langue* over *langage*.

This new development, to the extent that it was reflected in new curricula, new pedagogies, and new material practices, was the source of a great deal of conflict and intellectual debate, as might be imagined. Jan Ziolkowski describes this shift in *Alan of Lille's Grammar of Sex*:

> In the twelfth century, the nature of instruction changed fundamentally: *rationes* formerly taught through the *auctores* were now taught autonomously. Partly because of the

---

26 Stephen C. Ferruolo, *The Origins of the University: The Schools of Paris and Their Critics, 1100–1215* (Stanford: Stanford University Press, 1985).

excitement that dialectic and new translations from Arabic generated, learning became less a matter of philology than of philosophy, especially logic. In the same towns where universities were evolving or soon to evolve, teaching could take any form on a spectrum that ran between two extremes, the one dominated by *ratiories* and logic and the other by *auctores* and *grammatica* (in the sense of belles-lettres). Matthew of Vendôme declared succinctly, "Parisius logicam sibi iactitet, Aurelianis / Auctores." [*Paris is proud of its logic while Orleans is proud of its authors*]. In the thirteenth century *rationes* forced many of the *auctores* from the curriculum.[27]

The second, and partly related, factor at work was a dramatic increase in demand and enrollments at the cathedral schools. John of Salisbury's *Metalogicon* is cited perhaps more than any other work for its description of the twelfth-century crisis in education. Like Steven, bishop of Tournai, who complained that beardless youths were stealing the chairs of the old professors right from under them, "neglecting the rules of the arts and discarding the books of good authority,"[28] John was preoccupied with what he perceived as the new generation's lack of respect for the *auctores* and the speed with which they promised to deliver the curriculum to their students. And speed, or more generally, the temporality of teaching and learning, was a major concern in high medieval discussions of grammatical pedagogy. Grammar went from being a sort of art, with a range of unquantifiable payoffs, to being considered rather more like a technical skill, necessary but better done cursorily in order to get to the interesting stuff as quickly as possible.

John of Salisbury writes about this increase in speed, describing the effect it had on his own teachers' grammatical pedagogy:

> But later, when popular opinion veered away from the truth, when men preferred to seem, rather than to be philosophers, and when professors of the arts were promising to impart the whole of philosophy in less than three or even two years, William and Richard [John's teachers] were overwhelmed by the onslaught of the ignorant mob, and retired. Since then, less time and attention have been given to the study of grammar. As a result, we find men who profess all the arts, liberal and mechanical, but who are ignorant of this very first one [i.e., grammar], without which it is futile to attempt to go on to the others.[29]

Although John seems to believe that the "onslaught of the ignorant mob" was the result of the newer, dialectic-oriented curricula offered by the youngest generation of professors, it seems more likely that it was the other way around. An

---

[27] Ziolkowski, *Alan of Lille's Grammar of Sex*, 87.
[28] Cited in Louis John Paetow, *The Arts Courses at Medieval Universities with Special Reference to Grammar and Rhetoric* (Champaign: University Studies of the University of Illinois, 1910), 521.
[29] *Metalogicon*, 71.

unprecedented upsurge of enrollments in the cathedral schools of John's time made it materially necessary for many teachers to rethink their methods, pedagogical genres, and disciplinary boundaries. These new constraints, which threatened to reduce the amount of classroom time spent on Latin grammar, in concert with the logicization of grammar that had begun in the eleventh century, set grammar up to be a frequent object of disciplinary and pedagogical debates in the twelfth and thirteenth centuries. One major debate, according to John, concerned the amount and quality of the time that should be spent learning grammar. John's opponent, Cornificius, asks whether eloquence should be favored over logic and factuality, whether form should matter more than content. John responds that the question creates a false opposition that misses the point about the relationship between language and learning. The latter's impatience with the painstakingly slow process of attaining eloquence through study assumes a specific understanding of the relationship between nature and language. John writes:

> In the judgment of Cornificius (if a false opinion may be called a judgment), there is no point in studying the rules of eloquence, which is a gift that is either conceded or denied to each individual by nature. . . .] The device of learning precepts in order to become eloquent fails to accomplish its object. Even the most diligent study of rules cannot possibly make one eloquent. The use of language and speech suffices for intercourse among fellow countrymen, whereas he who most assiduously employs his faculty of speech becomes most fluent. This is evident with the Greeks and Latins; the Gauls and Britons will also bear witness to it; nor is it otherwise among the Scythians and Arabs. . . . Finally, [Cornificius argues,] what can eloquence and philosophy possibly have in common? . . . Philosophy (or wisdom, its object) is concerned not with words, but with facts.[30]

As John would have it, Cornificius follows the logic that speakers of vernaculars do not need to learn grammatical rules in order to become eloquent in their languages. If eloquence can be acquired naturally, the study of language is perhaps less important than the study of whatever it is that language conveys, what he calls "facts." In the Cornifician model, language is instrumentalized and nature becomes somehow knowable independently of language. Cornificius might represent the new student who, aware of universal categories across the range of individual languages, no longer perceives the discipline of grammar to be the same as the mastery of the Latin language. One can now learn the "facts" of grammar—universal categories such as subject and predicate, noun and verb, and so on—without mastering the language, or as John might say, without

---

30 *Metalogicon*, 24–25.

learning the art of grammar. But as soon as the mastery of language and the study of linguistic categories become separate, it becomes possible for such a student to imagine that neither the language nor the linguistic categories need to be learned at all, since they are both rooted in natural principles; we can and do learn the vernacular without the artifice of instruction. Grammatical categories are natural and are thus knowable on the same order as trees and animals.

John responds by defending grammar on as many grounds as possible (its practical and ethical utility, its epistemological centrality, etc.) but his response concerning the relationship between nature and grammar undergirds his argument throughout the *Metalogicon*. It also highlights the fact that the stakes of his argument are, at least partly, tied to questions of sexual ethics:

> Since grammar is arbitrary and subject to man's discretion, it is evidently not a handiwork of nature. . . . However, we have already seen that nature is the mother of the arts. While grammar has developed to some extent, and indeed mainly, as an invention of man, still it imitates nature, from which it partly derives its origin.[31]

Against the reductive tendencies of the Cornificians, John produces a much more nuanced response to the question, almost too nuanced for a polemic. Grammar is a product of human artifice that imitates nature. It is not a handiwork of nature but it does originate "partly" in nature. These hedged formulations make more sense if you place them in a neo-platonic framework. He compares substance and accident to nouns and adjectives; for example:

> and that the devices of reason may cleave even more closely to nature, since the substance of a thing is not susceptible of greater or less intensity, a noun does not admit of degrees of comparison . . . is this not a clear footprint of nature impressed on [the devices of] human reason?[32]

The similarity of grammatical categories (such as nouns and adjectives) to physical categories (such as substance and accident) John takes as proof that some prior principle—Nature, as the case may be—determines both. As he formulates it, nature impresses its footprint on the devices of human reason, on both logic and on grammar. But the question of orthopraxy remains unresolved. Does nature provide a model for correct speech and behavior? Are the correct and the natural one and the same? Certainly, the use of the adjective "natural" as an orthodox ideal would suggest so, but John explains that the natural as an

---

31 *Metalogicon*, 39.
32 *Metalogicon*, 40–41.

orthodox ideal is not perfectly consonant with the natural world. Simply put, Nature, like mankind, is in a post-lapsarian state. As John explains:

> We will grant that the genitive force originally implanted in things [nature] is powerful and effective. But, certainly, just as it can be canceled or hindered by defects, so it can, on the other hand, be restored or helped by *aids*. *Care* is accordingly not superfluous. Rather, it *assists* nature, and makes easier something that is already possible in one way or another. Socrates, we are told, was naturally wanton and overly susceptible to women (to use history's own word). But he *subdued* and *controlled* his passionate nature, which he *corrected* by philosophy and the exercise of virtue.[33]

Following this logic, the study of grammar can bring us closer to understanding nature's originary state but it can also, just as easily, lead us astray. Some other principle—here, it is "care," that is, the irreducible presence of a pedagogical authority, but elsewhere "reason" and "tradition"—must be invoked to help determine what constitutes a defect and what should be considered correct. John's reference to the sex life of Socrates here to explain the fallenness of nature is not, of course, incidental. Sexual desire is frequently imagined by John's contemporaries in teleological terms as a natural necessity that became deformed or excessive over time. Desire is part of nature but not all of nature is "natural." One thus needs to employ the artifices of reason and magisterial "care" to recover desire in its original form.

Much like John of Salisbury, Alan of Lille believed that grammar reflected nature darkly, that desire and grammar were shaped by the same underlying laws, and that an intervention via some form of *auctoritas* was necessary to parse "natural" grammar from "fallen" grammar, orthodox from perverse. And, like John of Salisbury, Alan of Lille was wary of many of the new methods being used in the grammar classroom and the speed with which grammar was increasingly being taught. However, unlike John of Salisbury, Alan did appear to appreciate and even delight in the new logic-inflected grammar; that the rules of grammar could reflect "deeper" logical categories certainly fits into Alan's particular brand of neo-platonic cosmology.[34]

---

[33] *Metalogicon*, 29–30.
[34] As Ziolkowski explains, "Whereas Alan evinced an unambivalent pleasure in the newfound usefulness of each *ars* to the others, he was not completely happy with all the other educational developments that occurred during his lifetime and that had a bearing upon grammar. He manifested special concern about two changes in pedagogical method: the increasing emphasis on methodology at the cost of readings in literature and the displacement of old texts from the syllabus by newer ones. Both changes in education came about partly in response to the predominance of dialectic over the other *artes*" *Alan of Lille's Grammar of Sex*, 86.

Although no single figure has been identified with Cornificius, we can cite pedagogical innovators such as Petrus Helias (who invents the *summa*) and Alexander de Villedieu (whose *Doctrinale* eliminates literature from the grammar curriculum) to understand that pedagogical models for the teaching of Latin grammar were moving away from those of the early medieval period, just as John feared. Traditional disciplinary boundaries began to erode under the ascendancy of Logic while economic pressure to train new professionals for new times (jurists and medical doctors) forced a sudden shift in the temporality of education, in particular the process of becoming lettered (or becoming *grammaticus*).

One telling symptom of the "crisis" in education John of Salisbury describes is the overwhelming success of the *summa* as a pedagogical genre. Petrus Helias's (1150) *Summa super Priscianum* very likely represented, for John of Salisbury, the new wave of quick and flimsy grammar teaching he complained about so bitterly. It was an instant success in large part because it responded to the new material demands of twelfth-century education. Unlike compendia or traditional commentary, heavily reliant on the primary text, the *summa* is "a commentary complete in itself without recourse to the primary text."[35] This innovation allowed students to work through material on their own without the mediating presence of a teacher. More precisely, the forms of textual mediation that usually took place in the grammar classroom (*lectio, progymnasmata, declinatio*) become the primary text; the importance of the "teacher function" is both amplified, to the extent that the original primary text—the *auctor*, in this case Priscian—is supplanted by its pedagogical mediation, and diminished, to the extent that the teacher's presence is no longer required in quite the same way as before. In Derridean terms, we might say the *summa* participates in the logic of the supplement, both accretion and substitution, "not a signified more than a signifier, a representer than a presence, a writing than a speech."[36] Just as Derrida saw the logic of the supplement at work in Rousseau's reflections on autoeroticism versus altereroticism, we can see a certain erotic economy at work in the transfer from magisterial presence to *summa*-as-supplement. John seems to have been concerned specifically with the loss of magisterial presence when he describes Bernard of Chartres's method, one that, he goes to great lengths to explain, cannot be replicated in writing. This is, incidentally, the same passage in which John describes Bernard's use of flogging in the classroom:

---

[35] Petrus Helias, *Summa Super Priscianum*, ed. Leo Alexander Reilly (Toronto: Pontifical Institute of Mediaeval Studies, 1993), 12.

[36] Jacques Derrida, *Of Grammatology* (Baltimore: Johns Hopkins University Press, 1998), 315.

[Bernard] would point out, in reading the authors, what was simple and according to rule. On the other hand, he would explain grammatical figures, rhetorical embellishments, and sophistical quibbling, as well as the relation of given passages to other studies. He would do so, however, without trying to teach everything at one time. On the contrary, he would dispense his instruction to his hearers gradually, in a manner commensurate with their powers of assimilation. . . . In view of the fact that exercise both strengthens and sharpens our mind, Bernard would bend every effort to bring his students to imitate what they were hearing. In some cases he would rely on exhortation, in others he would resort to punishments, such as flogging. Each student was daily required to recite part of what he had heard on the previous day. Some would recite more, others less. Each succeeding day thus became the disciple of its predecessor.[37]

John uses heavily qualified, sometimes paradoxical, formulations to insist on the irreducibility of the teacher's presence. Good grammar teaching is about adhering to the rules but also about learning when to suspend the rules; it points to the connectedness of different areas of knowledge without totalizing; it involves an indefinable combination of regularity and spontaneity; it is tailored to the level of the student and yet rigid enough that any student can master Latin grammar within a year's time; it calls on both inspiration and intimidation to elicit good work from the students. He insists moreover on the fragile contingency of a day's lesson. That "[s]ome would recite more, others less" suggests again that the day's lesson depends on the mnemonic capacities of the particular students present or on the ups and downs of their everyday. And by personifying "each succeeding day" as a "disciple of its predecessor," conflating the student with a successive measure of time, John suggests that teaching is bound to a genealogical (metonymic, contingent) notion of time that the bound book, which operates in a more timeless (allegorical, monumental) modality, cannot adequately reproduce. We can look at it as a defense of a guarded tradition defined by a set of pedagogical practices handed down through generations, defined by its long continuities and communitarian practice and characterized by contingency and nuance. We can also look at it as a panicked, and essentially elitist, response to the opening of education to a larger public. In either scenario, John's defense of magisterial presence strangely naturalizes the already-queer quality of medieval grammar education. In other words, the genealogical model implied by the various metaphors to describe both the teacher–student relation and the chain of relations connecting the *auctores* to the *moderni* (most famously Bernard of Chartres's metaphor of dwarves on the shoulders of giants, cited by John in the *Metalogicon*) is itself a supplement, and a very queer one at that, to "natural" genealogy. The chain of relations John describes functions as an alternative

---

37 *Metalogicon*, 70.

genealogy, one that might even be construed as a queer supplement to the reproduction of familial wealth and power. In rejecting the newer pedagogical modalities, those that eschew magisterial presence and the queer filiation of teacher and student, that is, in rejecting a supplement of a supplement, John paradoxically naturalizes the queer filiation of teachers and students.[38]

The "old" model of grammar teaching that John advocates is thus deeply coursed with a language of homosocial intimacy. And this is because, for John, Latin grammar is also a discipline of orthopraxy, geared to the formation of good ethical subjects. Linguistic rectitude, for John and his grammar teachers, was one and the same as moral rectitude. Through grammar, boys become men. And to this end, the pagan *auctores*, with their many representations of sexual excess and disorder, were in fact useful. A grammar teacher could engage erotic literature as a sort of prophylactic by harnessing his students' charged response to the literature, arousing productive anxieties but driving ultimately toward orthopraxy. Petrus Helius may not have been motivated by a desire to eliminate erotic content from the grammar classroom, and he doesn't completely, but the *summa* does interrupt the tradition of grammar as an ethical practice transmitted largely via the homosocial bond between male teachers and students that John of Salisbury so cherished.

Beyond the threat it seemed to pose to the irreducible presence of the *magister*, the *summa* also harked a new sense of disciplinarity connected to the emerging institution of the university. If the *summa*'s purpose was to summarize a particular field of knowledge, it also had to delimit the boundaries of that field. The *auctores* could no longer be simply cited to explain the divisions of knowledge. More fundamental principles had to be found. As Copeland and Sluiter explain, "[t]he twelfth century is the period of the first great systematic commentaries and encyclopedic overviews of the disciplines that go beyond simply describing the doctrine contained in each area and attempt to explain the intellectual and cognitive principles that justify the divisions of knowledge."[39] As subjects became more compartmentalized their value relative to one another became necessarily hierarchized. Whereas the liberal arts curriculum was once imagined in quasi neo-platonic

---

[38] Cf. Canto XV of the *Inferno* where Brunetto Latini addresses Dante as "filgiuol mio." Arnd Bohm notes in his essay, "Increasing Suspicion about Browning's Grammarian" (*Victorian Poetry* 44.2 –[2006]: 165–82): "Brunetto's addressing of his pupil as 'my son' implies an unnatural procreation, both of the pupil as a person and, ultimately, because they will incorporate traces of the teacher's instruction, of the pupil's own works. Giving intellectual birth, particularly in the overwhelmingly male world of medieval learning, could be construed as part of a man-to-man transmission" (168).

[39] *Medieval Grammar and Rhetoric*, 368.

terms as a seamless whole, in the twelfth century it becomes a power struggle, ideologically volatile, both institutional and counter-institutional, an epistemological battlefield. In this sense, John of Salisbury and Alan of Lille are conservative for their time. They both put forward arguments for the unity of knowledge, a position that requires them to accord significant importance to grammar understood as the *fundamentum*, the material anchoring of language to the world.

Thus, reading Petrus Helias's *Summa super Priscianum* against John of Salisbury's *Metalogicon* allows us to see how this pedagogical shift, which relegated much grammatical learning to a space *outside* of the classroom, might have also threatened an aspect of grammar pedagogy that was proper to the classroom, although not in the curriculum. The slow and intimate mode of teaching grammar that both John of Salisbury and Alan of Lille advocate understands grammar as a fundamentally ethical art in which the erotic and morally dubious pagan content of the literary texts under analysis can in fact be channeled to teach moral continence, to train desire through a highly mediated encounter with pagan sexuality. Of course we can only make educated guesses as to how such mediations might have been undertaken, but first-hand accounts such as John of Salisbury's do suggest that, before the mid-twelfth century when this shift in grammar pedagogy took place, grammar teachers spent a great deal of time mediating the alterity of the classical works studied for their students. Certainly the elimination of certain classical works from grammar curricula (now replaced with literary works of *moderni* such as Gautier de Chatillon's *Alexandreis*) and the increasing popularity of *summae* and versified grammars suggest that less time in the grammar classroom meant less time to grapple with pagan sexuality, thus diminishing or altogether eliminating the training of desire.

In the Grammar Classroom of Life

However, it is also possible to follow a different line of causality here. Alexandre de Villedieu, for example, explains that his versified grammar, the *Doctrinale puerorum*, is motivated by a desire to eliminate erotic and morally dubious content from the grammar classroom. Could it be that new, less open attitudes toward sexuality might have motivated some of the pedagogical innovations of this period as well? It may not be possible to answer this question with archival documentation, but we might learn something just by paying attention to Alexandre de Villedieu's comments on the danger of teaching erotic pagan literature to children. His *Prooemium*, which opens the *Doctrinale* (ca. 1200), aligns the inaccessibility of the *auctores* with the "nonsense" of Maximianus, referring to the inassimilable erotic content of the works of the *auctores*:

> I am getting ready to write a Doctrinale ["book of instruction"] for newer
> students ["Scribere clericulis paro Doctrinale novellis"]
> and will adopt many works of my teachers.
> Instead of the nonsense of Maximianus boys will read
> those things which the ancients did not want to make accessible to their dear
> fellows. ["Iamque legent pueri pro nugis Maximiani / quae veteres sociis
> nolebant pandere caris"]
> May the Grace of the nurturing Spirit be present to this work.
> May it help me to complete something that may be of use.
> If the boys should be unable to pay full attention to it at first,
> let him then at least pay attention, who fulfills the tasks of a teacher,
> who reads it to the boys, and will disclose it to them in the language of the laity
> [i.e., the vernacular];
> Words [*voces*], which you must give different forms in different cases,
> I will first of all teach you to decline, in as easy a way I can. . . .
> Although this doctrine is not really general enough,
> yet it will be more useful than the nonsense of Maximianus.[40]

Unlike John of Salisbury, Alexandre seems to show a degree of disdain for the *auctores*. As he puts it, his *Doctrinale* will make available that which the *auctores* failed to make accessible to their contemporaries. Just as Marie de France famously made Priscian a synechdoche for the *auctores* (who wrote, in her words, "assez oscurement," quite obscurely) in her prologue, Alexandre cites Maximianus as a synechdoche, suggesting a broader concern with the value of pagan classical literature in the grammar classroom. Maximianus was a sixth-century Roman poet whose elegiac lamentations about old age fondly reconstruct the sexual adventures of his youth with a deliciously amoral sensibility. His Elegies were part of a set of six elementary Latin texts favored in thirteenth-century grammar curricula that came to be known as the *Sex Auctores*. This bundle of readings included the *Distichs* of Cato, the *Eclogue* of Theodulus, the fables of Avian, Statius's *Achilleid* and Claudian's *Rape of Proserpina*. For largely moral reasons, as the name implies, the *Sex Auctores* were soon revamped into what would become the *Octo Auctores morales*, a much more suitably Christian curriculum with the addition of modern works such as Bernard de Cluny's *De Contemptu Mundi* (On Contempt for the World), and which eliminated all but Cato and Theodulus from the original six. Alexandre's denigration of Maximianus in his *Prooemium* may have contributed to the elimination of

---

40 *Medieval Grammar and Rhetoric*, 576–77.

the latter from the grammar curriculum, especially given the huge and immediate popularity that the *Doctrinale* enjoyed.[41]

Perhaps influenced, then, by grammarians like Petrus Helias who had begun to divorce grammar from literature, Alexandre proposes an efficient method of learning Latin grammar that will be more easily memorized, thanks to its versification, and less encumbered by potentially morally dubious citations of the *auctores*. He does cite Cicero frequently but also includes even more examples from Scripture and from the Church Fathers. Indeed, Alexandre seems to believe that grammar can be "cleaned up" and that the eroticism of the grammar classroom is located in literal representations of love, sex, and desire in the *Sex Auctores*. It does not seem to occur to him, however, that there might be something intrinsically erotic about grammatical structures in and of themselves. However, dozens of Latin parodic poems, roughly contemporaneous with the *Doctrinale*, use grammatical terminology in sexually suggestive ways that seem to run counter to Alexandre's project. One of these, in particular "Scribere clericulis" (which appears in two German manuscripts), is a direct parody of the *Doctrinale*, and suggests a critique of Alexandre's project to clean up grammar:

> Scribere clericulis
> paro novellis omnibus
> per hoc tempus vernale.
> Renunciemus emulis
> nostris sevis doctoribus.
> Ad me, scolares, currite
> et hoc lete suscipite,
> quod scribo, doctrinale.
>
> Non posco manum ferule,
> non exigo sub verbere
> partes orationis.
> Proiciantur tabule,
> queramus, quid sit ludere
> cum virginale specie,
> que primule, non tercie
> sit declinacionis.
>
> Jam tempus est cognoscere
> quid feminini generis
> composita figura:
> quid sit casus inflectere

---

[41] *Medieval Grammar and Rhetoric*, 573–76.

> cum famulabus Veneris;
> quid copulat, coniunctio;
> quid signat interiectio,
> dum miscet cruri crura.
>
> Sunt silve resonabiles
> philomenosis cantibus,
> iam flores sunt in pratis;
> sunt virgines placabiles
> nostris novis amplexibus.
> Que cuius modi, discite,
> cuius sint forme, querite,
> cuius sint qualitatis.
>
> Et prima coniugatio
> cum sit presentis temporis,
> hec: amo, amas, amat
> sit nobis frequens lectio.
> Scola sit umbra nemoris,
> liber puelle facies,
> quam primitiva species
> legendam esse clamat.
>
> Dum ad choream tenditur
> gradu pluralis numeri;
> dum cantu conclamatur;
> dum sonus sono redditur,
> iungatur latus lateri,
> quod fixum sit vel mobile,
> quod Veneri flexibile,
> dum cantu conclamatur.
>
> Hic instat disputacio,
> vincant promissis precibus,
> non tandem ludo pari
> amoris sit relacio,
> sit fervor in amplexibus,
> dum demum verno tempori
> iam pratis, campis, nemori
> potestis colluctari![42]

I am getting ready to write to all new clerics in this springtime. Let us renounce our harsh (and diligent) schoolmasters. Hurry to me, scholars, and receive joyfully the *doctrinale* that I write./ I am not asking for, not demanding, the parts of speech by means of the rod or with blows. The tablets are thrown out. We ask [instead] what,

---

[42] Paul Lehmann, *Die Parodie Im Mittelalter* (Stuttgart: A. Hiersemann, 1963), 147–55.

of the virginal species, to play with, whether those of the first or those of the third declension./ Now it is time to learn what the composed figure of the feminine gender is, what it is to inflect case endings with the servants of Venus, what a copula, a conjunction, and an interjection signify, while mingling thigh with thigh./ All this is reasonable material for poems of easy friendship now that the flowers are in the fields. These virgins—allowing of our surprising embraces—you must learn: of which sort are they? what are their forms? you must ask: what qualities do they possess?/ And may this first conjugation—*amo, amas, amat*—when it is in the present tense be our regular study. May the shade of the wood be our school, and may the face of a girl be the book, which the primitive instinct of the kind is goaded to read./ While one is directed to a dance by the plural sum of degree [dance step]; while one is summoned by a song; and one sound is echoed by another sound, and while one is connected by conjunction, side by side, let what is firmly established be mobile instead, what is of Venus be flexible, while one is summoned by the song./ This one insists on a debate/ with their prayers (seduction) they will overcome promises/ a match of equals for not much longer/ may the grammar lesson be one of love/ may the passion be (found) in embraces,/ for at least as long as springtime lasts,/ then you all can wrestle in the/ meadows, fields, and groves.[43]

The opening lines duplicate the first line of the *Doctrinale*, nearly word for word. However, in the lines that follow the students are quickly exhorted to renounce, not Maximianus, but the harsh schoolmasters, perhaps figures for Alexandre de Villedieu himself, described in terms of the physical punishment they inflict on their grammar students. The classroom itself is transformed into a lush outdoor space, the pages of books become the faces of beautiful maidens, a lesson in logic is transformed into dance steps, classroom *disputatio* becomes a lovers' quarrel, and the lesson on verb tense and conjugation becomes that of *amo, amas, amat*, in an eternal and erotic present tense. Grammatical terms such as *flexus*, which denotes inflections in tense, mood, person, number, case, and gender, and *casus*, which denotes grammatical cases, nominative, genitive, dative, and so on, take on multiple erotic meanings. *Flexus*, derived from the verb *flecto*, to bend, bend over, bend to one's will, becomes *inflectere* and *flexibile* in the poem. *Casus*, derived from *cado*, to fall, to fall over, becomes sexually suggestive in the line "quid sit casus inflectere."

We can read this parody as operating along the logic of a "return of the repressed." However, the repressed eroticism that "returns" is not in the form of Virgilian or Ovidian, or even Maximianian, perversions. Rather, it is grammar itself in its most elementary structures that turns out to be erotic. As the author of

---

43 Translation mine.

this parody—and dozens of other similar erotic grammar poems that survive from the period—would suggest, Alexandre's attempt to "clean up" the grammar classroom backfires, producing an even more erotically charged pedagogical framework that, now stripped of literary content, isolates and foregrounds grammar's intrinsically erotic focus on connections, disjunctions, and substitutions.

This subversive parody of the *Doctrinale*, although it urges the young students to leave the space of the classroom, finally reminds its readers that the erotic intensities found out in the world nonetheless originate in the grammar classroom. The grammar classroom channels the inherent eroticism of grammatical language and shapes it. Trains it. The erotic grammatical metaphor, whether used playfully or seriously, is a perpetual reminder of this training.

In effect, Alan of Lille allegorizes the notion of the grammar classroom as a space for the training of desire by making Venus (i.e., Desire) a student in Lady Nature's grammar classroom. What's more, the making of Venus into a grammar student is itself contained within a larger grammar lesson; the narrator is already positioned as a student in Nature's grammar classroom. As Mark Jordan notes, the citation of Boethius's *Consolation of Philosophy* indicates that what is at stake, above all, is the reeducation of the narrator.[44] Indeed, the entirety of prose sections four through eight is written, as though in a classroom, in the form of a pedagogical dialogue in which Nature speaks as the authoritative *magister* while the dreamer-poet speaks as the eager and obsequious student. This means that the classroom becomes a kind of recursive *mise-en-abime* for Alan. Nature explains that, just as responsibility over the union of matter and form was delegated to her, she herself delegated responsibility over the continuation of this union, by means of sexual reproduction, to Venus. This delegation—or, in neoplatonic terms, emanation[45]—is described significantly as a grammar lesson. Thus, a second grammar lesson is contained within the narrator's lesson, suggesting an infinite regress or a spiraling effect that situates the reader in the next circle out as a grammar student. The grammar classroom thus expands infinitely to encompass all things. This expansive quality of the grammar classroom in Alan's *Plaint* conveys the same idea expressed in the parodist's calquing of the language of the grammar classroom onto the fields, girls, dances, trees, outside of the classroom. If the grammar classroom is a space in which student desire is trained, it must also by definition be expansive, transferable, infinitely if necessary, so that "all things" can become objects on which to attach one's desire.

---

44 Jordan, *Invention of Sodomy*, 72.
45 On Alan of Lille's cosmology, see Jeffrey Bardzell, *Speculative Grammar and Stoic Language Theory in Medieval Allegorical Narrative: From Prudentius to Alan of Lille* (New York: Routledge, 2010).

Of course, the expansiveness of the grammar classroom also accounts for the expansive multiplication of perverse desires since expansion implies a kind of degradation in Alan's cosmology. These perverse desires (re)appear in the classroom as monstrous grammatical combinations, an inverse movement that brings what is "outside" of the grammar classroom to the always already inside. Nature does not shy away from enumerating varieties of sexual coupling in her grammar lesson—somehow more vivid, more imaginatively suggestive because expressed via grammatical euphemisms rather than via literal designation. But what purpose could such a florid enumeration of sexual configurations have in Nature's training of the narrator's, and by extension the reader's, desire? Nature's list of perverse desires (what she terms humanity's "grammatical" errors) begins with examples taken from classical literature, from Helen's infidelity and Medea's infanticide to Narcissus's destructive self-love. She then goes on to describe a whole catalogue of sexual perversions entirely through use of grammatical metaphors. As her lesson explains, some men "embrace those of masculine gender only" while others "those of feminine gender," and some prefer "those of common, or epicene gender." Others are described as "belonging to the heteroclite class," reclining (=declining) with "those of female gender in winter and those of masculine gender in summer."[46] Here, again, a comparison with the *Doctrinale* and its parody is called for: Nature's movement from pagan eroticism to purely grammatical eroticism inversely mirrors Alexandre's quasi-expulsion of the *auctores* set against his parodist's needling insistence that the erotics of grammar cannot be removed from the classroom as long as grammatical categories retain their erotic metaphoricity. Nature allows for both levels of eroticism in her classroom, both erotic classical allusions and erotic grammar metaphors. Although it is not always obvious which sexual practices these metaphors refer to—for example, what is the difference between men who embrace epicene gender and those who are themselves heteroclite?—the underlying assumption Nature makes here is that grammatical categories are transferable to the realm of sexuality.[47] The classroom becomes transferable to the world, an ever-dilating expanse of potential objects

---

46 Alan of Lille, *The Plaint of Nature*, trans. James Sheridan (Toronto: Pontifical Institute of Mediaeval Studies, 1980), 136.
47 The transferability of grammatical categories outside of the once-narrow purview of grammar was, of course, one of the difficult questions in contemporaneous debates about the liberal arts curriculum. Nature does not offer a clear-cut response to these debates. On the one hand, she uses grammatical categories to describe a whole number of perversions, implying that language itself is full of perverse categories and should not be used as a guide in sexual ethics. On the other hand, in the next prose section she grounds her lesson in sexual orthodoxy with "fundamental" grammatical categories.

of desire. In a word, Nature's grammar classroom *grammaticalizes* desire. And although grammaticalized desire might always potentially increase the quality and quantity of sexual couplings, it also simultaneously inscribes desire with a drive to limit its expression, a drive to orthodoxy. And so, although Nature's classroom is expansive, and thus prone to perversion or degradation, it is also a space where desire can be effectively disciplined.

Although Alan and the *Doctrinale* parodist both invoke the grammar classroom as a figurative image, we can still draw some conclusions concerning the place of desire in contemporaneous grammar instruction. For one, the parody suggests that the place of desire in the grammar classroom is in question, an object of polemic. For another, both Alan and the parodist suggest that grammar cannot be conceived of separately from desire. Grammatical structures are desirous and human sexual desire is structured like a grammar. By focusing on these transitional figures and on the question of grammar's ethical value in the mode of debate, we are able to reconstruct obliquely what was imagined to have been lost in the shift from grammar-as-orthopraxy to grammar-as-sodomy and the concurrent shift from early medieval pedagogical grammar to high/late medieval speculative/modistic grammar. Essentially we glimpse a sophisticated, although in some ways contradictory, account of the linguistic nature of desire and the desirous nature of language, a willingness to engage ambiguity in the grammar classroom and a canny awareness of the fact that the same facet of grammar conditions *both* the disorderly nature of desire and the drive to inscribe limits. One can easily understand, therefore, the strong sense of loss expressed in John of Salisbury's writing. A loss, not simply of an old homosocial pedagogical tradition, but also of a sophisticated and artful understanding of desire and language.

Bibliography

Aelius Donatus. *The Ars Minor of Donatus: For One Thousand Years the Leading Textbook of Grammar*. Translated by Wayland Johnson Chase. Madison: University of Wisconsin Press, 1926.

Alan of Lille. *The Plaint of Nature*. Translated by James Sheridan. Toronto: Pontifical Institute of Mediaeval Studies, 1980.

Alford, John. "The Grammatical Metaphor: A Survey of Its Use in the Middle Ages." *Speculum* 57.4 (1982): 728–60.

Alighieri, Dante. *The Divine Comedy: Inferno 2*. Commentary. Translated by Charles S. Singleton. Princeton: Princeton University Press, 1989.

Bardzell, Jeffrey. *Speculative Grammar and Stoic Language Theory in Medieval Allegorical Narrative: From Prudentius to Alan of Lille*. New York: Routledge, 2010.

Boswell, John. *Christianity, Social Tolerance, and Homosexuality: Gay People in Western Europe from the Beginning of the Christian Era to the Fourteenth Century.* Chicago: University of Chicago Press, 1980.
Cestaro, Gary P. *Dante and the Grammar of the Nursing Body.* Notre Dame: University of Notre Dame Press, 2003.
Cleaver, Laura. "Grammar and Her Children: Learning to Read in the Art of the Twelfth Century." *Marginalia* 9.1 (2009): n. p. http://www.marginalia.co.uk/journal/09education/cleaver.php.
Derrida, Jacques. *Of Grammatology.* Baltimore: Johns Hopkins University Press, 1998.
Desmond, Marilynn. *Ovid's Art and the Wife of Bath: The Ethics of Erotic Violence.* Ithaca: Cornell University Press, 2006.
Ferruolo, Stephen C. *The Origins of the University: The Schools of Paris and Their Critics, 1100–1215.* Stanford: Stanford University Press, 1985.
Gautier de Coinci. *De Sainte Leocade: Au Tans Que Sainz Hyldefons Estoit Arcevesques De Tholete Cui Nostre Dame Donna L'aube De Prelaz: Miracle Versifié / Vilamo-Pentti, Eva.* Suomalaisen Tiedeakatemian Toimituksia. Annales Academiae Scientiarum Fennicae. Helsinki: Suomalainen Tiedeakatemia, 1950.
Petrus Helias. *Summa Super Priscianum.* Edited by Leo Alexander Reilly. Toronto: Pontifical Institute of Mediaeval Studies, 1993.
Holsinger, Bruce. *Music, Body, and Desire in Medieval Culture: Hildegard of Bingen to Chaucer.* Palo Alto: Stanford University Press, 2001.
Irvine, Matthew. *The Making of Textual Culture: Grammatica and Literary Theory, 350–1100.* Cambridge: Cambridge University Press, 1994.
John of Salisbury. *Metalogicon.* Translated by Daniel D. McGarry. Berkeley: University of California Press, 1962.
Jordan, Mark. *The Invention of Sodomy in Christian Theology.* Chicago: University of Chicago Press, 1997.
Lehmann, Paul. *Die Parodie Im Mittelalter.* Stuttgart: A. Hiersemann, 1963.
Lenzen, Rolf. "'*Altercatio Ganimedis et Helene*' Kritische Edition mit Kommentar." *Mittellateinisches Jahrbuch* 7 (1972): 161–86.
Lombardi, Elena. *The Syntax of Desire: Language and Love in Augustine, the Modistae, Dante.* Toronto: University of Toronto Press, 2007.
Martianus Capella and the Seven Liberal Arts: The Marriage of Philology and Mercury. Translated by William Harris Stahl, Richard Johnson, and E. L. Burge. New York: University of Columbia Press, 1992.
Medieval Grammar and Rhetoric: Language Arts and Literary Theory, AD 300–1475. Edited by Rita Copeland and Ineke Sluiter. Oxford: Oxford University Press, 2009.
Moser, Thomas C. *A Cosmos of Desire: The Medieval Latin Erotic Lyric in English Manuscripts.* Ann Arbor: University of Michigan Press, 2004.
Paetow, Louis John. *The Arts Courses at Medieval Universities with Special Reference to Grammar and Rhetoric.* Champaign: University Studies of the University of Illinois, 1910.
Stehling, Thomas. *Medieval Latin Poems of Male Love and Friendship.* New York: Garland, 1984.
Stock, Brian. *Augustine the Reader: Meditation, Self-Knowledge, and the Ethics of Interpretation.* Cambridge: Harvard University Press, 1996.

The Etymologies of Isidore of Seville. Edited and translated by Stephen A. Barney, W. J. Lewis, J. A. Beach, and Oliver Berghof. Cambridge: Cambridge University Press, 2006.

Vance, Eugene. *Mervelous Signals: Poetics and Sign Theory in the Middle Ages.* Lincoln: University of Nebraska Press, 1989.

Ziolkowski, Jan. *Alan of Lille's Grammar of Sex: The Meaning of Grammar to a Twelfth-Century Intellectual.* Cambridge: Medieval Academy of America, 1985.

Will Rogers
Chapter 2
Failed Orientations: The Spaces of Sexual Histories and Failures

The twelfth-century dream vision *Altercatio Ganimedis et Helene*, or *Ganymede and Helen*, depicts a debate between Helen who is in love with Ganymede, who seems uninterested in a female lover. These cross-purposes – Helen in love, Ganymede without interest – introduce a debate: whom do men want? The answer is given through images of disgust which Helen and Ganymede use to debate each other, and these images – the very center of the *Ganymede and Helen* – nevertheless lead to their marriage at the end. This debate, voiced in this dream space, almost seems prophetic – the objects of men's desire find themselves reoriented toward each other and the marriage seems an abrupt, if fitting end. While the marriage orients the poem toward what is normative, this poetic dream space with its debate centered around disgusting images of the body and sex and twisting of time and knowledge maintains a core of queerness that cannot be fully erased and a failure of Ganymede and Helen that must be explained.

Contextualizing the poem by way of Jack Halberstam's "queer art of failure" offers the opportunity to view some of the ways *Ganymede and Helen* anticipates and voices queerness. The queer art of failure is not simply losing or defeat, but the articulation of a different relationship to identity and success, even a kind of style or way of existing. In this way, failure might be decoupled from success and made into a queer term, where "under certain circumstances, failing, losing, forgetting, unmaking, undoing, unbecoming, not knowing may in fact offer more creative, more cooperative, more surprising ways of being in the world."[1] Indeed, in the revision of Ganymede and Helen as interlocutors before they wed each other, the poet shows how their failures – Helen's inability to see the sodomite, Ganymede's failure to win the debate – animate the tensions between Helen and Ganymede in the poem. We might first look at the end of the poem, seeing in Ganymede's failure to act normatively as a "man" the kind of "queer failure" that opens up new opportunities for identity for the cupbearer of Zeus. Even further, the failure of both Helen and Ganymede to recognize each other as somehow

---
[1] Jack Halberstam, *The Queer Art of Failure* (Durham: Duke University Press, 2011), 2.

other than expected – Helen as dominant, Ganymede as submissive – presents a chance to revise and review these characters before and beyond their marriage and the loss of their subversive characters. These more "surprising ways of being in the world" are ones where these two figures are centered not as objects of rapacious desires but as interlocutors who claim poetic space and authority through their frank speech and revel in their orientations toward those who desire them. Their marriage, perhaps meant to close this debate and excise what is queer about their interactions, itself fails to save the Dreamer who sees them quarrel and then wed. The poet's ending repentance is full of potential for sins which might have been committed or which might yet occur.

For this essay, which builds on this notion of queer art of failure, I want to think about the number of ways this poem might queer itself, and anticipate important directions in queer theory, including considerations on space and orientation, what Sara Ahmed calls "queer phenomenology," and examinations of time and history, building on Elizabeth Freeman's explorations of "chrononormativity," "erotohistoriography," and "temporal drag," as well as Heather Love's "feeling backward." All three of these queer approaches – failure, orientation, history – seem bound up in the figure of Ganymede in the poem, pointing to the numerous ways the poem looks at the queer and we might look at the poem.[2] Together with failure, these categories of queer study build upon each other in this poem, suggesting that this medieval work serves as a test case for locating what is queer, across time, in both medieval and postmedieval materials. Indeed, failure is implicitly central to Ahmed's, Freeman's, and Love's discussion of space/orientation, time, and history, respectively (if one can even separate these three concepts). For Ahmed, calling queer a sexual orientation recalls the word's etymology – as a kind of twisting – and that identity's spatial relations. One is queer *in relation* to what is not queer, what is straight, itself a word and condition which recalls a point in space – not twisted but direct between two points. As a reflection of space, straight too encapsulates ease and the absence of pain – the shortest way between two points, two identities, two lovers is a straight line, in other words. To be queer is to feel the burden of space and distance. For Freeman and Love the study of queer pasts and queer histories is necessarily one which suggests something like failure – Freeman notes there might be something pleasurable in being out of time – her "temporal drag" complicates some of the narratives of progress that a larger term like

---

[2] This approach is borrowed somewhat from Masha Raskolnikov's reading of the *Clerk's Tale*, itself guided by Wallace Steven's "13 Ways of Looking at a Blackbird," which she presented at the 43rd Sewanee Medieval Colloquium at the University of the South in 2017.

"queer" might suggest, as the nostalgia for identities of the past pulls subjects back to them. But for Love, the pleasure might be found in what is painful, as negative affects and the erasure of queer history can motivate political progress in the present. These citations of modern queer theory and their usefulness in interpretations of *Ganymede and Helen* also show just how modern the poem can be, a characteristic that I further emphasize through the poem's comparison to *Angels in America*, a play that has been the subject of medievalist inquiry for a few decades. Together these theories and play might open up the past in order to begin reading the future of the queer past in *Ganymede and Helen*.[3]

But before I discuss the present and the future, a turn to the past is helpful. Perhaps little known today, *Ganymede and Helen* does offer productive connections with other discussions of premodern queerness and examinations of the normative in language and sexuality. Whether the poem maintains any space for queerness in its ultimate condemnation of homosexuality is itself debatable, it does certainly feature in debates on the effect of sodomy on language, reproduction, and nature. Indeed, many examinations of the poem center on its relation to Alan of Lille's *Plaint of Nature* where Ganymede appears too in a rebuttal of the exchange between Nature and the Dreamer, a scene that is instructive for reading Ganymede in *Ganymede and Helen*. In responding to Nature's claims about the "strange and profane language" she must use to describe the unnaturalness fleshed out by poets, the Dreamer responds

> I wonder why, when you consider the statements of the poets, you load the strings of the above attacks against the contagions of the human race alone, although we read that the gods, too, have limped around the same circle of aberration. For Jupiter, translating the Phyrigian youth to the realms above, transferred there a proportionate love for him on his transference. The one he had made his wine-master by day he made his subject in bed by night.[4]

This sole direct reference to Ganymede in *Plaint* suggests a number of ideas not only about Ganymede's larger depictions but also about the similarities between *Plaint* and *Ganymede and Helen* which demand some attention here.

---

3 See, for example, Benilde Montgomery, "*Angels in America* as Medieval Mystery," *Modern Drama* 4 (1998): 596–606. Montgomery also notes the critical response to the play, especially from queer theorists such as Leo Bersani (596). Also of interest is Steven F. Kruger's "Identity and Conversion in *Angels in America*," in *Approaching the Millennium: Essays on Angels in America*, ed. Deborah R. Geis and Steven F. Kruger (Ann Arbor: University of Michigan Press, 1997), 151–71.

4 Alan of Lille, *Plaint of Nature*, trans. James J. Sheridan (Toronto: Pontifical Institute of Mediaeval Studies, 1980), 137–39.

Ganymede is the Dreamer's response to Nature's condemnation of poetic treatments of sodomy and the unnatural, one which, while not an excuse for human sodomy, seems to use the divine sins of Jupiter to mitigate the force of Nature's critique against human sin. In this somewhat ambiguous condemnation the Dreamer is necessarily calling attention to the rape and abduction of Ganymede, a story whose ubiquity is signaled by the lack of any direct naming for Ganymede, other than the Phyrigian youth. And like Helen in *Ganymede and Helen*, Nature echoes (if one takes an earlier date for *Ganymede and Helen* and a later one for *Plaint*) Helen's apparently contrived reluctance to speak in terms that are graphic.[5] Indeed, like Nature, Helen worries that "I don't know which way to turn, for if I do not speak on a par with the vicious,/ I shall be called the loser."[6] For both *Ganymede and Helen* and *Plaint*, language and sexuality seem connected in their construction as either normative and natural or nonnormative.

These connections between *Ganymede and Helen* and *Plaint* certainly help frame how Ganymede might be a repository for nonnormative sexuality and its effects on nature and language. Like *Ganymede and Helen*, *Plaint* emphasizes some aspects of Ganymede's nonnormative identity clearly although Alan of Lille more forcefully condemns the same-sex activities embodied by Ganymede, even if the Dreamer attempts to halfheartedly debate the culpability for sodomy. Nevertheless, the ties between the two dream visions are made apparent in Ganymede, who enjoys a robust afterlife in the Christian Middle Ages. Indeed, Ganymede, as V. A. Kolve shows, has an afterlife in the high Middle Ages during which Zeus's cupbearer is often a symbol for other kinds of attachments beyond queer desire, even as that queerness inheres

---

5 Barbara Newman, *God and the Goddesses: Vision, Poetry, and Belief in the Middle Ages* (Philadelphia: University of Pennsylvania Press, 2005), 91. Arguing for an earlier date for *Ganymede and Helen* (*Altercatio*), Newman suggests that *Plaint* echoes *Ganymede and Helen*.
6 *Ganymede and Helen*, 201–2. For a translation of *Altercatio Ganimedis et Helene*, see John Boswell's *Ganymede and Helen*, 381–89. For this essay, I have cited this edition by line number and Boswell's title, while nevertheless consulting Rolf Lenzen's critical edition of the Latin manuscripts in "'Altercatio Ganimedis et Helene': Kritische Edition mit Kommentar," *Mittellateinisches Jahrbuch* 7 (1972): 161–86. Boswell's edition is based primarily on Lenzen's text but, according to his footnote (on 381), he nevertheless consulted a manuscript (Houghton Library MS Lat. 198) at Harvard University for his translation. Thomas Stehling's translation, printed in *Medieval Latin Poems of Male Love and Friendship*, trans. Stehling (New York: Garland Publishing, 1985) was also consulted but not used or cited in the essay. I have checked Lenzen's Latin edition against Boswell's translation.

nevertheless. Kolve's "Ganymede/*Son of Getron*: Medieval Monasticism and the Drama of Same-Sex Desire" traces

> a late-twelfth-century St. Nicholas play called *Filius Getronis* (*The Son of Getron*) that has been little studied, and never in this context. I want to set it against the anxiety occasioned in medieval monasteries concerning same-sex desire, especially across generations, between men and youths or boys, and the ways in which the monastic community sought to control such desire and rechannel it into acceptable forms. My subject is not man/boy love in the modern criminalized sense of that term, but rather the ways in which medieval monasticism acknowledged the possibility of such emotion, sometimes (as in this play) allowed it an unusual degree of dignity, and urgently sought viable forms for its transcendence.[7]

In Kolve's wide-ranging article, one can see why Ganymede becomes a flashpoint, if you will, for affections and desires that might map onto Ganymede's own mythological story, especially in monastic contexts. Novices and monks in a community could model, problematically, the kinds of dynamics of abduction and servitude which the ancient myths centered on Ganymede depict. In the space of such highly charged homosocial spaces, where intergenerational bonds might be formed between monastic figures, the echoes of Ganymede have the power, according to Kolve, to redirect these homosocial, and homoerotic, elements to paper over the troublesome desires which these spaces almost certainly produced.[8] And while the author of the poem cannot be known with any certainty – Boswell mentions evidence of an author from southern France – the material, like many of the other expressions of same-sex love from the high Middle Ages that Boswell includes in *Christianity, Social Tolerance, and Homosexuality* (*CSTH*) is certainly legible in a monastic context.[9]

So while at first glance it does seem odd to include this poem as any indication of premodern queer identity, for its apparent condemnation of sodomy and same-sex desire, it is a rich source for fleshing out what premodern queerness means. This short Latin dialogue, with its 270 lines, nevertheless reflects much of the critical discourse surrounding sodomy, pederasty, and the role of passivity in

---

[7] V. A. Kolve, "Ganymede/*Son of Getron*: Medieval Monasticism and the Drama of Same-Sex Desire," *Speculum* 73.4 (1998): 1014–67 at 1018.
[8] See also Mathew Kuefler, "Male Friendship and the Suspicion of Sodomy in Twelfth-Century France," in *The Boswell Thesis: Essays on Christianity, Social Tolerance, and Homosexuality* (Chicago: University of Chicago Press, 2006), 179–212. In discussing some of the afterlives of Ganymede, although not his main focus, Kuefler asserts the "image of Jove and Ganymede [in *Roman d'Énéas*] itself depends on the parallels between the mythical rapture of the adolescent male by an adult male for domestic and sexual service and the contemporary 'theft' of boys into military household as foster-sons" (189).
[9] John Boswell, *Christianity, Social Tolerance, and Homosexuality: Gay People in Western Europe from the Beginning of the Christian Era to the Fourteenth Century* (Chicago: University of Chicago Press, 1980), 258.

the twelfth century. And, according to John Boswell in *CSTH*, while short the poem is remarkable, for many reasons. "Modern scholarship has largely ignored this poem, but it was extremely popular in the Middle Ages: it survives wholly or in part in manuscripts all over Europe, from Italy to England, and it was recited aloud to students and known by heart by many educated persons. Its influence on subsequent literature was profound."[10] The extant manuscripts seem to demonstrate the reach of this particular text, and the poem's echoes in similar poems, many of which Boswell includes in *CSTH*, speak to Ganymede's versatility as a symbol for same-sex love and premodern queerness.[11] In this way, the poem also serves to encapsulate both the desire for a queer past and the difficulties in finding it. Rather than reproduction and the energies of marriage that consume the end of the poem couched in the citation of Nature's creations and future considerations, the poem implicitly gives voice to concerns for those who desire a queer past, a past which we might try to recover. According to Heather Love, that

> effort to recapture the past is doomed from the start. To reconstruct the past, we build on ruins, to bring it to life, we chase after the fugitive dead. Bad enough if you want to tell the story of a conquering race, but to remember history's losers is worse, for the loss that swallows the dead absorbs these others into even more profound obscurity. The difficulty of not reaching the dead will not keep us from trying.[12]

The motif of loss here is different from Halberstam's formulation, of course. Love is speaking to the destruction of the histories, mythologies, and narratives of those who have been conquered, but in her promise here we might see glimpses of Halberstam's queer failures. In Love's queer historiography, the absence or loss of traditional evidence gives rise to desire to see, and implicitly I think the ability to see beyond what counts as traditional evidence and record. Likewise, for *Ganymede and Helen*, if Ganymede does lose to Helen in the poem's debate, it is that loss that will recover some of what is gone. For the poem, losing offers both a challenge to the enforced productivity of proto-heterosexual logic and an anticipation of queer historiography, reading in the gaps and filling in lost desires from the past.

---

10 Boswell, *Christianity, Social Tolerance, and Homosexuality*, 255–56.
11 See, for example, Boswell's inclusion of "Ganymede and Hebe" (392–400) and "Ganymede" (401) in *CSTH*.
12 Heather Love, *Feeling Backward: Loss and the Politics of Queer History* (Cambridge: Harvard University Press, 2007), 21.

In thinking through how this queer historiography is connected to "queer failure," we might return to Halberstam and see how Love's characterization of history's losers above connects to failure as style. According to Halberstam,

> Failing is something queers do and have always done exceptionally well; for queers, failure can be a style, to cite Quentin Crisp, a way of life, to cite Foucault, and it can stand in contrast to the grim scenarios of success that depend upon "trying and trying again."[13]

What I suggest Ganymede, as a figure, and as a figure in the *Ganymede and Helen*, might show is just how we can map the queer, with respect to time, desire, and failure, and to see, again, the similarities to and differences from queers, medieval and postmedieval. The use of Halberstam's theoretical framework – which builds upon animated movies and CGI creations – might be met with multiple objections here. *Ganymede and Helen* is no trifle, it seems, no silly *tour de force* centered on animated beings, but it was popular, and, like the animated works Halberstam tracks, uses fictive beings to hint at somewhat eternal or moral truths. These popular works might hide their subversive critiques, as the comparison between *Ganymede and Helen* and *Angels in America* demonstrates.

Ganymede in Heaven: *Angels in America*

As a Latin poem that survives in a number of manuscripts, *Ganymede and Helen* seems to celebrate the normative in a somewhat authoritative context. In order to trace how *Ganymede and Helen* maintains queerness in this authoritative context and to flesh out the medieval poem's handling of queer time and space, all while making sense of the failure of Ganymede to win the debate, I am drawn first to *Angels in America*. *Angels in America* is a text where this union of normative and nonnormative echoes and whose treatment of queerness is likewise ambiguous: as a meditation on AIDS, homosexuality, and religion in the late twentieth century, the play makes clear how the narrative of *Ganymede and Helen* moves – how a figure of queerness (Ganymede) and spurned woman (Helen) eventually become husband and wife, a relationship that, in its development, reflects two separate moments in *Angels in America*. The debate between Helen and Ganymede is enlivened and its revelatory power exposed set alongside Prior's first meeting with Harper, the wife of a closeted Mormon, in a dream-like space. This space reveals Prior's homosexuality and

---

[13] Halberstam, *Queer Art of Failure*, 1.

centers on his bodily infirmity, a moment that implicitly rehearses the homophobic attack Helen uses against Ganymede. While Harper and Prior discuss, Helen and Ganymede debate in their *altercatio*, as Helen emphasizes Ganymede's obsession with youth:

> "Tell me, youth, when youthful good looks change,
> When you grow a beard, when your face gets wrinkles,
> When your chest turns bushy, when your hole grows tough,
> What anxious stud will dream of you then?"[14]

Helen's provocative question – which anxious stud will dream of Ganymede once he is no longer young, when age has made him mature, even old? – anticipates, first, some of the interactions between Harper and Prior and then an argument – even *altercation* – between Harper and her husband, Joe. Compare for example *Angel*'s example of another coming out in a dream space:

> Prior: Something surprising.
> Harper: Yes.
> Prior: Your husband's a homo.[15]

This brief dialogue offers the first glimpse of the unraveling of Harper's marriage to Joe, the chiseled Mormon lawyer, a closeted gay man whose appearance suggests something of the embodiment of Reagan's America, defined by its whiteness, compulsory heterosexuality, and lack of sickness or impairment. While Prior reveals what surely Harper already suspects, the dream space of the play in large part undoes the totality of the fiction of her marriage and Joe's orientation. Indeed, in the "threshold of revelation," the liminal space of their shared hallucination, Harper reveals the extent of Prior's illness and suffering from AIDS and his inner freedom from the ravages of the disease – the human cost of which now seems almost incalculable and somewhat obscured by mainstream appeal and success of the play. And likewise, in *Ganymede and Helen*, the dream space where the Dreamer first sees Helen and Ganymede offers a threshold of revelation for these two mythological figures, where they both first misrecognize each other and then debate their relative worth to men. Even so, this space erases some of their earlier literary contexts: there are no direct connections between this Ganymede and that of mythology, where Ganymede is

---

14 *Ganymede and Helen*, 177–80.
15 Tony Kushner, *Angels in America: A Gay Fantasia on National Themes: Revised and Complete Edition 20th Anniversary Edition* (New York: Theatre Communications Group, Inc., 2013), 33.

often presented as the cupbearer for Zeus.[16] While the source of Helen or Ganymede cannot be known with any certainty in this poem, there are, especially concerning Helen, signal differences from the Homeric tradition and the depiction of Helen from Ovid's *Heroides*, even as there are similarities. Menelaus is not present nor is Paris, even as her condemnations of Ganymede strike a similar moral tone to her condemnations of Paris in *Heroides*.[17]

The absence of Helen's husband and her lover, and the intimacy she desires to enjoy with Ganymede, along with her surprise and disgust at the unveiling of Ganymede as a lover of sodomy, are striking when read alongside Harper and Prior. Indeed, the collapse of Harper's marriage in her hallucination which follows her surprise seems to echo Helen's own surprise of Ganymede's submissive sexual behavior. Harper articulates the mutual disgust Joe and she feel toward each other, especially in the bedroom, giving something of a conclusion to what *might* have happened in the poem's ending marriage between Helen and Ganymede:

> Yes, I'm the enemy. That's easy. That doesn't change. You think you're the only one who hates sex; I do; I hate it with you; I do. I dream that you batter away at me till all my joints come apart, like wax, and I fall into pieces. It's like a punishment. It was wrong of me to marry you. I knew you. . . . It's a sin, and it's killing us both.[18]

The "it" here, that thing between them, is the unspeakable for both characters, for the majority of the play, until Harper asks Joe if he's a "homo." Absolutely erased, absolutely highlighted, Joe's homosexuality becomes the excuse for this failure of heterosexual pleasure and reproduction. It is a moment that seems absolutely modern: the thirty-something couple, pulled apart by religion and identity in a 1980s New York riven by a "gay plague." Indeed, it's a queer place to be: writing about a twelfth-century monastic text with reference to a modern American play. As many have noted, the play itself has been and continues to be a success and it is wise to question its queer potentiality and its place in an essay that opens a volume on new views of historicized queerness.[19]

---

16 For a discussion of Ganymede's abduction, see Ovid, *Metamorphoses*, Bk X:143–219.

17 Ovid's *Heroides* 17 characterizes Helen as outraged at Paris's acts and as faithful to her husband. For a discussion of Ovid's influence and readership in the Middle Ages, see Marilynn Desmond, "Ovid's *Ars Amatoria* and the Wounds of Love," in her *Ovid's Art and the Wife of Bath: The Ethics of Erotic Violence* (Ithaca: Cornell University Press, 2006), 35–54 but especially 53–54.

18 Kushner, *Angels in America*, 37.

19 In particular, Montgomery's "*Angels in America* as Medieval Mystery" cites David Savran's critique of the play's ambivalent critique, even support, of Reagan's politics. I am indebted to one of the reader's suggestions to view this play and its inclusion here with suspicion.

But the seemingly hegemonic success of the play and its handling of sodomy, same-sex attraction and the interplay between normative and nonnormative sexuality positions the play as somewhat of an ideal entry into *Ganymede and Helen*, with the medieval poem's debate between Helen and Ganymede, following Ganymede's submission to Helen, and their competition for male attention.

Nature's Failures?

The very structure of *Ganymede and Helen* calls attention to the structural failure of a kind of proto-heterosexuality to contain what is queer. Indeed, one of the signal ways the poem registers the failure of its ending is in the framing of its debate – not just in the actual framing and orientation of Helen's and Ganymede's bodies but also in the contextualization of the poem as one extolling nature and Nature personified. Indeed, as Barbara Newman has argued,

> these excerpts from the "Altercatio" suggest the general tenor of debates about homosexuality in the later twelfth century. Appeals to animal behavior could backfire, as Helen discovers. Most animals are obviously not monogamous, but more to the point, there was no other ethical context in which clerics taught that rational humans should imitate irrational beasts. Boswell has shown that two contradictory ideas about "natural sexuality" seem to have taken hold among writers at about the same time: first, the notion that certain creatures – such as the hare, the hyena, and the weasel – were "innately" homosexual and therefore to be shunned, and second, the belief that homosexuality is "unnatural" because it does not occur at all among animals. Alan of Lille alludes to both ideas in *De planctu*.[20]

The poem ends, as one supposes it must, with the union of Ganymede and Helen. This ending and its celebratory tone of proto-heterosexual marriage is anything but a victory, at least for Ganymede. Ganymede loses both the debate and his desires. Then, it is clear that if the twelfth-century dream vision is an effort at supporting a kind of premodern heterosexuality and reproductive futurity, it fails completely. Ganymede, whose passivity disgusts Helen, is still conquered by Helen at the end of the poem, and merely becomes her bottom. Even if that failure can be overlooked and their marriage celebrated, then the final ending of the dream vision, too, hints at failure. I would suggest just as "the apparent victory of Helen should be viewed cautiously," so then should the Dreamer's ending repentance.[21] The Dreamer awakes to find whatever solutions are available to Ganymede for nonnormative desire are not available to him. If

---

20 Newman, *God and the Goddesses*, 92.
21 Boswell, *Christianity, Social Tolerance, and Homosexuality*, 258.

a monastic author, then in his homosocial environment there is no room for marriage. If not, failure seems perpetual, as the potential for sodomy seems eternal in his ending repentance. In light of these layers of failure, how might failure actually be reinterpreted? How does failure actually become a way to interrogate and criticize those structures which render Ganymede a loser? In the lines that describe Ganymede's loss, Ganymede's submissive nature in fact remains, even as he seems to change and become a figure of normative sexuality:

> He is silent. Reason rises to speak.
> She prudently limits herself to a few words:
> "There is no need of a judge," she says, "the matter speaks for itself.
> "I say to the boy, enough. The boy is conquered."[22]

The reclamation of Ganymede for marriage, for the active role, suggests a kind of ambiguity that rewrites time, space, and victory in ambivalent ways. Even losing, Ganymede's position, voice, and history are articulated in the poem, and the poet's descriptions of all three suggest a rather hollow victory for Helen and heterosexuality. Indeed, the debate between Ganymede and Helen probably best exemplifies what might be read as ambivalence on the subject of homosexuality. The poet makes Ganymede lose the debate, and at the poem's conclusion abjures homosexual acts: "Let the Sodomites blush, the Gomorrhans weep/ Let everyone guilty of this deed repent."[23] His poem *eventually* stands as a condemnation of homosexuality, even as the poem's structure gives equal time to arguments on both sides of the question, and in the body of the debate the poet lets both Ganymede and Helen "score points."[24] If anything, Ganymede gets lines that are more repulsive and wounding to Helen. He describes her vagina and those of other women as "a yawning cave" and a "sticky bush" and as a "hole whose stink is worse than anything else in the world."[25] These insults are given in response to Helen's claim that

> Your Venus is sterile and fruitless,
> And highly injurious to womankind.
> When a male mounts a male in so reprobate a fashion,
> A monstrous Venus imitates a woman.[26]

---

22 *Ganymede and Helen*, 251–54.
23 *Ganymede and Helen*, 268–69. Boswell's note in *CSTH* following these lines (389) is instructive, as he notes they are part of an expanded ending, found only in the Houghton manuscript.
24 Boswell, *Christianity, Social Tolerance, and Homosexuality*, 258–59.
25 *Ganymede and Helen*, 230–31.
26 *Ganymede and Helen*, 225–28.

Helen's weapon, of course, is Ganymede's ejaculate – the "tear of Venus between your thighs" – and he is silenced.[27] Echoing or anticipating Alan of Lille's dream vision (Michael Johnson's essay in this collection touches more on the relationship between the two poems), these lines seem to match those of Nature personified in the *Plaint of Nature*. The poem begins with radical sameness: both Helen and Ganymede are touched by the divine in their appearance, and even Ganymede misrecognizes Helen, and this perceived sameness hints at the sterility and waste of Ganymede's ejaculate later in the poem. Difference is necessary to avoid this "monstrous Venus." But as a boy and a woman, sitting alone in a field, they begin to debate – the poet/monk notes they talk of many subjects, but he gives voice to their competition. What do men want? Ganymede says it's him. Helen counters it's her. Indeed, it is the reliance on Nature, personified in the poem, and nature, as a space and place governed by a kind of reproductive time, that actually twists and opens a space for queerness. And yet, it is in this space of nature that the anxieties of queerness surface.[28] Far from seeing Nature as a strict moral authority, one which polices and regulates normative behavior, Nature and, by extension, what is natural contains vice and virtue. Indeed, as Joan Cadden has shown,

> Nature was, in many respects, the source, judge, and enforcer of right living and proper social relations in the view of both academic and social elites in the late Middle Ages. It directed the production of desire and its regulation under the auspices of reason, both crucial to the psychological dynamics of virtue and the political dynamics of hierarchy. But, if natural desire and pleasure were necessary elements in the dialectic of moral goodness and perhaps also of justice, they were dangerous forces that necessarily subverted the orders they supported.[29]

Cadden's focus here – the tensions inherent in a system dominated by nature where nature's "fragility" and its "lapses" make virtue and vice possible – helps to clarify how the depiction of nature as the setting for *Ganymede and Helen* might highlight what the Dreamer and Helen eventually see: the figure of Ganymede is beautiful and perfect, even as he is an unrepentant sodomite. Nature's wild attributes and Ganymede's freedom to exist introduce how space might control, reflect, or create positions that are not normative. As Sara Ahmed makes clear, queerness

---

[27] *Ganymede and Helen*, 244.
[28] William Burgwinkle, *Sodomy, Masculinity and Law in Medieval Literature: France and England, 1050–1230* (Cambridge, Cambridge University Press, 2004), 7.
[29] Joan Cadden, "Trouble in the Earthly Paradise: The Regime of Nature in Late Medieval Christian Culture," in *The Moral Authority of Nature*, ed. Lorraine Daston and Fernando Vidal (Chicago: The University of Chicago Press, 2004), 207–31 at 208.

and its etymology make evident how space might be central not only to orientation but also to orientation of what is sexual:

> We can turn to the etymology of the word "queer," which comes from the Indo-European word "twist." Queer is, after all, a spatial term, which then gets translated into a sexual term, a term for a twisted sexuality that does not follow a "straight line," a sexuality that is bent and crooked. . . . The spatiality of this term is not incidental. Sexuality itself can be considered a spatial formation not only in the sense that bodies inhabit sexual spaces, but also in the sense that bodies are sexualized through how they inhabit that space.[30]

Ahmed here highlights the consequences of spaces, which in their layout can force bodies to twist and turn in order to fit, to exist. These spaces, then, seem to create or influence the orientation – strictly understood – of bodies. But this orientation, as Ahmed notes, goes further: the physical positioning of bodies creates sexual positions and positions of sexuality, connections that I explore next in linking Ahmed's theories of spaces that queer to the spaces, places, and times of *Ganymede and Helen*.

Ganymede and Helen at first seems never queer in time or place: an encomium in many ways of the beauty and normativity of nature, it would seem to challenge any queer readings one might apply to the apparently timeless scenes of nature it depicts, both the poem's framing of the Dreamer resting in spring or in the romantic scene of Helen and Ganymede which he sees in his sleepy state. The two settings for the poem – the grasses upon which the Dreamer lies, and the "summer grass beneath a lovely pine," where Helen and Ganymede stand – are both spaces where desire blooms, often in wild and unrestrained ways.

> The sun had entered the House of the Bull, and spring, blossom laden,
> Had reared its lovely, flowered head.
> Under an olive tree I lay, on a bed provided by the grass,
> Amusing myself by recalling the sweetness of love.[31]

The discussion here of the position of the Dreamer in time (on a bed of grass), in spring, and in the middle of a sort of astrological time (the so-called House of the Bull signals the ruling astrological sign is Taurus, so April and May) presents a time so deeply embedded in procreative love that even this Dreamer is swept away by the regimes of time here, but there are other regimes of time in the Middle Ages, such as monastic time and its scheduling. As I've argued above, Ganymede's frequent appearance in the high medieval ages, especially in monastic or religious

---

30 Sara Ahmed, *Queer Phenomenology: Orientations, Objects, Others* (Durham: Duke University Press, 2006), 67.
31 *Ganymede and Helen*, 1–4.

materials, makes this poem legible in a monastic context, a claim that Kolve's examination of *Getron* implicitly supports. The poem might be considered within this experience of monastic time, which is regimented, prescribed, and regulated, just as surely as allegorical spring and the Zodiac signs regulate the seasons and the emotions and activities which they direct.[32]

And here, modes of procreative, natural time and monastic time don't seem that different from the modern rhythms of time that Elizabeth Freeman describes in *Time Binds*:

> Chrononormativity is a mode of implantation, a technique by which institutional forces come to seem like somatic facts. Schedules, calendars, time zones, and even wristwatches inculcate what the sociologist Evitar-Zerubavel calls "hidden rhythms," forms of temporal experience that seem natural to those whom they privilege.[33]

It might seem odd to link this kind of modern regulation to medieval modes of time – sacred, natural, monastic. But what remains similar among all these modes, medieval and postmedieval, is the way in which, according to Freeman, "naked flesh is bound into socially meaningful embodiment through temporal regulation" and this "binding is what turns mere existence into . . . *chrononormativity*, or the use of time to organize individual human bodies toward maximum productivity."[34] Indeed, in her fleshing out of how time binds, drags, or otherwise organizes modern life, especially queer life it seems, one might see in the Dreamer's desire "that it [the sight of spring] had never left [his] eyes," voiced at the beginning of the poem, a challenge to the regimes of time that unite the homosocial and sterile environment of the monastery with the regimes of time that Helen feels as she reaches out to Ganymede.[35] Before we

---

32 See J. D. North, "Monastic Time," in *The Culture of Medieval English Monasticism* (Woodbridge: Boydell Press, 2007), 203–12 for a clear account of time and its accounting in religious communities in the Middle Ages. "The Jews had the custom of praying three times a day at the third, sixth and ninth hours, and the early Christians later extended that scheme, adding prayers at midnight (when Paul and Silas sang in prison) and at the beginning of day and night. It was St. Benedict himself who added a seventh hour of prayer, compline, so completing this rule of the Church for the times of prayer, although one that was subject to much local variation. I will not even try to explain how matins could move around, as one moved from place to place, how lauds was occasionally combined with it, how sext and none could be joined, or vespers with compline. The important thing is that the canonical hours mattered greatly, and that some means of deciding on the times of service was of crucial importance" (207).
33 Elizabeth Freeman, *Time Binds: Queer Temporalities, Queer Histories* (Durham: Duke University Press, 2010), 3.
34 Freeman, *Time Binds*, 3.
35 *Ganymede and Helen*, 8.

hear any of the words they exchange, the poet reports that Ganymede and Helen begin to debate and argue, as "the impudent youth compares himself to the female."[36] One might wonder whether Helen actually notices because, following this description of their exchange, the poet describes Helen's own rush to lust and love:

> She, already longing for the male and ready for bed,
> Has for some time felt the proddings of love.
> The singular beauty of Ganymede inflames her,
> And already the warmth within proclaims itself without.[37]

These lines, and their connection to time and haste, signal a kind of anticipation of Freeman's notions of how time binds – "the use of time to organize individual human bodies toward maximum productivity." But this haste and citation of time and waste – Helen kisses the boy when she is not asked and waits for no frivolous courtship – also returns to orientations and how space orients actual bodies into different orientations.

But before these lines quoted above, in view of the gods and goddesses, Helen and Ganymede relax and recline:

> Both are stretched out upon the verdant grass,
> And might have been blessed with union,
> But Ganymede, not knowing the role expected of him,
> Presses himself against her as if he wishes to be passive.[38]

The two failed lovers are in the orientation of the Dreamer – reclining upon the verdant grass, and, like the Dreamer, both are oriented to ask for the impossible: Helen demands to submit; Ganymede presses his body into position, ready to be mounted. These spatial clues, following Ahmed's lead, might be read as an implicit indictment of the fluidity of nature – here on the grass, in the very bed and foundation of nature, both ask not just for what is impossible but also for what is unnatural. It is no surprise, then, that we next see the would-be lovers come to the house of Nature, where they find Nature, along with Reason and Providence,

> Ruminating over the secrets of things to come,
> Weaving thread into countless figures
> And creating things with precise scales and balances.[39]

---

36 *Ganymede and Helen*, 20.
37 *Ganymede and Helen*, 21–24.
38 *Ganymede and Helen*, 29–32.
39 *Ganymede and Helen*, 46–48.

As created beings, Ganymede and Helen challenge the order and layout of this space – Nature, Reason, and Providence work together on creation and the future, handling each with care and precision, but it is precisely the dominant woman and the submissive man who upset the "precise scales and balances" of creation. And this is where part of the poem ends – the indirect reporting and the voice of the Dreamer. Following the introduction of the pair's dilemma, Ganymede's and Helen's words take center stage, as the poem shifts from looking at the pair with a Dreamer describing their appearances to the direct speech of both Ganymede and Helen. It seems appropriate to think about the claims of history and the erasure of queerness that this trip to Nature appears to inaugurate. The invocation of the future in this distant, dreamy past offers a glimpse into the past, where the Dreamer and his readers can see and recuperate histories, present and lost, to find where silence might be read, where queer pasts meet feminist figures, and where exempla can be found to guide the present and future. Indeed, what this loss looks like is an orientation (something akin to an inclination) toward failure for both Ganymede and Helen. The submissive man and dominant woman, therefore, anticipate and enliven the very notion of alternate histories, partially erased, told from a queer or feminist perspective, as "queer and feminist histories are the histories of those who are willing to risk the consequences of deviation."[40]

But who really loses? In the course of debating, Helen feels her desire come alive, and she longs – both with her body and mind – for Ganymede. Ganymede, shamed for his desires, asks for forgiveness, accepting the original advances of Helen. But, as Freeman's notion of "temporal drag" implies, the pull of previous depictions, imagery, and convention cannot be erased here. Ganymede is a mythological figure known for having no choice or voice, and is abducted – raped would be more accurate – by Zeus as an eagle, and taken to Olympus. As this poem and its early articulations of queer space, time, and failure indicate, Ganymede reverts to an object of desire at the end, and Ganymede, as with *Angels*'s Joe, cannot hide his nonnormative desires, even in heterosexual marriage. Nor can the poem escape the drag of previous histories of Ganymede. This failure to make Ganymede straight, to change his orientation, is made clear in the poet's discussion of Helen's conquest of Ganymede in debate. Reinforcing his submissive orientation both in the poem and in mythology, and echoing how Ganymede approaches Helen as a dominant sexual partner at the opening of the poem, the apparent deletion of his queer desires makes them clear and present. In this way, the ending of the poem reflects the troublesome logic, or non-logic,

---

[40] Sara Ahmed, *The Promise of Happiness* (Durham: Duke University Press, 2010), 91.

of sodomy and the fear of it: "[Sodomy] was nowhere, yet everywhere threatened society with destruction. It was blotted out of the annuals of the past, unrecorded in the present, forbidden to exist in the future."[41]

As this poem and its early articulations of queer space, time, and failure indicate, Ganymede looks queerly at procreation, seeing the continuation of his face and person as a waste. Likewise, he looks queerly at Helen, whom he first sees implicitly as one of his "anxious studs."[42] Simultaneously, he also looks queer to Helen and at Helen, that is, she first sees a potential partner rather than competition for men and he sees her at first in a similar fashion. And, finally, the Dreamer, the poet inside the poem and, arguably, the same poet outside, looks queer by the end – his ending and shame appear unavoidable. The poem ends with the "blessed union" which joins Ganymede to Helen, at Ganymede's request, and, seemingly, Ganymede is the dominant figure, asking for Helen's hand and their nuptials occur in the penultimate stanza. Here, at the end, I unsettle the supposedly harmonious end of the poem and instead concentrate on Ganymede's failure to win the debate and Helen's highlighting of his failure to procreate. How might these failures be coded as queer failure? Before marriage, after defeat, Ganymede is reminded of his ejaculation and his position, as a bottom, and this reminder anticipates that the dream functions similarly for the poet who remains, as he awakens, fearful of his own potential and penitential position as a sodomite both literally – as he likely is laying just as Ganymede and Helen are at the beginning of the poem – and figuratively, because if we read this author and his work as monastic, then he is fixed in a homosocial environment. In the monastery, as Kolve makes clear, Ganymede remains a potent symbol and the specter of sodomy is not gone. And sodomy, the ending of the poem reminds us, will forever haunt the Dreamer/poet:

> The vision befell me by the will of God.
> Let the Sodomites blush, the Gomorrhans weep.
> Let everyone guilty of this deed repent.
> God, if I ever commit it, have mercy on me![43]

This dream seems to remind the poet and reader that the queer failure of Ganymede's sexual appetites cannot be forgotten nor cured – for outside the poem, he cannot dispel sodomy with a marriage to Helen, or anyone for that

---

41 Warren Johansson and William A. Percy, "Homosexuality," in *Handbook of Medieval Sexuality*, ed. Vern L. Bullough and James A. Brundage (New York: Garland Publishing, Inc., 1996), 155–89 at 175.
42 *Ganymede and Helen*, 180.
43 *Ganymede and Helen*, 267–70.

matter. The ending lines, with the ambiguity about the sin of the Sodomites and the potential or history of such a sin for the Dreamer, haunt this poem. Ganymede, in this poem as in others, speaks to an archaeology of feeling and affect – that of the queer failing – and rather than let failure stand in opposition to winning might it be useful to see how Ganymede stands for a rejection or critique of this system of winning and losing, as well as all kinds of premodern hierarchies and ideologies, from marriage to monasticism? And this enduring influence of Ganymede is where we might see queer time and space converge, especially in the queer failure he can represent in various poems and texts.

Ganymede Wins?

Emphasized in John Boswell's book, these narratives of Ganymede seemingly announce the failure of queer love and the necessity for heterosexual procreation. Yet, as John Boswell's aforementioned work demonstrates, debate follows Ganymede. Indeed, in *CSTH*, Boswell devotes an entire chapter to what he calls "The Triumph of Ganymede," which is followed by a section called "The Rise of Intolerance."[44] Part of the controversial "Boswell Thesis" (not so named by Boswell), this chapter interrogates a body of literature – among which he briefly includes *Altercatio* – centered on expressions of love for youths largely by those figures in positions of authority in institutions such as the medieval Church which gave them a certain amount of safety.[45] According to Boswell, "none was accused of entertaining unorthodox opinions, either during his lifetime or subsequently."[46] And these texts centered on Ganymede – Boswell includes three poetic treatments of Ganymede in an appendix that includes eighteen translations

---

[44] Boswell, *Christianity, Social Tolerance, and Homosexuality*, 243–66.
[45] Mathew Kuefler, "The Boswell Thesis," in *The Boswell Thesis: Essays on Christianity, Social Tolerance, and Homosexuality*, ed. Mathew Kuefler (Chicago: University of Chicago Press, 2006), 1–31 at 2. In his edited volume centered on Boswell's *CSTH*, Matthew Kuefler outlines the contours of what might be described both as the central and ancillary arguments of the book and the Boswell Thesis itself: "There were four main points that form the narrative for the book: First, that Christianity had come into existence in an atmosphere of Greek and Roman tolerance for same sex eroticism. Second, that nothing in the Christian scriptures or early tradition required a hostile assessment of homosexuality; rather, that such assessments represented a misreading of scripture. Third, that early medieval Christians showed no real animosity toward same sex eroticism. Fourth, that it was only in the twelfth and thirteenth centuries that Christian writers formulated a significant hostility toward homosexuality, and then read that hostility back into their scriptures and early tradition."
[46] Boswell, *Christianity, Social Tolerance, and Homosexuality*, 244.

in total – show the full spectrum of responses toward his myth, a point Boswell makes in the *CSTH* itself: "use of the Ganymede figure was not necessarily a sign of participation in or even approval of the gay subculture."[47] But *Ganymede and Helen* shows how queerly the poem construes time and space/orientation in highlighting the failure of Ganymede even in the apparent condemnation of Ganymede's same-sex love and subsequent rewriting as Helen's husband. By seeing how the twelfth-century dream vision anticipates Ahmed's, Freeman's, and Love's formulations of queer space, time, and history, we can see how the past is the future for queerness in some ways, a twisting of progress, time, and success – indeed, this poem shows how "History is about to crack wide open."[48]

Bibliography

Ahmed, Sara. *The Promise of Happiness*. Durham: Duke University Press, 2010.

Ahmed, Sara. *Queer Phenomenology: Orientations, Objects, Others*. Durham: Duke University Press, 2006.

Alan of Lille. *Plaint of Nature*. Translated by James J. Sheridan. Toronto: Pontifical Institute of Mediaeval Studies, 1980.

Boswell, John. *Christianity, Social Tolerance, and Homosexuality: Gay People in Western Europe from the Beginning of the Christian Era to the Fourteenth Century*. Chicago: University of Chicago Press, 1980.

Burgwinkle, William. *Sodomy, Masculinity and Law in Medieval Literature: France and England, 1050–1230*. Cambridge, Cambridge University Press, 2004.

Cadden, Joan. "Trouble in the Earthly Paradise: The Regime of Nature in Late Medieval Christian Culture." In *The Moral Authority of Nature*, edited by Lorraine Daston and Fernando Vidal, 207–31. Chicago: University of Chicago Press, 2004.

Desmond, Marilynn. "Ovid's *Ars Amatoria* and the Wounds of Love." In *Ovid's Art and the Wife of Bath: The Ethics of Erotic Violence*, 35–54. Ithaca: Cornell University Press, 2006.

Freeman, Elizabeth. *Time Binds: Queer Temporalities, Queer Histories*. Durham: Duke University Press, 2010.

Ganymede and Helen. Translated by John Boswell. *Christianity, Social Tolerance, and Homosexuality: Gay People in Western Europe from the Beginning of the Christian Era to the Fourteenth Century*. Chicago: University of Chicago Press, 1980.

Halberstam, Jack. *The Queer Art of Failure*. Durham: Duke University Press, 2011.

Johansson, Warren and William A. Percy. "Homosexuality." In *Handbook of Medieval Sexuality*, edited by Vern L. Bullough and James A. Brundage, 155–89. New York: Garland Publishing, Inc., 1996.

Kolve, V. A. "Ganymede/*Son of Getron*: Medieval Monasticism and the Drama of Same-Sex Desire." *Speculum* 73.4 (1998): 1014–67.

---

47 Boswell, 251.
48 Kushner, *Angels in America*, 118.

Kruger, Steven F. "Identity and Conversion in *Angels in America*." In *Approaching the Millennium: Essays on Angels in America*, edited by Deborah R. Geis and Steven F. Kruger, 151–71. Ann Arbor: University of Michigan Press, 1997.

Kuefler, Mathew. "The Boswell Thesis." In *The Boswell Thesis: Essays on Christianity, Social Tolerance, and Homosexuality*, edited by Mathew Kuefler, 1–31. Chicago: University of Chicago Press, 2006.

Kuefler, Mathew. "Male Friendship and the Suspicion of Sodomy in Twelfth-Century France." In *The Boswell Thesis: Essays on Christianity, Social Tolerance, and Homosexuality*, edited by Mathew Kuefler, 179–212. Chicago: University of Chicago Press, 2006.

Kushner, Tony. *Angels in America: A Gay Fantasia on National Themes: Revised and Complete Edition 20th Anniversary Edition*. New York: Theatre Communications Group, Inc., 2013.

Lenzen, Rolf. "'Altercatio Ganimedis et Helene': Kritische Edition mit Kommentar." *Mittellateinisches Jahrbuch* 7 (1972): 161–86.

Love, Heather. *Feeling Backward: Loss and the Politics of Queer History*. Cambridge: Harvard University Press, 2007.

Montgomery, Benilde. "*Angels in America* as Medieval Mystery." *Modern Drama* 4 (1998): 596–606.

Newman, Barbara. *God and the Goddesses: Vision, Poetry, and Belief in the Middle Ages*. Philadelphia: University of Pennsylvania Press, 2005.

North, J. D. "Monastic Time." In *The Culture of Medieval English Monasticism*, edited by James G. Clark, 203–12. Woodbridge: Boydell Press, 2007.

Raskolnikov, Masha. "Chaucer's *Clerk's Tale* on the Borders of the Queer." Paper presented at 43rd Annual Sewanee Medieval Colloquium, Sewanee, TN, March 2017.

Part II: **French Kisses: Queer Romance**

Joseph Derosier
Chapter 3
Guillaume de Lorris's Unmaking of the Self: The Dreamer's Queer Failures

All of us know, whether or not we are able to admit it, that mirrors can only lie, that death by drowning is all that awaits one there.[1] There seems to be something queer – something ill at ease – in Guillaume de Lorris's *Roman de la Rose*. The Dreamer, figure for the narrator and the reader, is an impossible character, torn between his own misguided interpretations and the text's glossing of itself. Guillaume embraces misinterpretation and the dangerous queer artifice of writing, which terrify his near-contemporaries Alan of Lille and Jean de Meun. Throughout the *Roman*, Guillaume gestures toward uncovering the hidden meanings of this dream vision, as promised in the prologue. His text disintegrates as the Dreamer, our slippery protagonist, fails to understand the hermeneutics of the text and himself, as his homosocial quest for the elusive rose leads to accusations of improper relations – *mauvais acointement*. In embracing the queer artifice of writing, Guillaume's text can only fail, flail, and disintegrate. It is this very impossibility, the improbability of the subject and the narrative, that asserts a space beyond and across binaries, illegible and imminently desirable at the same time. The queerness of this romance rests in its refusal to satisfy the expectations of its protagonist and eventually its readers. As Tison Pugh writes, "[w]hen backgrounds of generic heteronormativity are shattered, the queer emerges with a vengeance for auditors and readers anticipating the pleasure of a heteronormatively inscribed genre but discovering something altogether different."[2]

The queerness embraced here frames desire as always seeking to uncover the uncoverable, to unmask the unmaskable. That is, the quest to find one's ideal beloved is problematically teleological, and the *Rose* offers a critique of how we seek to fulfill and understand those desires. The thrust of the text is perhaps an iteration of the genealogical parody of reproduction in the "unlimited" or "impersonal intimacy" of barebacking described by Leo Bersani in *Intimacies*, which Adam Phillips glosses as "believ[ing] in the future without personalizing it."[3] That is, the future can be sought without having a fixed or

---
[1] James Baldwin, The Fire Next Time (New York: Vintage, 1963), 95.
[2] Tison Pugh, *Queering Medieval Genres* (New York: Palgrave Macmillan, 2004), 2.
[3] Leo Bersani and Adam Phillips, *Intimacies* (Chicago: University of Chicago Press, 2008), 43–53; 117.

expected telos. Bersani is specifically invested in "self-divestiture," which "has to be rethought in terms of a certain form of self-expansiveness, or something like ego-dissemination rather than ego-annihilation."[4] For Bersani, this is accomplished in impersonal acts of unprotected anonymous sex as the receiving partner "enters into an impersonal intimacy" with his partners: "His subjecthood is, we might say, absorbed into the nameless and faceless crowd that exist only as viral traces circulating in his blood and potentially fatally infecting him."[5] This is the nature of the futurity Bersani and Phillips seek: impersonal yet mythologized and romanticized. There is a kind of impersonal intimacy in Guillaume's notion of interpretation, wherein the end is desired but never articulated. Posterity emerges not as a fixed legacy but as something that must be continually examined and reinterpreted. Guillaume shows, through his protagonist's quest and failure, that even impersonal futurities are fraught. The Dreamer seeks his rose, at the expense of himself, and his quest for conquest leads to his, and the narrative's, disintegration.

The impersonal for Bersani opens up the possibility of radical forms of desire, akin to desire in the *Phaedrus*. Here, the impersonal nature of this desire is formulated in the projection of a godlike persona onto one's lover:

> the self the boy sees and loves in the lover is also the lover's self, just as the lover, in remembering and worshipping his own godlike nature in the boy, is also worshipping the boy's real (ideal) soul. Narcissistic love in both the lover and the beloved (can they even still be distinguished?) is exactly identical to a perfect knowledge of otherness.[6]

Bersani sees impersonal narcissism as a radical gesture toward otherness and against the individualism and ego of modernity. This gesture is performed in the *Rose* as the Lover seeks out a beloved that is at once other (a plant) and impersonal (a fetish). Thus, Guillaume de Lorris can help us trace these desires, and his retelling of the Narcissus myth offers a critique of fetishizing desires and a lesson on idealized desire.

Intimacies is primarily the work of Bersani, with a gloss and continuation by Phillips, seeming all the more germane to the *Rose*. I will note that, for the purpose of this chapter, Guillaume's text will be read independently of Jean de Meun's continuation. This allows us to approach Guillaume's text without reading it as part of or prologue to Jean's version of the *Rose*, which reframes and repurposes Guillaume's text. Jean's vision and version is very much at odds with Guillaume's: he fundamentally reimagines what Guillaume's *Rose* offers

---

4 Bersani and Phillips, *Intimacies*, 56.
5 Bersani and Phillips, *Intimacies*, 53.
6 Bersani and Phillips, *Intimacies*, 84–85.

us in his continuation. My reading of Narcissus in the *Rose,* and its critique of our misguided reliance on certain tropes to understand relationality, suggests that this type of impersonal narcissism can only lead to our obliteration, and not in the sexy-shattering-of-the-ego manner espoused by Bersani. The *Rose* opens the possibility for a novel hermeneutics of queer desire, a continuous unlayering and undoing of identity. This is continuous self-fashioning and revision, reproduced and mirrored in the Dreamer *cum* interpreter *cum* reader. This always feels "improbable," to cite Michel Foucault.[7] This improbability, a resistance to attempting to find coherent identities, seeks alternate ways to think through desire and identity as linear or teleological concepts.

The *Roman de la Rose* is a thirteenth-century best-seller that offers its reader a *roman,* which is at once a text in *romans,* the vernacular, as well as a nascent form of vernacular literature, "romance," which eventually leads to the modern French novel, the *roman.* This *roman* is also a dream-vision, highlighting the fraught yet tight relationship between fiction and mysticism. As Guillaume explains, this is an ambitious *ars amatoria,* an art of love, in the wake of Ovid:

> Ce est *li romanz de la rose*
> Ou l'art d'amours est toute enclose.
> La matiére est bone et nueve:
> Or doint dieus qu'an gre le reçoive
> Cele pour cui je l'ai empris. (vv. 37–41)

This is *The Romance of Rose*,
Where the art of love is entirely enclosed.
The subject is good and novel,
So may it please god that it be well received
By her for whom I undertook this task.

Guillaume de Lorris's hubristic description tells us that this art of love is entirely new – and entirely good – both of which we soon see to be lies. The narrator is split in his roles as our narrator, as the Dreamer whose vision is the *roman,* and as the Lover who pursues the rose, both euphemism for vulva and metonym for his disembodied love interest. Guillaume never finishes his art of love, and Jean de Meun rebaptizes the *roman* as the "mirror for lovers" – *le miroer aus amoureus* (v. 10655) – and thus shifts from an ostensibly encyclopedic work to an explicitly didactic text.

---

[7] Michel Foucault, "De l'amitié comme mode de vie" (interview with R. de Ceccaty, J. Danet and J. Le Bitoux), in *Dits et Écrits,* vol. 2, text no. 293 (Paris: Gallimard [Quarto], 2001), 982–83; trans. John Johnston, "Friendship as a Way of Life," in *Ethics: Subjectivity and Truth,* ed. Paul Rabinow (New York: New Press, 1998), 137.

Guillaume retells the story of Narcissus, an exemplum familiar to his contemporaries from Ovid's *Metamorphoses*, as well as vernacular translations.[8] He retells this story to frame the Dreamer's gazing into a fountain, which leads to him falling prey to Amor, the god of love. Guillaume both misreads Ovid and then in turn misreads his own reading of Ovid, using allegory against itself, forcing the reader to question the very process of reading a text, to question the role – and danger – of interpretation in extracting meaning from a source. What does it mean for an author to misread his own work, and then to encourage his reader to engage in misinterpretation? Guillaume's *Rose*, in these misreadings, interrogates the role of interpretation in reading and in retelling, and assumes the foreclosure of a singular reading of his work. These various hermeneutic failures – or provocations – suggest an ever-present danger for language to be misinterpreted and for literature to be translated, transformed, and transfigured at each step of its production. Guillaume's *Rose* becomes a perilous mirror of itself, reflecting, refracting, and disintegrating as it goes on, ultimately collapsing abruptly.

Guillaume's misreading of Ovid asks the question of what it is to rewrite Narcissus. As David Hult points out, the "paradox of Narcissus is not 'Why one cannot possess oneself' but rather 'Why one needs to go beyond oneself.'"[9] Guillaume's Narcissus loses himself in the mirror and doesn't need to seek a lover outside of this illusion. If Ovid's Narcissus doesn't need to seek love beyond himself, he dies realizing this; Guillaume's Narcissus fails to recognize this illusion, as if lost in a dream. Guillaume's misreading feels jarring, as a reader might very well recognize that she or he was being tricked by this new version of Narcissus. Walter Benjamin asks, "[i]s translation meant for readers who do not understand the original?"[10] whereas Guillaume's text seems to ask a different question: What is the task of the translator for readers who *do* understand the original, or have heard this tale before? Benjamin is concerned with the afterlife in a work of art, with the relationship between form and sense, with the translator at odds with the poet: "[t]he intention of the poet is spontaneous, primary, graphic; that of the translator is derivative,

---

[8] Guillaume de Lorris and Jean de Meun, *Le Roman de la Rose*, ed. Armand Strubel (Paris: Lettres Gothiques, 1992); Guillaume's *Rose* is based on Ms. BN fr. 12786 (s. xiii^{ex}/xiv^{in}), the only manuscript without reference to Jean de Meun or to his text (Strubel, "Principes d'édition," 38–40).
[9] David F. Hult, *Self-fulfilling Prophecies: Readership and Authority in the First* Roman de la Rose (New York: Cambridge University Press, 1986), 285.
[10] Walter Benjamin, "The Task of the Translator," in *Illuminations*, trans. Harry Zorn (New York: Schocken, 2007), 69–82 at 69.

ultimate, ideational."[11] If fidelity to the sense of words is at odds with fidelity to the whole, the translator is working with as well as against the original. Thus, "[m]eaning is served far better – and literature and language far worse – by the unrestrained license of bad translators."[12] Guillaume fights against both of these trajectories, embracing the "bad translation" in making misreading and failure so apparent. His dream vision appears thus destined to be cast into a future where it may never become fully legible. As Marta Powell Harley notes, Guillaume's "abbreviated" version maintains details such as Narcissus hunting before the episode, suggesting knowledge of his source.[13] As Eric Hicks notes, "si l'on n'ose affirmer que Guillaume de Lorris ait connu le texte, il semble difficile d'admettre qu'il ait ignoré la tradition dont il est issu" (if one dare not admit that Guillaume may have known the text, it seems difficult to suggest that he could have not known the tradition from whence it came), citing Latin and French adaptations of Ovid that would have been available to Guillaume as didactic or moralized versions of Ovid.[14]

Importantly, there are many other uses of Narcissus before the *Rose* in twelfth-century vernacular literature: Chrétien de Troyes compares the hero Cilgès to Narcissus, for his beauty compares to that of Narcissus, but his hero surpasses Narcissus in wisdom:

> Mes tant [Clygés] ert biaux et avenanz
> Que Narcisus, qui desoz l'orme
> Vit an la fontainne sa forme,
> Si l'ama tant, si com an dit,
> Qu'il an fu morz quant il la vit,
> Por tant qu'il ne la pot avoir.
> Molt ot biauté et po savoir;
> Mes Clygés en ot plus grant masse,
> Tant con li ors le cuivre passe
> Et plus que je ne di encor.

> For Cligès was as handsome and worthy
> As Narcissus, who under the elm
> Saw in the fountain his figure,

---

11 Benjamin, "Task of the Translator," 76–77.
12 Benjamin, "Task of the Translator," 78.
13 On Guillaume's Ovidian influence, see also Marta Powell Harley, "Narcissus, Hermaphroditus, and Attis: Ovidian Lovers at the Fontaine d'Amors in Guillaume de Lorris's *Roman de la Rose*," PMLA 101.3 (1986): 324–37, esp. 327.
14 Eric Hicks, "La mise en roman des formes allégoriques: hypostase et récit chez Guillaume de Lorris," in *Études sur le Roman de la Rose de Guillaume de Lorris*, ed. Jean Dufournet (Paris: Honoré Champion, 1984), 53–80 at 57.

And loved it so much – as they say –
That he died when he saw it
But yet could never possess it.
Great was his beauty but little was his intelligence,
But Cligès head a much greater wealth of it,
Just as gold weighs more than copper,
And much more of which I will not tell.[15]

Elsewhere, Aimon de Varennes's Florimont is warned against the folly of Narcissus by his tutor, Floquart.[16] In Benoît de Saint-Maure's *roman antique*, the *Roman de Troie*, Achille also compares himself to Narcissus, loving not only his reflection but also loving death itself.[17] In these instances Narcissus is used as a reference, as a point of comparison for protagonists. Thus, we can see Narcissus as a trope, as representative of madness, vanity, and foolishness. These examples help to establish Narcissus as fitting a certain mold in medieval literature in French, one which Guillaume defies.

Alan of Lille refers to the youth in his twelfth-century Latin prosimetrum *Plaint of Nature*. He says of Narcissus that "[b]elieving himself to be this other self, he brought upon himself through himself a perilous love."[18] That is, his

---

[15] Chrétien de Troyes, *Cligès*, ed. Laurence Harf-Lancner (Paris: Honoré Champion, 2006), vv. 2748–57.

[16] "Volez vos sembler Narcisus | De folie ou Piramus? | Cist dui furent mort per amor" (Do you want to be like Narcissus or Piramus? Those two died on account of love); Aimon de Varennes, *Florimont, ein altfranzösischer Abenteuerroman*, ed. Alfons Hilka (Göttingen: Gedruckt für die Gesellschaft für romanische Literatur, 1932), vv. 3959–61.

[17] Achille cries out:

> Narcisus sui, ço sai e vei,
> Qui tant ama l'ombre de sei
> Qu'il en mourut sor la fontaine.
> Iceste angoisse, iceste peine
> Sai que jo sent: jo raim mon ombre,
> Jo aim ma mort et mon encombre.

I am Narcissus, I know it and I see it, he who loved his own shadow so much that he died of it at the fountain. This anguish, this pain – I know what I feel: I'm in love with my shadow, I love my death and my failure.

Benoît de Saint-Maure, *Le Roman de Troie*, ed. Léopold Constans, 6 vols. (Paris: Firmin-Didot et c[ie], 1904–1912), 3: vv. 17690–94.

[18] "seipsum credens esse se alterum de se sibi amoris incurrit periculum" (Alan of Lille, *The Plaint of Nature*, in *Literary Works*, ed. and trans. Winthrop Wetherbee [Cambridge: Dumbarton Oaks Medieval Library, 2013], 8§10).

misrecognition is what causes his death. These twelfth-century Latin and vernacular sources, with references to Narcissus that seem to need little glossing, suggest that a reader would be expected to recognize the figure of Narcissus, and would be familiar with his story, rather than encountering it as novel. Chrétien and Aimon both note that Narcissus falls in love with his image in the fountain and, like Guillaume, their Narcissus does not overtly identify with this reflection. Nevertheless, he sees "sa forme" (his form, 2750) in *Cligès* and "tant ama l'ombre de sei" (so loved his own reflection, 17692) in the *Roman de Troie*, whereas in the *Rose* he falls for "un enfant bel a desmesure" (an outrageously handsome child, 1485). In contrast, a twelfth-century vernacular translation of "Narcissus" maintains the moment of recognition, Ovid's *iste ego sum*:

> Le cors, le vis que je la voi,
> Ce puis je tot trover en moi.
> J'aim moi meïsme, c'est folie!
> Fu onques mais tes rage oïe?

> The body, the face that I see:
> I can find it all in myself.
> I love myself, it's madness!
> Was there ever such madness heard of?[19]

This is reprised in the early fourteenth century in the vernacular translation of the *Metamorphoses*, the *Ovide moralisé*, which also retells the Narcissus story.[20] In this version, which is particularly concerned with referencing the original and in faithful translation,[21] Narcissus recognizes himself:

> J'aim moi meïsmes, et, sans faille,
> Je pors le brandon et la faille
> Dont je meïsmes sui espris. (1, bk. 3: vv. 1729–31)

> I love myself, and without fail,
> I bear the torch and the flare
> With which I set myself on fire.

---

[19] *Narcisse*, in *Pyrame et Thisbé, Narcisse, Philomena*, ed. Emmanuèle Baumgartner (Paris: Folio, 2000), vv. 869–72; this text is faithful in the *iste ego sum* moment, but it makes other alterations: Echo is replaced by "Dané."

[20] *Ovide moralisé: Poème du commencement du quatorzième siècle*, ed. C. de Boer, 3 vols (Amsterdam: Johannes Müller, 1915–1938).

[21] For example "se la letre ne ment"; "Ensi com la fable recite"; "si com la fable recite" (1, Bk. 3: vv. 1464, 1525, 1576).

Given Narcissus being a common figure across genres, and his association with what has since been defined as "narcissism"[22] – or with sodomy, according to Alan of Lille[23] – it seems reasonable to assume that Guillaume's reader would have expected Narcissus to recognize himself, especially in a work as learned as the *Rose*. As Nicholas Ealy argues in *Narcissism and Selfhood in Medieval French Literature*, "selfhood is always infiltrated by otherness, that subjectivity is always intersubjective in nature," and the Narcissus tales we see across medieval French literature expose that.[24] Guillaume's version refuses recognition, encourages misrecognition, and offers a critique of the genre. As Ealy notes, "the unavoidable imperative to deny Narcissus as our reality is the only way we can accept him, accept our desire, accept our very self. *Iste ego sum!*"[25] Guillaume fights the telos of identity: the idea of self, desire, and the other are always unfolding and being rewritten, rather than a stable concept. Thus, Narcissus operates as a mirror for the Dreamer and for us readers, as Guillaume encourages us to make the same failures. The tale is altered in that recognition becomes impossible and the closest one can come to *being* is a penultimate, rather than definite, identity.

Our protagonist – the Dreamer – falls asleep and finds himself wandering along a river which leads him to an enclosed garden whose walls are adorned with portraits of the Vices (vv. 129–462). He wanders through the garden, stalked by Amor, and happens upon a fountain, upon which is engraved that Narcissus died here (vv. 1432–35). In the span of fifty-eight lines (vv. 1436–93), Guillaume's narrator, the Lover, recalls the story of Narcissus, his memory triggered by the epitaph:

> Si vit en l'yaue clere et nete
> Son vis, son neis et sa bouchete.
> Icil maintenant s'esbaï
> Car ses ombres tout le traï,
> Qu'il cuida veoir la figure
> D'un enfant bel a desmesure. (vv. 1480–85)

---

22 In 1914 Freud writes: "The word narcissism . . . denote[s] the attitude of a person who treats his own body in the same way as otherwise the body of a sexual object is treated" ("On Narcissism: An Introduction," in *General Psychological Theory* [New York: Simon and Schuster, 1991], 41–69 at 41).

23 Alan of Lille, *Plaint of Nature*, 8§10; Guillaume also makes references to homosexuality: Male Bouche accuses the Lover of having a "mauvais acointement" with Bel Acueil (vv. 3519–23).

24 Nicholas Ealy, *Narcissism and Selfhood in Medieval French Literature: Wounds of Desire* (New York: Palgrave Macmillan, 2019), 227–28. For a detailed analysis of echoes of Ovid's Narcissus in medieval French romance, and trauma and wounds in relation to selfhood, see this excellent volume.

25 Ealy, *Narcissism and Selfhood*, 231.

> So (Narcissus) saw his face, his nose, and
> His mouth in the clear, clean water.
> Now he was stunned,
> For his shadow betrayed him,
> Since he thought that he saw the face
> Of an outrageously handsome child.

Narcissus's legacy soon becomes fraught and bleeds into the present, mapping onto our protagonist. Guillaume's Narcissus falls prey to the fountain's illusion and never recognizes himself; the Dreamer, not recognizing his own weakness, doesn't see that he too will fall prey to the folly of Love.

Let us recall that Ovid's Narcissus falls in love with his image, and calls out: "Why, O peerless youth, do you elude me?" (3: vv. 454–55) but soon realizes his mistake and dies knowing his blunder, crying out *iste ego sum!* – "I am he!" (3: vv. 463–64).[26] As Nicholas Ealy writes, "Ovid's myth of Narcissus establishes itself as a narrative about selfhood," and the *iste ego sum* moment "establishes a central understanding of how selfhood emerges from the tense interplay with something *other.*"[27] Ovid's Narcissus dies knowing that he can only love this image of himself: the result is self-annihilation, death, and vegetal rebirth. On the other hand, Guillaume's Narcissus has been tricked (*trai*) by his shadow, and falls in love with the *enfant bel a desmesure*: he never recognizes himself in the reflection. He dies soon thereafter, and that is, quite simply, the end of the story: "Ce fu la some de la chose" (v. 1493). There is no narcissus flower, just a legacy of misrecognition and fatal desire. Guillaume's retelling – at fifty-eight lines – is a fraction of Ovid's 141 lines (3: vv. 370–510), and Narcissus neither speaks nor recognizes himself. His transformation into madness is explained once he is dead – for he never would be able to satisfy his desire:

> Si en fu morz a la parclose:
> Ce fu la some de la chose.
> Quar quant il vit qu'il ne porroit
> Acomplir ce qu'il desirroit
> Et qui l'avoit si pris par fort
> Qu'il n'en porroit avoir confort
> En nule fin ne en nul sen
> Il perdi d'ire tout son sen
> Et fu morz en pou de termine. (vv. 1492–1500)

---

26 Ovid, *Metamorphoses*, ed. G. P. Goold, trans. Frank Justus Miller, Books I–VIII (1921; Cambridge: Harvard University Press, 1984).
27 Ealy, *Narcissism and Selfhood*, 7–8.

And so in the end he died:
That was the whole story.
For when he saw that he could not
Fulfill that which he desired,
Which had taken him so strongly,
That he could not have any solace
Neither in any resolution nor any feeling,
He lost all reasoning by anger
And died soon thereafter.

Amor avenges Echo by exploiting Narcissus's *grant orgueil* – great pride – and his contempt for and power over Echo, but we don't see Narcissus realizing this (v. 1487), just as the Dreamer will later refuse to acknowledge the danger in which he places himself (v. 1519).

The Dreamer does not explain where or when he has learned the story, but the memory is strong enough that he is afraid to look again:

> Quant li escriz m'ot fet savoir
> Que ce estoit trestout pour voir,
> La fontaine au bel Narcisus,
> Je me trais lors ·i· pou en sus,
> Que dedenz n'osai regarder,
> Ainz commençai a coarder,
> Et de Narcisus me sovint
> Cui malement en mesavint.
> Mes je pensé que a seür,
> Sanz paor de mauves eür,
> A la fontaine aler porroie
> Par folie m'en esmaioie. (vv. 1508–19)

When the inscription informed me
That this was entirely in truth
The fountain of the handsome Narcissus,
I went a bit further up,
But I did not dare look inside,
And I began to act cowardly
And I recalled Narcissus,
Who experienced such horrible misfortune.
But I thought that I could safely,
Without fear of bad luck,
Go to the fountain,
And that it was folly to be alarmed.

He assures himself that he is safe – it would be mad to worry about sharing Narcissus's fate. But the Dreamer *does* share Narcissus's fate of failing to recognize the object of his desire. Furthermore, Guillaume's misreading of Ovid asks the question of what it is to rewrite Narcissus, for other twelfth-century Latin and vernacular sources containing references to Narcissus attest to the fact that a reader could easily have encountered a more faithful adaptation. Moreover, Guillaume's version writes Narcissus as a mirror for the Dreamer, but the tale is soon confusingly glossed. Guillaume misreads his own retelling of the tale, and finishes it with a lesson, a warning to women:

> Dames, cest essemple aprenez,
> Qui vers vos amis mesprenez,
> Car se vous les laissez morir,
> Dieus le vos saura bien merir. (vv. 1504–7)

> Ladies, you who mistreat your lovers,
> Learn from this exemplum,
> Because if you let your lovers die,
> God knows well how to pay you back.

The female reader, in this exemplum, is discouraged from spurning her lover and letting him die, for God will repay her in kind. But, as Guillaume has already explained, it is Echo who dies after having been spurned by her would-be lover (vv. 1450–60). The reader cannot help but be surprised at this seemingly contradictory glossing of the tale. The tale is reversed again and the reader is asked to accept this incompatible moral – to misread what she or he has just read. Narcissus – and in turn the Dreamer – are both mirrors for us, the readers. This mismatched moral lesson – which the Dreamer accepts (and uses to justify his own invulnerability to the fountain) – also encourages the reader to take part in these misreadings, to go forward under false pretenses. The Lover assumes that he cannot be Narcissus, a boy who unwittingly falls for his own reflection, rendered sodomitical in his love for the unidentified *enfant bel a desmesure* and then feminized in the warning for women. He is tricked by language, much like a cuckolded husband of a fabliau: in accepting the exemplum's mismatched lesson, he ignores the very real possibility of losing himself in the fountain, in a reflection of himself or of his desire.

The mismatched morals of this narcissine fable might have been part of the very fabric of the tale. Alan of Lille's *Plaint of Nature*, a twelfth-century prosimetrum in which Nature bemoans the perversion of grammar and sex in the contemporary world, uses Narcissus as a warning tale against effeminacy and sodomy. Nature explains to Alan's Dreamer that

> Believing himself to be this other self, [Narcissus] *brought upon himself through himself a perilous love*. And many other young men, endowed with glorious beauty through my favor, but drunk with the thirst for wealth, have converted their hammers of Venus to perform the function of the anvil.[28]

Nature has already warned that hammers must only perform their natural, creative function, lest they transgress the natural order.[29] Alan thus warns that narcissism leads to sodomy, and that men have traded in their hammers, or penises, for anvils, or vaginas.[30] Narcissus thus functions as a figure for inversion, for misgendered relations.

Meanwhile, Guillaume's Dreamer falls prey to the fountain and to Narcissus's folly: first he sees two crystals (v. 1535), which inexplicably become one (v. 1546), and then he sees a reflection of the Garden of Deduit (Pleasure) in the perilous mirror. As Suzanne Conklin Akbari writes, "the crystals mark a liminal moment in Guillaume's allegory of vision, for after the Lover looks into them, he passes from the realm of reflected vision, *intuition*, into that of refracted vision, *detuitio* or *deduit*."[31] A warning follows, explaining that even the most noble have succumbed to the perilous mirror:

> C'est li mireors perilleus
> Ou Narcisus li orgueilleus
> Mira sa face et ses yauz vers,
> Dont il jut puis mort toz envers.
> Qui enz ou mireor se mire,
> Ne puet avoir garant ne mire
> Que tel chose a ses ieulz ne voie
> Qui d'amors l'a tout mis an voie.
> Maint vaillant home a mis a glaive
> Cil mireors, car li plus saive,
> Li plus preu, li plus afaitie
> I sont tost pris et agaitie. (vv. 1568–79)

---

[28] "Narcisus etiam sui umbra alterum mentita Narcisum, umbraliter obumbratus, seipsum credens esse alterum se, de se sibi amoris incurrit periculum. Multi etiam alii iuvenes mei gratia pulchritudinis honore vestiti, siti debriati pecuniae, suos Veneris malleos in incudum transtulerunt officia." Alan of Lille, *The Plaint of Nature*, 8§10.
[29] Alan of Lille, *The Plaint of Nature*, 10§2.
[30] Cf. Jan Ziolkowski, *Alan of Lille's Grammar of Sex: The Meaning of Grammar to a Twelfth-Century Intellectual* (Cambridge: Medieval Academy of America, 1985), 30.
[31] Suzanne Conklin Akbari, "Guillaume de Lorris's *Roman de la Rose*," in *Seeing Through the Veil: Optical Theory and Medieval Allegory* (Toronto: University of Toronto Press, 2004), 45–77 at 67.

> This is the perilous mirror
> Where Narcissus the haughty
> Saw his face and his bright eyes
> For which he fell dead, backwards.
> And he who looks at himself in the mirror
> Cannot have security nor a doctor
> To assure that his eyes do not see that
> Which it placed in the way to love.
> This mirror has led many a valiant
> To the sword, for the wisest,
> The most noble, and the most adroit
> Have been taken and ambushed here.

Narcissus dies both *toz envers* – reversed – and *en vers*, in verse: he dies at the fountain and he dies in translation, rewritten as a different figure, a refraction of Ovid's figure. This, as Ealy notes, is echoed in Réné d'Anjou's *Livre du cœur d'Amour épris*, although Réné's "alter ego appears to be the true literary manifestation of his tormented experiences with love."[32] In Guillaume's version, the Dreamer will soon follow suit, and his fall pulls him away from Guillaume-as-narrator and away from the Ovidian tradition. Instead of being transformed into a flower, he becomes a trite warning to haughty dames. The Dreamer soon realizes that he too has been deceived – "Cil mireors m'a deceü" – and realizes that which Narcissus fatally failed to do (v. 1606); nevertheless he too is lost in the mirror, mesmerized by the reflections of rosebushes. Amor strikes him with an arrow, and the Dreamer then performs Narcissus's death, falling to the ground and passing out (vv. 1697–99). Now *tantost versez*, the Dreamer has performed Narcissus's death (*mort toz envers*). He has been distracted by the reflection in the fountain and has fallen prey to Amor. The Dreamer continues his refusal to recognize himself as mirroring Narcissus.

This is decidedly not Ovid's Narcissus, but neither is it Alan's. As a reader, the gloss which maps Narcissus onto brutal female lovers encourages the reader to misgender Narcissus, and thus we are encouraged to misplace and swap our own hammers and anvils. The repetition of *mireor* ("miror") and *mirer* ("to look," cf. vv. 1568–79 above), with the addition of the homophone *mire*, or doctor, focuses the reader on visual aspects, despite a warning in the prologue that in dreams one sees *Maintes choses covertement / Que l'en voit puis apertement*, that one sees "all sorts of hidden things that one later understands overtly" (vv. 19–20). If we, the readers, keep waiting for an overt understanding

---

[32] Ealy, *Narcissism and Selfhood*, 104.

of the text, then we are moving forward as clueless as Narcissus. As Jonathan Morton notes, part of the intrigue of the *Rose* is that this promise of overt resolution is never fulfilled.[33] In other words, the *roman* is perhaps more about the process of uncovering meaning and decoding, rather than in actually finding that hidden truth, as I also argue here. I see Guillaume's fountain as both a mirror and a crystal, and thus it not only reflects but it alters and refracts: Guillaume's Narcissus is distracted, and his Dreamer's search for the rose results in what Male Bouche names a *mauvais acointement* – an inappropriate relationship – between Bel Acueil and the Dreamer (3519–23). When Jalousie imprisons Bel Acueil (3624–26), the Dreamer is stricken and once again performs Narcissus's fall: "Et je sui cil qui est versez!" (And I am he who is turned upside-down [3989]), crying out that Bel Acueil is both his joy and his salvation ("ma joie et ma garison | Est tout en lui et en la rose" [my joy and my cure is entirely in him and the rose] [3995–96]). Bel Acueil becomes a mirror of the rose, a substitute for the desired object. The tale then abruptly ends as the Dreamer loses all confidence (*fiance*) in others.

There is a radical failure of the text to provide narrative coherence or resolution, and Guillaume's failure to finish the text may be, as scholars have only recently accepted, part of its textuality. In other words, as scholars such as Paul Strohm, Suzanne Conklin Akbari, David Hult, and Peter Haidu have argued, the first part of the *Rose* can be read as a complete document, its "unfinished" nature integral to this reading of the work.[34] This also allows for Guillaume's version to be read outside of the admittedly fraught but pervasive focus on heterosexual reproductivity in Jean's continuation. Furthermore, Jean's scholasticism and references to Alan of Lille serve in certain ways to recover meaning and to rehabilitate what Jean sees as the mediocrity of Guillaume's version. Hult's influential *Self-fulfilling Prophecies* argues that *Rose* is complete, "insofar as it can be seen to form an artistic whole consistent with stylistic and narrative standards of judgment as well as with medieval poetic traditions."[35] He also asserts that the "misreading" of Guillaume's text as unfinished, and as needing to be finished, results from accepting Jean de Meun's claims. The art of the *Rose*, he argues, is

---

[33] Jonathan Morton, "État-présent: Le roman de la rose," *French Studies* 69.1 (2015): 79–86 at 79.
[34] Paul Strohm, "Guillaume as Narrator and Lover in the *Roman de la Rose*," *Romanic Review* 59.1 (1968): 3–9; Peter Haidu, "Problematizing the Subject: *Rose I*," in *The Subject Medieval/Modern: Text and Governance in the Middle Ages* (Stanford: Stanford University Press, 2004), 215–38; Hult, *Self-fulfilling Prophecies*; Akbari, "Guillaume de Lorris's *Roman de la Rose*."
[35] Hult, *Self-fulfilling Prophecies*, 6.

that it is an "elaborate *trompe d'œil*": "Guillaume's *trompe d'œil* is the unfinished edge that becomes a part of what is from another point of view a completed masterpiece."[36] Haidu sees the *Rose* as an exercise in retreating to an internal space of love, freed from the constraints of courtly violence: "[w]arrior violence, even its submission to love, is elided in the *Rose Novel*. Only love's desire remains, rather than 'honor,' to propel the narrative."[37] Thus, "[i]n the place of the subject, it leaves only *d'amer volonté pure*: the pure desire to love, the pure will to love. That purity itself dissolves the subject," which would have led the author to abandon the *Rose* and never write again.[38]

Hult's and Haidu's proposals are compelling, but what seems to be happening in this work is even more complicated. Haidu sees the *Rose* as attempting to create a space outside of politics and Hult sees this as a *trompe d'œil*. As this chapter demonstrates, in using misreading as a device for translation and for allegorical production, Guillaume interrogates the use of allegory itself, and embraces the artifice of identity and the slippery nature of posterity. Rendering the Narcissus myth courtly, and then rendering it a fabliau, is at the center of the work, suggesting that meaning shifts in contexts and that interpretation is often a trap. Ovid is neither read simply as an exemplum – as a classic source providing a Christian lesson – nor is he rendered entirely comic in the narcissine fabliau. Guillaume uses Ovid as the material with which he interrogates allegory and interpretation: the levels of mirroring, decoding, and interpretation in *Rose* force the reader to acknowledge their own complicity in falling into Guillaume's trap. His *Rose* finishes as the Dreamer mourns his friend Bel Acueil, losing sight of the rose just as Narcissus lost sight of himself in the fountain. As Masha Raskolnikov writes, Jean, in mourning for Guillaume in his continuation, "self-consciously places himself in the future impossible, into a queer future, giving an unrestitutable continued life to Guillaume, letting him be the one who gets the girl."[39] And thus Jean perhaps finds himself as lost as we, as readers, find ourselves, in navigating Guillaume's text.

The Dreamer becomes non-viable in this narrative, he is unable to navigate the twists and turns of the text and to understand the fables within the *roman*. Just as Narcissus dies before recognizing himself, the Dreamer's final plaints prevent him from seeing his own downfall. The Narcissus exemplum, repeated in his multiple misrecognitions, leads to a failure to take up a life independent

---

[36] Hult, *Self-fulfilling Prophecies*, 8–9.
[37] Haidu, "Problematizing the Subject," 218.
[38] Haidu, "Problematizing the Subject," 238.
[39] Masha Raskolnikov, "Between Men, Mourning: Authorship, Love, and the Gift in the Roman de la Rose," *GLQ: A Journal of Lesbian and Gay Studies* 10.1 (2003): 47–75 at 69.

of Narcissus. Concerning translation and the "afterlife" of a work of art, Walter Benjamin writes:

> The idea of life and afterlife in works of art should be regarded with an entirely unmetaphorical objectivity. . . . The concept of life is given its due only if everything that has a history of its own, and is not merely the setting for history, is credited with life.[40]

Concerned with the "kinship of languages,"[41] Benjamin notes that there is always a near-impossibility in reproducing the meaning of the original, given the differences between languages and their socio-historical contexts. Thus, "[t]he task of the translator consists in finding the intended effect [Intention] upon the language into which he is translating which produces in it an echo of the original."[42] Producing an "echo of the original" reduces the text to linguistic analysis; thus Benjamin's earlier comment about the "bad translator." But this echo is always problematic: Ovid's Echo replies "adest" to Narcissus's "equis adest" (3: v. 380), for the echo never fully captures the first speech act. Guillaume is aware of this: an echo reflects but it also refracts, breaking the sound into parts that return in such a way that the intended effect of the first sound is lost in the distortion. But for his *Rose*, the echo is purely a literary device: Echo is mute in his version. For the Narcissus fable to take on a new life of its own in the *Rose*, the fable needed to reflect the ways in which Ovid's intention might be lost on readers more than a millennium later. Thus, the only way to read Ovid is through misreading, for the context of the original is but a hypothesis to the later reader. Guillaume thus "misreads" Ovid, his Dreamer misreads the misreading, and the reader is forced to take part in the game: either we fall into the many traps, knocked over in the tumult of interpretation – becoming lost *toz envers* and *toz en vers* – or we are left wondering what we can ever glean from a text without falling prey to our own Narcissism of interpretation. The *Rose* ultimately collapses as the interpretive game reaches its climax: the Dreamer is lost in his affection for Bel Acueil, a mirror of his desire for the rose, and the narrative itself disintegrates *en vers*, breaking off until Jean de Meun attempts to resuscitate the poem, itself a project of interpretation, misreading, and echoing of the original.

The narcissism of Guillaume's Narcissus arises in the wake of both Ovid and Alan of Lille, and offers a version that falls out of line with both. The narcissism of Ovid's Narcissus is predicated on that *iste ego sum!* moment of recognition, on, as Freud would later excavate, a libidinal desire to "[seek oneself] as

---

40 Benjamin, "Task of the Translator," 71.
41 Benjamin, "Task of the Translator," 72.
42 Benjamin, "Task of the Translator," 76.

a love-object" in opposition to the Oedipal desire for one's mother.[43] The failure of Guillaume's Narcissus to recognize himself dislodges, paradoxically, his queer desire from the narcissism of Freudian Oedipal socialization. The homosexual, as Guy Hocquenghem has trenchantly argued, is a product of capitalism and Freudian oedipalization,[44] just as, one could argue, the sodomite is a different but equally artificial construct of rhetoric. Moreover, as Jonathan Morton notes of both Alan of Lille and Jean de Meun, the very act of writing is a queer activity, for, as he notes, "the only way to remain totally straight is to abolish the ego, and to avoid writing, speaking, or thinking, to be no more than an unindividuated sex-machine."[45] The sexual poetics and politics in Jean de Meun's *Rose* are absent from the less scholastic *Rose* by Guillaume. What Guillaume offers is an impossible subject, one who is mapped back onto the reader through a series of gestures that collapse allegorical figure, lover, dreamer, narrator, writer, and reader. What makes Guillaume's Dreamer/Lover queer is this refusal to accept failure, in the face of failure. This might be akin to Lauren Berlant's "cruel optimism": "A relation of cruel optimism exists when something you desire is actually an obstacle to your flourishing."[46] Guillaume's Dreamer certainly has this quality: when he falls flat on his back, accused of sodomy and failing to secure his fetish-object, that unattainable rose, the narrative dissolves only to be repaired with Jean de Meun's verbose series of conflicting adventures and narratives that likewise fail to provide a coherent account of love. And yet he continues in our reading, and misreading of his tale. As José Esteban Muñoz writes, "[q]ueerness is utopian, and there is something queer about the utopian";[47] the queerness of the Dreamer's journey is not about sexual identification, rather it is in how Guillaume shows that fixation on one future, on one clear identity, is an impossible venture. "The present is not enough," Munõz writes: "Opening oneself up to such a perception of queerness as manifestation in and of ecstatic time offers queers much more than the meager offerings of pragmatic gay and lesbian politics."[48]

---

43 Freud, "On Narcissism: An Introduction," 54–55.
44 Guy Hocquenghem, *Le désir homosexuel* (1972; Paris: Fayard, 2000), 23–29.
45 Jonathan Morton, "Queer Metaphors and Queerer Reproduction in the *De planctu naturae* and the *Roman de la rose*," in *Dante and Desire in the Middle Ages*, ed. Manuele Gragnolati, Tristan Kay, Elena Lombardi, and Francesca Southerden (Oxford: Legenda, 2012), 208–26.
46 Lauren Berlant, *Cruel Optimism* (Durham: Duke University Press, 2011), 1.
47 José Esteban Muñoz, Joshua Chambers-Letson, Tavia Nyong'o, and Ann Pellegrini, *Cruising Utopia, 10th Anniversary Edition: The Then and There of Queer Futurity* (New York: New York University Press, 2019), 26.
48 Muñoz, Chambers-Letson, Nyong'o, and Pellegrini, *Cruising Utopia*, 27, 32.

If the point of Guillaume's *Rose* is not to provide answers, but rather to provoke our desire for them, how can we make sense of the queer figures of Narcissus and the Dreamer, of the Lover and the reader? The *Rose*, despite its failure to imagine any future, does not embrace a resistance to futurity; rather, it always gestures toward a difficult, perhaps unattainable, but always indecipherable next step. There is something improbable, something impossible, in the fractured figure of our protagonist, at once and at times dreamer, lover, reader, writer. The didacticism of the *Rose* is pervasive in the lessons that it attempts to teach but insidious in its constant attempts to dupe the reader as he or she is watching the protagonist fail at decoding his dream world. The queerness of the Dreamer is in his failure to navigate the courtly codes of the romance: the rose – at once abstraction, metonym, and fetish-object – is lost as the Dreamer's journey to conquer the rose becomes more of a journey with Bel Acueil, leading to Male Bouche's aforementioned accusation that the two are involved in a *mauvais acointement*, perhaps sodomy (vv. 3519–23).

In a 1981 interview, Foucault attempts to reimagine *askesis*, to return to its classical origins in reflection and self-fashioning. This move is a sort of reparative reading of the *askesis* described in the third volume of his *History of Sexuality*. Here, Foucault speaks of an art of existence that is predicated on self-fashioning, on "taking care" of oneself.[49] Foucault imagines a "homosexual ascesis" in an attempt to imagine friendship outside of institutional, familial, and professional relations. He argues that

> L'ascétisme comme renonciation au plaisir a mauvaise réputation. Mais l'ascèse est autre chose: c'est le travail que l'on fait soi-même sur soi-même pour se transformer ou pour faire apparaître ce soi qu'heureusement on n'atteint jamais. Est-ce que ce ne serait pas ça

---

[49] "On peut caractériser brièvement cette 'culture de soi' par le fait que l'existence – la *technē tou biou* – s'y trouve dominé par le principe qu'il faut 'prendre soin de soi-même'; c'est ce principe du souci de soi qui en fonde la nécessité, en commande le développement et en organise le pratique. Mais il faut préciser; l'idée qu'on doit s'appliquer à soi-même, s'occuper de soi-même (*heautou epimeleisthai*) est en effet un thème fort ancien dans la culture grecque" (Foucault, *Le souci de soi* [Paris: Gallimard, 1984], 60–61) ("This 'cultivation of the self' can be briefly characterized by the fact that in this case the art of existence – the *technē tou biou* in its different forms – is dominated by the principle that says one must 'take care of oneself.' It is this principle of the care of the self that establishes its necessity, presides over its development, and organizes its practice. But one has to be precise here; the idea that one ought to attend to oneself, care for oneself [*heautou epimeleisthai*], was actually a very ancient theme in Greek culture") (*The Care of the Self*, trans. Robert Hurley [New York: Pantheon, 1986], 43); N.B.: This is in contrast to the Christian asceticism described in the 1981 lectures at Louvain, where penitence and confession are shown to be a new form of ascesis in which the truth of the self ceases to be self-fashioned and becomes textual and external with the rise of Christianity.

notre problème aujourd'hui? Congé a été donné à l'ascétisme. À nous d'avancer dans une ascèse homosexuelle qui nous ferait travailler sur nous-mêmes et inventer, je ne dis pas découvrir, une manière d'être encore improbable.

Asceticism as the renunciation of pleasure has bad connotations. But ascesis is something else: it's the work that one performs on oneself in order to transform oneself or make the self appear which, happily, one never attains. Can that be our problem today? We've rid ourselves of asceticism. Yet it's up to us to advance into a homosexual ascesis that would make us work on ourselves and invent – I do not say discover – a manner of being that is still improbable.[50]

This feeling of crisis and desire for the unknown or unrecognizable is echoed a decade later in the memoirs of queer artist David Wojnarowicz, who fears, but also celebrates, that "one of the last frontiers left for radical gesture is in the imagination."[51] This queerness of fiction and writing is hardly modern, as Alan of Lille's Natura worries about the creative potential of the pen, and explains that Venus must use her stylus correctly, lest she produce *falsigraphia*, or false writing:

> For the purpose of inscription I bestowed upon [Venus] a most powerful pen, that she might depict the different kinds of creatures, according to the rules of my orthography, on pages, provided through my kind generosity, that were prepared to await the inscriptions of this pen, so that she might never stray from the past of truthful description into the sidetracks of false writing.[52]

Writing this poses the existential danger of undoing truth, of inviting the "improbable," in Foucault's terms, of being open to radical gestures without the guidance of Natura and faithful attention to orthography and grammar.

Guillaume's Dreamer reads, rereads, and misreads out of his own narcissism and refusal to see himself as echoing Narcissus. Thus, much like barebacking for Bersani, there is "impersonal intimacy" in hermeneutical desire.

---

50 Foucault, *Le souci de soi*, 82–83; *The Care of the Self*, 137.
51 "I'm beginning to believe that one of the last frontiers left for radical gesture is the imagination. At least in my ungoverned imagination I can fuck somebody without a rubber, or I can, in the privacy of my own skull, douse Helms with a bucket of gasoline and set his putrid ass on fire or throw congressman William Dannemeyer off the empire state building. These fantasies give me distance from my outrage for a few seconds. They give me momentary comfort. Sexuality defined in images gives me comfort in a hostile world. They give me strength" (David Wojnarowicz, *Close to the Knives: A Memoir of Disintegration* [New York: Vintage, 1991], 120).
52 "Ad officium etiam scripturae, calamum praepotentem eidem fueram elargita, ut in competentibus schedulis ejusdem calami scripturam poscentibus, quarum meae largitionis beneficio fuerat compotita, juxta meae orthographiae normulam, rerum genera figuraret, ne a propriae descriptionis semita in falsigraphiae devio eumdem divagari sustineret" (Alan of Lille, *The Plaint of Nature*, 10 § 2).

Bersani's impersonal narcissism is predicated on Socratic pederasty, wherein the beloved is a godlike phantasm of the lover, a composite of projection and idealization. "The similarities between the theological notion of 'pure love' and the dangerous sexual practice of barebacking may not, to say the least, be immediately clear," Bersani writes. "And yet both can be thought of as disciplines in which the subject allows himself to be penetrated, even replaced, by an unknowable otherness."[53] Like the idealized love in the *Rose*, this impersonal intimacy seeks to replace, to render incomprehensible, the self. For Bersani, the Platonic ideal becomes a form for the fantasy of "impersonal narcissism," a love relation that he considers to be "revolutionary":

> The boy we madly love does not simply remind us of the Beauty we saw before being imprisoned in a body. Remember that every soul followed a particular god in his heavenly flights; on earth, "every one spends his life honoring the god in whose chorus he danced." This entails seeking a boy "whose nature is like the god's." . . . The boy's beauty is a likeness of an ideal Beauty; more specifically, he also has a particular nature that is the type of being most fully realized in a particular god. . . . The beloved loves the lover's image of him, which is of course the version of himself that makes the lover remember both heavenly Beauty and the god with whom the lover's soul had flown. . . . In a sense, the lover recognizes *his* ideal ego in the boy, desiring the boy is a way of infusing the boy with an ideal self that is both the boy's and the lover's.[54]

Adam Phillips glosses:

> The similarities between the theological notion of "pure love" and the dangerous sexual practice of barebacking may not, to say the least, be immediately clear. And yet both can be thought of as disciplines in which the subject allows himself to be penetrated, even replaced, by an unknowable otherness.[55]

The *Rose* unveils the danger of this fetish – embodied in the disembodied rose – as it asserts the impossibility of escaping Narcissus's fate. The falling *toz envers* and *en vers* is a thrust forward toward a different iteration of ourselves and our desires, but we cannot ever reach the Dreamer's rose – or Bersani's boy – in Guillaume's world.

As Lee Edelman notes, "the social order exists to preserve for [the] universalized subject, [the] fantasmic Child";[56] Alan of Lille would push that further, I argue, and say that writing itself exists to preserve for reproductive futurity.

---

53 Bersani and Phillips, *Intimacies*, 53.
54 Bersani and Phillips, *Intimacies*, 81, 83–84.
55 Bersani and Phillips, *Intimacies*, 117.
56 Lee Edelman, *No Future: Queer Theory and the Death Drive* (Durham: Duke University Press, 2004), 11.

Guillaume preemptively undoes this by demonstrating how the reader is always reproducing him- or herself in failed ways. This is our *only* manner of interpretation, in his view. The constant uncovering in the *Roman de la Rose* reminds us that interpretation is not the revealing of truth but rather hermeneutical layering, supplementing, and buggering of a text or situation that always evades us at present and is only revealed as a reflection, refracted like the rose seen in two crystals at the bottom of Narcissus's fountain. The fountain, Guillaume assured us, was a mirror that showed us things *sanz coverture* (v. 1554) – openly – and yet this is also the perilous mirror of perception, deception, interpretation, and the means by which we construct our plastic and contentious identities. Penultimately – for there cannot be a final interpretation with Guillaume – what the *Rose* teaches us is that the traps of coherence and identity politics will be our downfall. We must resist, and become *encore improbable*.

Bibliography

Aimon de Varennes, *Florimont, ein altfranzösischer Abenteuerroman*. Edited by Alfons Hilka. Göttingen: Gedruckt für die Gesellschaft für romanische Literatur, 1932.
Akbari, Suzanne Conklin. "Guillaume de Lorris's *Roman de la Rose*." In *Seeing Through the Veil: Optical Theory and Medieval Allegory*, 45–77. Toronto: University of Toronto Press, 2004.
Alan of Lille. *Literary Works*. Edited and translated by Winthrop Wetherbee. Cambridge: Dumbarton Oaks Medieval Library, 2013.
Baldwin, James. *The Fire Next Time* (New York: Vintage, 1963).
Benjamin, Walter. "The Task of the Translator." In *Illuminations*, trans. Harry Zorn, 69–82. New York: Schocken, 2007.
Benoît de Saint-Maure. *Le Roman de Troie*. Edited by Léopold Constans. 6 vols. Paris: Firmin-Didot et c^{ie}, 1904–1912.
Berlant, Lauren. *Cruel Optimism*. Durham: Duke University Press, 2011.
Bersani, Leo and Adam Phillips. *Intimacies*. Chicago: University of Chicago Press, 2008.
Chrétien de Troyes. *Cligès*. Edited by Laurence Harf-Lancner. Paris: Honoré Champion, 2006.
Ealy, Nicholas. *Narcissism and Selfhood in Medieval French Literature: Wounds of Desire*. New York: Palgrave Macmillan, 2019.
Edelman, Lee. *No Future: Queer Theory and the Death Drive*. Durham: Duke University Press, 2004.
Foucault, Michel. *The Care of the Self*. Translated by Robert Hurley. New York: Pantheon, 1986.
Foucault, Michel. *Dits et Écrits*, vol. 2. Paris: Gallimard (Quarto), 2001.
Foucault, Michel. *Ethics: Subjectivity and Truth*. Edited by Paul Rabinow. New York: New Press, 1998.
Foucault, Michel. *Le souci de soi*. Paris: Gallimard, 1984.
Freud, Sigmund. "On Narcissism: An Introduction." In *General Psychological Theory*, 41–69. New York: Simon and Schuster, 1991.

Guillaume de Lorris and Jean de Meun. *Le Roman de la Rose*. Edited by Armand Strubel. Paris: Lettres Gothiques, 1992.

Haidu, Peter. "Problematizing the Subject. In *The Subject Medieval/Modern: Text and Governance in the Middle Ages*, 215–38. Stanford: Stanford University Press, 2004.

Harley, Marta Powell. "Narcissus, Hermaphroditus, and Attis: Ovidian Lovers at the Fontaine d'Amors in Guillaume de Lorris's *Roman de la rose*." *PMLA* 101.3 (1986): 324–37.

Hicks, Eric. "La mise en roman des formes allégoriques: hypostase et récit chez Guillaume de Lorris." In *Études sur le Roman de la Rose de Guillaume de Lorris*, edited by Jean eu: Honoré Champion, 1984.

Hocquenghem, Guy. *Le désir homosexuel*. Paris: Fayard, 2000.

Hult, David F. *Self-fulfilling Prophecies: Readership and Authority in the First* Roman de la Rose. New York: Cambridge University Press, 1986.

Morton, Jonathan. "État present: Le roman de la rose." *French Studies* 69.1 (2015): 79–86.

Morton, Jonathan. "Queer Metaphors and Queerer Reproduction in the *De planctu naturae* and the *Roman de la rose*." *Dante and Desire in the Middle Ages*, edited by Manuele Gragnolati, Tristan Kay, Elena Lombardi, and Francesca Southerden, 208–26. Oxford: Legenda, 2012.

Muñoz, José Esteban, Joshua Chambers-Letson, Tavia Nyong'o, and Ann Pellegrini. *Cruising Utopia, 10th Anniversary Edition: The Then and There of Queer Futurity*. New York: NYU Press, 2019.

Ovid. *Metamorphoses*. Edited by G. P. Goold. Translated by Frank Justus Miller. Books I–VIII. Cambridge: Harvard University Press, 1984.

Ovide moralisé: Poème du commencement du quatorzième siècle. Edited by C. de Boer. 3 vols. Amsterdam: Johannes Müller, 1915–1938.

Pugh, Tison. *Queering Medieval Genres*. New York: Palgrave Macmillan, 2004.

Pyrame et Thisbé, Narcisse, Philomena. Edited by Emmanuèle Baumgartner. Paris: Folio, 2000.

Raskolnikov, Masha. "Between Men, Mourning: Authorship, Love, and the Gift in the Roman de la Rose." *GLQ: A Journal of Lesbian and Gay Studies* 10.1 (2003): 47–75.

Strohm, Paul. "Guillaume as Narrator and Lover in the *Roman de la Rose*." *Romanic Review* 59.1 (1968): 3–9.

Wojnarowicz, David. *Close to the Knives: A Memoir of Disintegration*. New York: Vintage, 1991.

Ziolkowski, Jan. *Alan of Lille's Grammar of Sex: The Meaning of Grammar to a Twelfth-Century Intellectual*. Cambridge: Medieval Academy of America, 1985.

Lynn Shutters
Chapter 4
Sodom, Bretons, and Ill-Defined Borders: Questing for Queerness with the *Knight of the Tower*

This essay examines queerness in a medieval text where we might least expect to find it: *Le Livre du Chevalier de la Tour Landry pour l'enseignment de ses filles* (*The Book of the Knight of the Tower for the Instruction of His Daughters*), a French conduct book written by the knight Geoffroy de la Tour Landry in the late fourteenth century. From a modern-day perspective, this work seems profoundly heteronormative. The Knight-narrator assumes that his daughters will marry; to prepare them for this role he focuses on the virtuous behaviors through which they can attract and maintain a husband. While he draws stark distinctions between virtuous and wicked women, his exempla hardly seem queer: both good and bad women desire men; the question is whether they seek that man within or outside marriage. Queerness, however, is not so much absent from the *Livre du Chevalier* as it is represented indirectly; for modern-day readers, the *Livre*'s queerness is particularly hard to discern, since, despite caveats to the contrary, we all too often conflate queerness with homosexuality, or, among medievalists who eschew "homosexual" as too anachronistic in its implications, with same-sex sex acts, particularly acts between men which, in surviving medieval records, receive more direct documentation than do sex acts between women.[1] Questing for queerness within this rigidly moralistic conduct

---

[1] Surviving medieval accounts of sexuality often present sodomy as one of the most dangerous, socially outlawed forms of sexuality; therefore formulations of sodomy have been of particular interest to scholars of medieval queer studies. While medieval formulations of sodomy are notoriously indirect, some of the clearest surviving accounts of medieval sodomy focus on same-sex sex acts between men; on this see Judith M. Bennett, *History Matters: Patriarchy and the Challenge of Feminism* (Philadelphia: University of Pennsylvania Press, 2006), 111. Consequently, some important studies of medieval sodomy have focused on same-sex sex acts between men; see, for example, Mark D. Jordan, *The Invention of Sodomy in Christian Theology* (Chicago: University of Chicago Press, 1997) and William Burgwinkle, *Sodomy, Masculinity, and Law in Medieval Literature: France and England, 1050–1230* (Cambridge: Cambridge University Press, 2004). Not only is it more challenging to locate and identify evidence of same-sex sex acts between women in medieval texts,

---

Note: I would like to thank Lynn Ramey for help with translations of Middle French.

https://doi.org/10.1515/9781501513701-005

book allows us to expand the term beyond same-sex sex acts between men; to consider how female queerness might be formulated *by men*; and to contemplate how queerness might exceed the regulatory contexts within which it is here conceived.² I argue that what ends up being most queer in the *Livre du Chevalier* is *fin amor*, a claim counterintuitive to modern-day associations of courtly love with the brave knight and the beautiful lady, with heteronormativity *tout court*. Yet, for the Knight, *fin amor* is an outdated mode of emotional and sexual behavior, and one which his book renders queer in temporal terms. In warning his daughters against *fin amor*, the Knight casts it as a queer practice to which women are particularly susceptible, even as he struggles to resist *fin amor*'s powerful pull.

The *Livre du Chevalier* in fact opens with the *fin amor* longings of the Knight, who appears in a springtime garden, lamenting the loss of the lady love of his youth. The twenty years that have transpired since her death have done nothing to mitigate the Knight's sorrow, nor should they, he claims, for a true, loyal lover always remembers his beloved. Here setting and sentiment locate the Knight within the world of *fin amor*, as does generic form. "[T]he Prologue," as Roberta Krueger observes, "begins not as a prose tract but as a lyric octosyllabic *dit* that has been set into prose."³ The Knight's musings come to an abrupt halt when his young daughters appear and inspire a different recollection of times past. The Knight recalls the companions of his youth, "beaux langagiers et emparlez" (eloquent speakers), who employed the language of love to seduce and deceive women (Prologue, p. 3).⁴ False knights, the Knight fears, continue to circulate and thus pose a risk to his daughters, a risk the Knight counters by

---

but it is challenging to recognize other forms of female queerness as well, since many medieval discussions of femininity focused on sexuality as a particular point of female weakness; therefore for women to go against naturalized prescriptions of sexuality was, paradoxically, viewed as part of female nature and would not necessarily be queer. As my essay demonstrates, it is possible to locate queerness within what might seem like normative constructions of female sexuality, and doing so might help us identify pressure points at which those constructions were most volatile or contested.

2 In formulating female queerness in the Middle Ages, my work draws on that of Karma Lochrie, *Heterosyncrasies: Female Sexuality When Normal Wasn't* (Minneapolis: University of Minnesota Press, 2005) and Robert Mills, *Seeing Sodomy in the Middle Ages* (Chicago: University of Chicago Press, 2015), 248–70.

3 Roberta L. Krueger, "Intergeneric Combination and the Anxiety of Gender in Le Livre Du Chevalier De La Tour Landry Pour L'Enseignement De Ses Filles," *L'Esprit Createur* 33 (1993): 61–72 at 63.

4 Geoffroy de la Tour Landry, *Le Livre du chevalier de La Tour Landry, pour l'enseignement de ses filles*, ed. Anatole de Montaiglon (Paris: P. Jannet, 1854; repr. Nabu Press, 2010). All subsequent quotations of this text are cited parenthetically by Prologue/chapter number and page number.

writing a book of instruction to prepare them for entrance into the larger world. Youthful reminiscence gives way to parental responsibility, and the Knight is propelled out of his garden and forced to recollect *fin amor* differently, as masculine deception resulting in feminine shame. Although the Knight distinguishes himself from his former companions, one cannot help but wonder if they function as the hypothetical friend who screens a guilty speaker. At the very least, these "other men" invite speculation regarding the possibility of the Knight's own youthful indiscretions, in which case, as Krueger notes, his aim is "to warn his daughters against men precisely like himself."[5] Notably, the Knight's solution to the perils of *fin amor* is not that men behave better but that women shield themselves from seduction. Men, the Knight implies, are unable or unwilling to learn from the past. Women, in progressing away from *fin amor* and toward love-based marriage, propel their society toward the present and future.

And yet the emotion from which the Knight so definitively turns at the opening of his treatise reemerges at its end when, after recounting multiple exempla excoriating *fin amor*, the Knight advocates in its favor in a debate with his wife, who here gives voice to the many arguments that the Knight rehearses earlier. The debate provides further fodder against *fin amor* by presenting the Knight's arguments in a different mode, dialogic, as opposed to narrative, and from a different perspective, a woman's, as opposed to a man's.[6] Certainly the Knight's backsliding from his earlier stance on *fin amor* proves a point from his Prologue: men, on their own, are incapable of abandoning this emotion and require female intervention to do so. While the Knight's recidivism is performative, I want to suggest that his ongoing investment in *fin amor* is more than a straw man stance. The Knight's preoccupation with his own youthful love practices opens up a temporal dimension to sexual transgression, and he consequently attempts to distinguish *fin amor* from virtuous marriage using temporal terms, associating *fin amor* with stasis, immaturity, and the past and marriage with progress, adulthood, and the future. By casting *fin amor* as a backward, superseded mode of emotion and sexuality, the Knight also casts it as queer.

The temporal queerness of the *Livre du Chevalier* aligns this medieval French conduct book with recent work in queer theory focusing on sequence and time. If, on the one hand, heteronormative regimes cast homosexuality as a derivative and failed copy of heterosexuality, then, on the other, to quote Heather Love,

---

[5] Krueger, "Intergeneric Combination," 63.

[6] As Glenn D. Burger convincingly argues, by advising her husband well, the Knight's wife is herself an exemplum of new models of virtuous female conduct. See Burger, *Conduct Becoming: Good Wives and Husbands in the Later Middle Ages* (Philadelphia: University of Pennsylvania Press, 2018), 88–104.

"queers have been seen . . . as a backward race. Perverse, immature, sterile, and melancholic: even when they provoke fears about the future, they somehow also recall the past."[7] Or, as Elizabeth Freeman argues, queers defy "chrononormativity," a term she coins for "the interlocking temporal schemes necessary for genealogies of descent and for the mundane workings of domestic life."[8] Societies, Freeman argues, ground themselves in temporality, in the histories and rhythms that establish where a people come from and where they are going, and therefore delineate who a people are. Individuals are expected to synchronize their own movements through time, in terms of maturation, work, and reproduction, with these histories and rhythms, such that "[m]anipulations of time convert historically specific regimes of asymmetrical power into seemingly ordinary bodily tempos and routines, which in turn organize the value and meaning of time."[9] Queers, however, march to the beat of a different drum, or they refuse to move on to a new beat when their society demands it.

Freeman explains this queer recalcitrance through the concept of temporal drag, a play on the familiar queer practice of drag performance to disrupt naturalized regimes. Freeman, however, invites us to consider drag "as a *temporal phenomenon*"; "as an excess . . . of the signifier 'history' rather than of 'woman' or 'man.'"[10] Temporal drag, she argues, involves performing outdated, anachronistic versions of gender and sexuality, and therefore constitutes "a countergenealogical practice of archiving culture's throwaway objects, including the outmoded masculinities and femininities from which usable pasts may be extracted."[11] *Fin amor*, in the Knight's *Livre*, can be understood as just such a cultural "throwaway object," a set of "outmoded masculinities and femininities" beyond which both the individual knight and the late medieval French nobility have allegedly evolved. Despite the Knight's best efforts to distance himself and his daughters from *fin amor*, he fails to do so, and his ongoing investment in *fin amor* constitutes a medieval version of temporal drag. The Knight, however, is a reluctant performer, and he attempts to alleviate his own temporal instability through a revision of categories, by reconceptualizing *fin amor* as adultery and sodomy. Sodomy emerges in the conduct book as the negative counterpoint through which the Knight seeks to enforce chrononormativity,

---

[7] Heather Love, *Feeling Backward: Loss and the Politics of Queer History* (Cambridge: Harvard University Press, 2007), 6.
[8] Elizabeth Freeman, *Time Binds: Queer Temporalities, Queer Histories* (Durham: Duke University Press, 2010), xxii.
[9] Freeman, *Time Binds*, 3.
[10] Freeman, *Time Binds*, 62.
[11] Freeman, *Time Binds*, xxiii.

a point I make by focusing the second and third sections of this essay on two of the Knight's exempla: the exemplum featuring Sodom and Lot's wife, and one featuring the bizarre sexual practices of a society of "Galois" (a term I consider in detail in Section 3).

Sodomy, as scholars frequently note, makes only oblique appearances in medieval texts, and must be teased out on a text-by-text basis. Thus, in his study of sodomy and medieval theology, Mark D. Jordan eschews casting a wide net across texts to instead home in on the complex interplay of meanings that a single text offers. Adopting theater as a metaphor, he advocates that "we . . . regard the terms [associated with sodomy] as protagonists in the plots of various classifications, arguments, or persuasions and the texts themselves as performances. We are to learn what kind of character each protagonist has by watching its actions in the performance."[12] Thus, with each new textual construction of sodomy, we must not only "learn anew" the terms for sodomy, but also identify that text's "resources for teaching readers how its central terms are to be used."[13] In her study of avant-garde queer art, Freeman adopts a similar methodology. "Reading closely," she argues, "means fixating on that which resists any easy translation into present-tense terms, any 'progressive' program for the turning of art into a cultural/historical magic bullet or toxin."[14] Like Jordan, Freeman focuses up close, on individual exemplars rather than an archive, "to treat . . . texts and their formal work as theories of their own."[15] In this essay I adopt a similar methodology: to connect my selected exempla to each other and the Prologue, I trace a chain of associations that include emotion (*fin amor*, conjugal love), sexual practices (adultery, sodomy), cultural entities (Sodom, ancient Britons, ducal Brittany), and temporal concepts and terms (looking backward, in the case of Lot's wife, and the term "temps" itself in the story of the Galois). In the first section of the essay, I introduce many of these terms and provide the historical context necessary to connect them. In addition to connections between terms and concepts, I am interested in the fluidity of terms and concepts themselves, how *fin amor* transmutes into adultery and sodomy, for example, or how the term "Galois" translates to both revelers and Bretons.

A key difference, I should note, between the queer artists Freeman studies and the Knight-narrator of the *Livre du Chevalier* is that while the former adopt strategies like temporal drag actively to resist their dominant culture, the Knight writes his conduct book to promote the dominant culture of his own era,

---

12 Jordan, *Invention of Sodomy*, 5.
13 Jordan, *Invention of Sodomy*, 5.
14 Freeman, *Time Binds*, xvi.
15 Freeman, *Time Binds*, xvii.

and the resistance his book registers marks moments where his project is beyond his control. I am consequently drawn to a question posed by William Burgwinkle in his examination of accounts of sodomy in high medieval France and England: "Could courtly love texts, which have so often been read as the bedrock of monolithic, monologic heterosexuality, not be read instead as laboratory texts, a failed ideological experiment in imposing seamless models of (hetero)sexuality and gender?"[16] *Mutatis mutandis*, the same question can be posed of the seemingly conservative genre of conduct books, in which case conduct books might be just the site for theorizing the late medieval queer.

Following the Knight's Chain

In identifying the Knight's backward glance toward the lost love of his youth as a frame for his pedagogical mission, we might note the centrality of this mission to the French aristocracy more generally, for whom the fourteenth century was a tumultuous era. Wracked by both the Hundred Years' War with England and political upheaval within France, the aristocracy sorely required renovation as far as their self-perception was concerned, a need by no means lost on Charles V (r. 1364–1380), whose rule coincides with the composition of the Knight's *Livre*. Charles undertook a two-pronged program to strengthen monarchical authority and centralize his kingdom's administration; his success on both fronts was partially due to his skillful manipulation of the rhetoric of domesticity.[17] Charles promoted the well-ordered household, which, for him, was not confined to his immediate family but radiated out to include his court and his kingdom at large. Charles's male subjects were simultaneously the family over which he ruled and rulers over their own families; overseeing an orderly household marked Frenchmen as virtuous emulators of their king. In addition to bolstering Charles's authority, this program of reform provided opportunities to gentry like the author of the *Livre du Chevalier*, Geoffroy IV of the Tour Landry (died ca. 1402–1406), a knight in the region of Anjou. Surviving records indicate that Geoffroy participated in multiple battles in the Hundred Years'

---

16 Burgwinkle, *Sodomy, Masculinity, and Law*, 7.
17 My account of Charles V and household management is drawn from Lynn Staley, *Languages of Power in the Age of Richard II* (University Park: Pennsylvania State University Press, 2005), 265–338.

War and was eventually awarded the title *chevalier banneret*.[18] He married twice, both times to wealthy women. He composed his *Livre* in the early 1370s, when married to his first wife, Jeanne de Rougé, with whom he had at least two sons and three daughters. For a provincial knight whose fortunes were on the rise, composing a conduct book was doubly beneficial: it not only educates his daughters but also performs the knight's own virtue as a responsible head of household and therefore marks him as a loyal subject who is *au courant* of social practices extending well beyond his home region. Whether Geoffroy consciously had this latter goal in mind when composing his *Livre* is a matter of speculation, but it is worth noting that the book circulated widely. The French text survives in twenty-one manuscripts, and the conduct book was translated into English and German, and printed in French and English.[19]

If the household was central to late medieval French culture, so too was marriage, the institution around which the household was built. At the time Geoffroy composed his book, marriage was rapidly transforming, with virtuous wifehood emerging as a pressing concern.[20] Although marital dynamics remained hierarchical, with a husband ruling over his wife, they nonetheless shifted, so that the conjugal couple was increasingly perceived as a partnership through which spouses negotiated their world together. The virtuous wife did not just obey her husband, she also advised him, although within a private sphere where she did not challenge his public authority. Ideally husbands and wives would consult and communicate with each other and, indeed, love each other; they would care for each other, and take their spouse's best interests to heart. As Burger notes, conduct books of this era departed from earlier constructions of femininity as an inherently deficient gender, one that virtuous women had to transcend to attain a semi-masculine status. Rather, women were imagined to possess gender-specific traits that complemented those of their husbands and could therefore be cultivated to mutually beneficial ends. Wifely virtue was construed as at once spiritual – by this point in history marriage ranked among the Church's sacraments – and practical, as wives were required to assess situations and determine how their behavior might be most beneficial to the conjugal household. In both registers, rote performance failed to suffice. The sanctity of marriage required that a wife's intentions be set toward virtue, that she desire to be not just an outwardly good wife but an inwardly good one as well. And the

---

18 For historical information regarding Geoffroy de la Tour Landry, see Montaiglon's preface to *Le Livre du Chevalier*, vi–xxvii.
19 Burger, *Conduct Becoming*, 89.
20 For an overview of medieval transformations in love and marriage, see Burger, *Conduct Becoming*, 1–32.

practicality of wifely virtue required a woman to view herself as her husband's partner, not his servant, and therefore to think deeply about what behaviors would best lend themselves to the greater good of the couple.[21]

If, in the *Livre du Chevalier*, wifely virtue is a cognitive, affective, and performative phenomenon, then its foil is *fin amor*. The Knight's rejection of *fin amor* is at once spatial – his conduct book begins when he exits the garden of *fin amor* – and temporal – he moves beyond the deceased lady of his own past to his present familial situation, complete with a living wife and their daughters, and to the future, as he educates the next generation of nobility. Yet, the rejection of *fin amor* involves more than an exit or reorientation; it also requires careful taxonomic orchestration on the part of the Knight, who must redefine marriage and *fin amor* and revise their intertwined histories. On the one hand, the Knight presents *fin amor* as an overwhelming, uncontrolled passion, but one emptied of the grandeur it accrues elsewhere in medieval literature. Thus, in his negative exempla, wives who are overcome by *fin amor* commit adultery with men specified as less worthy than their husbands; these women lose their marriages, lives, and souls as a result. On the other hand, the Knight casts *fin amor* as a hollow performance of courtliness; its practitioners attend to their fine clothes, eloquent language, and physical beauty in a rote, perfunctory way that fails to take practicality or context into account.[22] For example, the Knight recounts two exempla, the first of a lady, the second of a lord, who both wear clothing that accentuates their beauty but poorly protects them from the winter weather. In both instances the cold transforms their skin to a deadly pallor, and the lovers they sought to impress turn their attentions to warmly dressed alternatives whose ruddy complexions indicate health. As either rote performance or overwhelming passion, *fin amor* becomes a case of either too little or too much. Marital affection represents the perfect balance of practicality, performance, and genuine emotional investment. The narrative drive of the Knight's *Livre* can in fact be summed up as a desire to promote wifely virtue and marital affection over and against *fin amor*, and to redefine precisely what "courtly love" is: for the Knight aristocratic affect is no longer characterized by the passionate throes of *fin amor* but rather by the more thoughtful and controlled emotion of marital affection.

Here, I argue, is where a third concept comes into play: sodomy, which further complicates the intellectual history underlying the Knight's *Livre*. If one strategy the Knight employs to denigrate *fin amor* is to equate *fin amor* with

---

21 See Burger, *Conduct Becoming*, particularly 1–7, 16–26.
22 On this portrayal of *fin amor* as a form of "rote repetition," see Burger, *Conduct Becoming*, 98.

adultery, then the Knight advances his attack by adding sodomy to this chain of associations. Certainly, the Knight's strategy is successful insofar as sodomy was perceived as sinful and unnatural, the very worst of sexual transgressions and likely to land its perpetrator in hell. Yet, if the wickedness of sodomy was indisputable, then what constitutes sodomy is notoriously difficult to pin down. Although "sodomia," or sodomy, derives its name from the biblical story of Sodom and Gomorrah (Genesis:18–19), the biblical Sodomites were not sodomites; they were guilty of grievous sin ("peccatum . . . adgravatum . . . nimis," 18:20), but the codification of that sin as sodomy only dates back to the eleventh century.[23] In the brief biblical narrative, God sends two angels disguised as men to Sodom to ascertain the residents' sinfulness, upon which discovery he plans to destroy both Sodom and Gomorrah. Arriving at Sodom, the angels are shown hospitality by Lot, who offers them shelter for the night. However, the men of Sodom demand that Lot relinquish his guests to them: "bring them out hither that we may know them" (educ illos huc ut cognoscamus eos [19:5]). Lot refuses, begging the men of the city to take his daughters instead: "I have two daughters who as yet have not known man: I will bring them out to you, and abuse you them as it shall please you, so that you do no evil to these men, because they are come in under the shadow of my roof" (habeo duas filias quae necdum cognoverunt virum educam eas ad vos et abutimini eis sicut placuerit vobis dummodo viris istis nihil faciatis mali quia ingressi sunt sub umbraculum tegminis mei [19:8]). The angels draw Lot back into the house, and the men outside are struck blind. The angels then instruct Lot to gather his family members and depart from the city before God destroys it. Lot, his wife, and their daughters depart from Sodom the next day, under instruction not to look back upon the city, lest they too be consumed. Lot's wife looks back and is turned into a pillar of salt. As Jordan notes, many contemporary biblical scholars read the story of Sodom as less targeted at a specifically sexual transgression than at arrogance, breach of hospitality, and rebellion against God.[24] In earlier Christian exegetical traditions, however, beginning with the Church Fathers and extending into the Middle Ages, the sin of Sodom was increasingly associated with sexual sin, and was eventually formulated as sodomy.[25]

The coining of this term, however, did not mitigate the ambiguity of the sin. Sodomy can include same-sex sex acts, sex acts involving penetration of

---

[23] The edition of the Bible quoted here is the Latin Vulgate; English translations are taken from the Douay-Rheims Bible; both can be found at *Vulgate.org, the Latin Vulgate Bible*, http://vulgate.org. On the eleventh-century codification of "sodomy," see Jordan, *Invention of Sodomy*, 1.
[24] Jordan, *Invention of Sodomy*, 30–32.
[25] Jordan, *Invention of Sodomy*, 34–44.

any orifice other than the vagina, autoeroticism, or sex acts in which a woman assumes an "active" position or the man a "passive" one. As this list suggests, sodomy was construed as a violation of gender roles as much as a performance of illicit sexuality; consequently, medieval sodomy encompassed any number of acts, both same sex and otherwise, believed to disrupt a binary construction of gender that promoted an idealized masculinity over and against an inferior femininity.[26] Sodomy, in short, imperils masculinity; therefore, when in the twelfth century sodomy emerged as a source of moral panic and a highly punishable offense, charges of sodomy, whether legal or literary, were most commonly leveled against men. However, with the emergence of a new model of femininity in the later Middle Ages, one that construed femininity not simply in terms of deficiency, it makes sense that sodomy might also imperil virtuous femininity, as is the case in the Knight's *Livre*.

To link sodomy, adultery, and *fin amor*, the Knight must revise *fin amor* discourses by highlighting some conventions while altering or omitting others. Certainly, a connection between *fin amor* and adultery is not hard to draw; the most famous literary *fin amor* affairs, those of Lancelot and Guinevere and Tristan and Isolde, were adulterous and non-procreative and therefore opposed to the institutions of marriage and inheritance on which nobility was based. The Knight's next step, equating *fin amor* with sodomy, is a bit more challenging; when *fin amor* first emerged in the twelfth century, it did so in contradistinction to the equally new discourse of sodomy. "Sodomy," as Burgwinkle argues, "surfaces as a charge and category at the very moment when heterosexual love becomes an essential theme and obligatory step in the development of exemplary knighthood."[27] Emphasis on distinct gender roles and idealized heterosexual coupling in *fin amor* discourse aligned it with another discourse to which it was frequently opposed: marriage.[28] Even as secular romance authors positioned sodomy as a threat to the heterosexual pairings of *fin amor*, the Church promoted marriage as a means to avoid sodomy and condemned sodomy for the danger it posed to marriage and procreation.

---

[26] On this point, see in particular Karma Lochrie, *Covert Operations: The Medieval Uses of Secrecy* (Philadelphia: University of Pennsylvania Press, 1999), 177–227. As Lochrie notes, "there would have been no medieval sodomite without certain medieval pathologies of femininity" (180).

[27] Burgwinkle, *Sodomy, Masculinity, and Law*, 4.

[28] I use the term "heterosexual" advisedly, in light of concerns regarding whether such modern terminology can be usefully applied to premodern formulations of gender and sexuality. Here I follow Sarah Salih, who argues that the historical investigation of premodern gender and sexuality "leaves room to discover forms of heterosexuality other than modern heteronormativity" ("Unpleasures of the Flesh: Medieval Marriage, Masochism, and the History of Heterosexuality," *Studies in the Age of Chaucer* 33 [2011]: 125–47 at 126).

To detach *fin amor* from marriage *and* idealized versions of gender and sexuality, the Knight must also revise the chrononormative narratives that, in the twelfth and thirteenth centuries, underpinned these connections. Central to these narratives are the biblical account of Eden and the relationship of Adam and Eve, which was construed as proof that marriage was instituted by God and formed part of his plan for humanity. Theologians largely agreed that Adam and Eve had sex before the Fall but believed that they did so in a wholly virtuous fashion. The Fall thus marks a before and after for marriage and sexuality, with their postlapsarian versions constituting a poor copy or derivative of their prelapsarian state. This was true of even the most tolerable versions of postlapsarian sex – between husband and wife, in the right position, and for procreative purposes – and was doubly true of sinful versions: sex for pleasure, outside marriage, or sodomitical. Thus, as Burgwinkle notes regarding twelfth-century constructions of sodomy, "the sodomite is associated with things 'new' and modern."[29] This strategy, of projecting ideal sexual practices and gender roles into a glorified past from which the world has since fallen away, is one that *fin amor* discourses appropriate. In the *Roman de la Rose*, for example, *fin amor* has its own Eden; Jean de Meun borrows from Ovid's account of a Golden Age to locate *fin amor* in an originary, lost epoch characterized by virtuous love and equality between the sexes. The advent of artificial social practices, marriage in particular, signals a falling away from *fin amor* and the idyllic state it here represents.

If, in the twelfth and thirteenth centuries, ideal versions of love, sex, and marriage were projected into the past, then, by the late fourteenth century, when the Knight was composing his *Livre*, we find different temporal configurations. These differences largely result from the increasing prominence of sacramental marriage within European societies. On the one hand, marriage continued to draw cultural capital from its status as a venerable institution decreed by God. Biblical relationships, including Abraham and Sarah, Jacob and Leah and Rachel, Esther and Ahasuerus, and Joseph and Mary, all exemplify the virtues of marriage and provide proof of its long history; it is therefore no surprise that the Knight includes them in his book. On the other hand, developments in sacramental marriage that have their roots in the twelfth century gained significantly in social prominence and intellectual theorization in the fourteenth and fifteenth centuries. These developments led to the sense that marriage in the fourteenth–fifteenth century "now" was different from past formulations of the institution, that marriage was in some way modern and new. Such formulations require a history of

---

29 Burgwinkle, *Sodomy, Masculinity, and Law*, 52.

progress rather than decline, and one strategy to establish such a history is to construct the modernity of marriage vis-à-vis an outdated and undesirable version of *fin amor*. This strategy is the impetus for the framing of the Knight's *Livre*, as the *fin amor* practices of his own past give way to the virtuous conjugal relations of his present and, he hopes, of his daughters' future.

Lot's Wife

The Knight's concern with *fin amor* and its backward pull becomes evident in chapter 54, "De la femme Loth" (Lot's Wife), a retelling of the sins of Sodom with a particular focus on female transgression. As this chapter constitutes one of the Knight's many biblical exempla drawn from the thirteenth-century *Miroir des bonnes femmes*, some commentary on the Knight's adaptation process is useful. John L. Grigsby notes that this process can include "cop[lying] an entire chapter almost verbatim"; "expand[ing] his source material" and "continu[ing a chapter] by inserting some personal anecdote or an *exemplum* from another source."[30] That the Knight employs the strategies of expansion and continuation in his chapter on Lot's wife allows us to pinpoint late-fourteenth-century concerns regarding femininity and *fin amor* that differ from those of the earlier *Miroir*. Close reading here proves a powerful strategy; to adapt Freeman, this chapter models the "'progressive' program" that the Knight advocates for his daughters even as it "resists any easy translation into present-tense terms."[31]

I begin by taking stock of the contents of the chapter, and noting which elements derive from the *Miroir* versus those which do not. Like the *Miroir*, the Knight interprets the backwards glance of Lot's wife toward the destruction of Sodom both literally, as an example of female disobedience, and allegorically, as the recidivism of a sinner who, despite receiving God's forgiveness, returns to past sins. The Knight expands and alters the *Miroir* exemplum as follows: 1) He compares the destruction of Sodom and Gomorrah to the destruction of Erbanges, a city in the region of Nantes allegedly destroyed through the intervention of St. Martin of Vertou (527–601 CE) for crimes identical to those of its infamous biblical counterparts. 2) The Knight specifies the sins of Sodom and Gomorrah as sexual acts committed outside the marriage bond. 3) The Knight

---

[30] John L. Grigsby, "A New Source of the *Livre du Chevalier de la Tour Landry*," *Romania* 84 (1963): 171–208 at 198.
[31] Freeman, *Time Binds*, xvi.

closes his chapter with an anecdote about a wife who runs away with her lover but is tracked down by her brothers and killed.

To a modern reader, focusing on Lot's wife as the primary sinner in the biblical account of Sodom might seem an odd choice, given the infamy of the Sodomites' sins. In medieval contexts, this focus makes more sense: for the Church Fathers and later medieval exegetes, the Sodomites are guilty of an abominable sexual transgression, frequently imagined in the Middle Ages as sex acts between men. Lot's wife is guilty of gender transgression; she literally refuses to follow her husband. Since sodomy was construed as a violation of the gender binary, Lot's wife's transgression is a logical extension of the sins of Sodom; just as a sexually penetrated man allegedly takes on a passive, feminine role, a self-determining wife takes on an active, masculine one. Furthermore, an association between wifely disobedience and sodomy, the most heinous of crimes, makes strategic sense in a conduct book for women. The Knight, however, expands this association well beyond what he finds in the *Miroir*; for him, wayward femininity *is* sodomy, an equivalency, I argue, that functions as a projection of his own ambivalence toward *fin amor*.

As noted above, once the Knight exits his garden and determines to educate his daughters regarding the dangers of *fin amor*, he directs his energies toward disparaging erotic desire, a goal achieved in several exempla by reconfiguring *fin amor* as adultery. Notably, in the chapter of Lot's wife, he also defines sodomy as adultery. After excoriating the sins of the Sodomites as foul, polluting, and unnatural – all predictable enough in medieval accounts of Sodom – the Knight less predictably directs his readers to interpret the story as follows: "Si est bel exemple comment l'en se doit garder du feu de luxure fors du fait de mariage, qui est commandement de Dieu et de sainte Eglise" (This is a good example of how one ought to keep oneself from the fire of lechery outside of marriage, which is a commandment of God and holy church [chapter 54, p. 114]). Some manuscripts of the *Livre* follow this sentence with the phrase: "Car aultrement que en mariaige on peche griefment" (Because otherwise than in marriage one grievously sins).[32] The closing anecdote of the chapter, the story of an adulterous wife, provides further evidence that the Knight equates sodomy and adultery and demonstrates the lengths he will go to when establishing this point. As noted above, this anecdote is an addition to the *Miroir* exemplum, one through which the Knight connects adultery to the disgust that the Sodomites inspire, as well as

---

32 This line is cited by M. Y. Offord in his notes to William Caxton's fifteenth-century translation of *The Book of the Knight of the Tower*: Geoffrey La Tour Landry, *The Book of the Knight of the Tower*, ed. M. Y. Offord, trans. William Caxton, Early English Text Society, Supplementary Series 2 (Oxford: Oxford University Press, 1971), 220.

to their harsh punishment.[33] When the lady's brothers catch up with their sister and her lover, they cut off his genitals and throw them in her face. They then place the two lovers in a sack weighed down with stones and throw them into a pond, where the two drown, a just punishment, from the Knight's perspective, "car c'est un pechié qui convient que une fois soit sceu ou pugny" (because it is a sin that is best punished immediately upon discovery [chapter 54, p. 115]).[34] The phrase "c'est un pechié" – it is a sin – is worth pausing on, for its construction suggests that the wife's crime has already been specified, yet it hasn't been. Clearly she is guilty of adultery, but, coming on the heels of the destruction of Sodom, which the Knight repeatedly attributes to "le pechié" of its inhabitants, the phrase "c'est un pechié" also appears to refer back to "le pechié" of Sodom, in which case the Knight does not just associate adultery and sodomy but appears wholly to conflate the two.

By reading this anecdote in terms of the Knight's larger mission to discredit *fin amor*, we can more closely connect it to the Knight's own attachment to the emotion as professed in the Prologue, an attachment that in turn ties the Knight to Lot's wife. The Knight's personal history constitutes a missing link between Lot's wife and the wayward lady, and Lot's wife can in fact be interpreted as a projection of the Knight's initial desires. As Robert Mills notes, "Lot's wife stealing a nostalgic glance toward the sins of Sodom, is stopped in her tracks and petrified . . . she is effectively essentialized by her transgression, transformed into the very embodiment of the backward glance that kills her."[35] The Knight also looks back, toward the desires of his youth, and, like Lot's

---

[33] The exemplum of Lot's wife in the *Miroir* concludes much more logically; after providing the allegorical interpretation of Lot's wife as relapsed sinner, the *Miroir* author ends with the statement: "Je voudroie que vous seussiez le conte de la dame qui perdi ennour pour ce qu'ele ne se voust garder de la compaignie a une personne dom ele avoit esté blamee aucune foiz" (I would like you to know the story of the lady who lost honor because she would not avoid a man whose company had frequently resulted in her censure). Quoted in John L. Grigsby, "*Miroir des bonnes femmes* – a New Fragment of the *Somme le roi* and a *Miroir des bonnes femmes*, a Hitherto Unnoticed Text," *Romania* 82 (1961): 458–89 at 470. This closing sentence convincingly demonstrates how the allegory of Lot's wife might apply to the women readers of the *Miroir*, who, like her, might likewise be drawn back to past sins. The Knight's anecdote makes no such connection, as the adulterous wife does not appear to be a recidivist.

[34] The use of the conjunction "ou," usually translated as *or*, seems odd, since clearly the knight does not intend discovering and punishing sodomy as alternatives but rather as a progressive event: when one discovers sodomy, one should punish it. This is the sense in which the fifteenth-century English translator William Caxton takes the phrase, which he translates as "it is a synne that nedes [needs] must at the last be knowen and punysshed [known and punished]" (de La Tour Landry, *Book of the Knight of the Tower*, 80).

[35] Mills, *Seeing Sodomy*, 176.

wife, risks being stopped in his tracks, essentialized as a *fin amor* lover, a risk underscored by the garden setting and lyric mode of the Prologue, both of which suggest stasis. In Freeman's terms, we might say that both Lot's wife and the Knight experience temporal drag and refuse the forward march of the family. For Lot's wife, this march is quite literal, as she refuses to follow her husband out of Sodom and toward a genealogical, chrononormative future. The Knight is spared a similar fate when his daughters rouse him from his reverie and redirect him toward the conjugal household. The chain of associations in this exemplum – sodomy leads to adultery leads to *fin amor* – suggests that the Knight, in looking back to his own "Sodom," could have been – perhaps almost was – Lot's wife, in which case she functions not only as an example of wifely disobedience for his daughters but also as a projection of the Knight's own temporal drag onto a figure from whom he is safely distanced. Nudging this interpretation a bit further, we might note that in the closing anecdote of the adulterous wife, the wife is married to a "moult bel chevallier" (very handsome knight [chapter 54, p. 114]). Might this married knight also be the Knight's double, in which case the Knight imagines himself as a virtuous victim (and a very handsome one at that)? And might such an identification be facilitated by the projection of the Knight's anachronistic desires onto the figure of Lot's wife?

The Galois and Galoise

If wayward women provide a means for the Knight to distance himself from his nostalgic leanings toward *fin amor*, then a second strategy for doing so is to project these desires upon an entire people, as happens in the exemplum of the "Galois" and "Galoise" – men and women "Galois," a term I return to below. Satan fans the flames of excessive, foolish love in these people, inspiring them to enact "une ordonnance moult sauvage et desguisée contre la nature du temps" (a very barbarous and bizarre ordinance against the nature of the seasons [chapter 122, p. 241]). This ordinance requires the Galois to behave in summer as if it were winter; despite the summer heat, they wear heavy clothes and light fires in their homes. Conversely, in winter they behave as if it were summer, wearing light clothing and lighting no fires. The ordinance further endorses and regulates adultery; when a Galois visits the home of a married couple, the husband must leave the home so that the visiting man can sleep with the wife. Such unnatural behavior reaps its just reward, from the Knight-narrator's perspective at least, when the inappropriately clad sinners succumb to the elements and freeze to death, many of them with their adulterous lovers, and subsequently burn in hell.

Before turning to the unusual sexual practices described here, I begin with what might seem like a simple question: Who precisely are the "Galois" and "Galoise"? The term can be defined as a joyous person, reveler, or pleasure-seeker, a definition which the *Dictionnaire du Moyen Français* illustrates by citing the *Livre du Chevalier*.[36] The *DMF* also notes that "Galois" can mean "Welsh," or refer to the region of Haut Bretagne, "Upper Brittany," the eastern region of the duchy where the romance language Gallo was predominantly spoken, as opposed to the western region of Bas Bretagne, Lower Brittany, where the people spoke Celtic. These two meanings are likely interrelated; the *DMF* quotes Gaston Paris's commentary on the appearance of "Galois" in a later Middle French text: "One most frequently finds this word in the plural form, suggesting the idea of a society. One can connect it here to the foolish brotherhood of 'Galois' mentioned by the Knight of the Tower Landry . . . as for this brotherhood, it was given its name because it aspired to revive the joyous and brilliant customs of Arthur's court."[37] I want to keep in play the possibility that the "Galois" of the Knight's exemplum might reference both the Britons and the Bretons, the people of Brittany, a duchy to which the Knight himself was connected.

The duchy of Brittany was the site of multiple conflicts during the latter part of the fourteenth century. When Duke John III of Brittany died childless in 1341, two scions of Breton nobility, the Penthièvres and the Montforts, laid claim to the duchy. Their dispute resulted in a twenty-five-year civil war (1341–1365), which served as a proxy for the war between France and England, each of which backed a claimant. As Shannon Godlove notes, "the civil war divided the nobility of Brittany between the pro-English Montforts in the western Celtic-speaking areas . . ., and the pro-French Penthièvres in the south and east, the regions closer to the kingdom of France."[38] John of Montfort, son of the deceased duke, eventually succeeded his father, although the political situation within the duchy and its foreign relations to England and France remained rocky for decades afterwards. These events were of some significance

---

[36] *Dictionnaire du Moyen Français*, s. v. "Galois," http://www2.atilf.fr/dmf/

[37] This is my translation of the French quotation appearing in the *Dictionnaire du Moyen Français*, s. v. "Galois": "Ce mot . . ., on le trouve surtout au pluriel, et important l'idée d'une société. On peut le rattacher à la folle confrérie des *Galois* dont parle le chevalier de La Tour Landry (ch. cxxii, p. 241), . . . Quant à cette confrérie, elle s'était donné ce nom parce qu'elle prétendait faire revivre les moeurs gaies et brillantes de la cour d'Artur."

[38] Shannon Godlove, "'Engelond' and 'Armorik Briteyne': Reading Brittany in Chaucer's *Franklin's Tale*," *The Chaucer Review* 51 (2016): 269–94 at 274.

Chapter 4 Sodom, Bretons, and Ill-Defined Borders: Questing for Queerness — **99**

to our knight, Geoffroy de la Tour Landry, whose lands in Anjou bordered on Brittany.[39] Notably, one document recording Geoffroy's service specifies that he fought in the king's wars over the land of Brittany ("ses guerres du pays de Bretagne").[40] Geoffroy's ties to Brittany were also more personal in nature; between 1352 and 1360, when the Breton civil war was fully under way, Geoffroy married Jeanne de Rougé, herself a Breton from a prominent pro-French family.[41] Jeanne died sometime between 1383 and 1391, and was therefore Geoffroy's wife at the time he composed his *Livre*. While we have no record of Geoffroy's personal feelings toward the Bretons, he likely partitioned them along similar lines to those that divided the duchy itself.[42] From a monarchical perspective, or, we might add, from the perspective of a provincial knight seeking to better himself and his line by espousing monarchical aims, there were two types of Bretons: good Bretons who aligned themselves with the French crown, and bad Bretons who did not.

It is through this latter category that I suggest we view the "Galois et Galoise" of the Knight's exemplum, which invites such association on a number of counts. If, as Paris suggests, "Galois" frequently indicates a "society," one characterized by the brilliance and revelry of King Arthur's court, then the term would likely recollect the Britons, over whom Arthur allegedly ruled. After the civil war, Duke John IV (John Montfort) certainly drew on longstanding associations between the Britons and Brittany to promote the autonomy of the duchy in relation to England and France. As Godlove notes, Geoffrey of Monmouth's *History of the Kings of Britain* proved central to this aim; not only does Geoffrey provide the Britons with an illustrious genealogy that includes King Arthur and the Trojans, but he also establishes the Britons as a distinct cultural entity with their own customs, laws, and institutions.[43] In the *Livre du Chevalier*, the Knight similarly portrays the "Galois" as a society that sets itself apart from others and establishes its own laws, although he presents these as acts of hubris rather than patriotism; if

---

39 See Montaiglon, *Livre du chevalier*, preface, vii–viii.
40 Montaiglon, *Livre du chevalier*, preface, xvi.
41 Jeanne's father, Bonabes de Rougé, viscount of la Guerche, was a close associate of King Charles V, whom he served as counselor and chamberlain.
42 According to Michael Jones, "the Civil War of 1341–1364 reopened and sharpened the division between Bretagne-Gallo or Haute-Bretagne, the area under Penthièvre influence, the region of the great seigneuries, and the Bretagne-Bretonnante or Basse-Bretagne, the area which was prepared to acknowledge Monfort's claim, the region of the lesser *noblesse*. It was a division which was recognized by the ducal administration even after the war" (*The Creation of Brittany: A Late Medieval State* [London: Hambledon Press, 1988], 12).
43 Godlove, for example, notes that "The Breton author of the fourteenth-century *Chronicon Briocense* . . . used Geoffrey of Monmouth's *History* as a source for his people's early history and

Brittany chafed under the rule of the French king, the Galois revolt against their heavenly ruler, and, in what is perhaps an oblique warning to their counterparts, pay an eternal penalty as a result. In his portrayal of the Galois, the Knight may also parody renewed Breton interest in legendary histories of the Britons by homing in on their less flattering details. The Knight's "Galois" parodically recollect the gallantry associated with the Arthurian court through their elaborate rules of love. Like the *fin amor* lovers whom the Knight upbraids elsewhere in his *Livre*, the Galois practice adultery, dress inappropriately in cold weather, and contemptuously look down upon those who do not follow their laws. *Fin amor*, I want to suggest, is the true target of the Knight's contempt, as he evokes but rejects the conventions that elevate lovers in other contexts. In a particularly smug statement, he doubts that the Galois achieve martyrdom for their love but instead surmises that these sinners who died from the cold will burn forever in hell. Even in comparison to most other sinners in the Knight's *Livre*, the Galois come across as particularly vile, and in fact bear the most resemblance to the sinners of Sodom, who likewise constitute a community of sexual transgressors.

If, in the account of Sodom, the Knight presents the unspecified transgressions of the Sodomites as adultery, then, in this later exemplum, he suggests that the Galois' adultery constitutes sodomy. The two exempla are linked through language, specifically the Knight's claim that the sins of the Galois and the Sodomites are against nature, a frequent circumlocution for sodomy in the Middle Ages. The Knight's description of the Galois law as "barbarous," "bizarre," and "against the nature of the seasons" evokes sodomy, as does the law's pairing of adultery with a willful perversion of the natural order. And we can add one more link to this chain of associations: the alleged sexual practices of the Britons, who were frequently accused of sodomy. This accusation has a long history, as attested to in works extending from Greco-Roman antiquity to

---

as a rallying point for the newly articulated Breton 'regional identity' promoted by the court of Duke John IV in opposition to both the English and the French" ("'Engelond' and 'Armorik Briteyne,'" 285). Geoffrey's *History* was particularly useful to this enterprise because he notes the Britons' diaspora from insular Britain to continental Brittany; as Godlove notes, many Briton characters in the *Historia* move back and forth between Wales and Brittany ("'Engelond' and 'Armorik Briteyne,'" 284). On Geoffrey's account, too, Brittany becomes the center of Briton culture after the Britons are defeated and exiled by the English. In Godlove's words, "Geoffrey of Monmouth's *History* thus explains how the Britons came to be seen (and, in part, saw themselves) as what Ingham calls 'a doubled people'" ("'Engelond' and 'Armorik Briteyne,'" 284; the phrase "a doubled people" is taken from Patricia Clare Ingham, *Sovereign Fantasies: Arthurian Romance and the Making of Britain* [Philadelphia: University of Pennsylvania Press, 2001], 41).

medieval texts like Gerald of Wales's *Journey through Wales*.[44] Of particular note is, once again, Geoffrey's *Historia*, in which Cadwallo, the penultimate king of the Britons, explains his people's defeats by citing their indulgence in "sexual excesses such as had never been heard of among other peoples."[45] Here the oblique rhetoric and alleged foreignness of the transgression almost certainly indicate sodomy. Again, the Knight is likely drawing on the very histories cited by the Montforts to bolster claims of Breton autonomy, but to different ends. Evidence that, for the Knight, the Bretons and sodomy are metonymically linked also appears earlier in the *Livre*; as noted above, the Knight compares the crimes and destruction of Sodom to those of Erbanges, a town he locates near Nantes, which in turn was the administrative hub of ducal Brittany under the Montforts.

To summarize thus far, in the story of the Galois the Knight further develops his associational chain to establish two, interrelated points: first, to imagine Bretons who resist the French crown as a community of sinful, sexual transgression similar to Sodom; and second, to reconfigure *fin amor* as adultery, and then, to go one step further, as sodomy. Unlike in the exemplum of Lot's wife, in which Lot's wife operates in part as an avatar for the Knight's own pull toward the past, in this exemplum the Galois are fully foreign, and, through their designation as a people or society, safely contained. Construing the exemplum of the Galois as a further revision of the earlier exemplum of Lot's wife, we can trace a linear progression for the Knight, as he pulls away from the *fin amor* sentiments characterizing his personal and cultural past. Along these lines, it is notable that the sexual transgression of the Galois is portrayed as both a social and a temporal disorder. Their sinful law is "contre la nature du *temps*," against the nature of the *temps*, a word with several meanings in play in the Knight's exemplum, including the "season," "weather," and "time" itself. The problem that unites the Galois, Lot's wife, and *fin amor* lovers is that they resist chrononormativity, that they "prefer to elaborate ways of living aslant to dominant forms of object-choice, coupledom, family, marriage, sociability, and self-presentation and thus out of synch with state-sponsored narratives of belonging and becoming."[46]

Taken together, the exempla of Lot's wife/Sodom and the Galois also expand upon the idea of what constitutes virtuous versus wayward femininity. By

---

44 On attributions of sodomy to the Britons, or Celts, see Burgwinkle, *Sodomy, Masculinity, and Law*, 22, 25–26.
45 Geoffrey of Monmouth, *History of the Kings of Britain*, trans. Lewis Thorpe (London: Penguin Books, 1966), 273.
46 Freeman, *Time Binds*, xv.

recasting *fin amor* as both adultery and sodomy, the Knight teaches his daughters that unfaithful, disobedient wives commit the most grievous of sins. Yet, if women like Lot's wife and the adulterous woman with whom her exemplum concludes demonstrate the dangers of wayward female agency, then the exemplum of the Galois demonstrates that too little female agency is equally problematic. Agency is of course a key concept in medieval constructions of gender and sexuality: according to Alan of Lille's influential metaphors, sexually active men are hammers and women or men who allow themselves to be penetrated are passive anvils.[47] Passivity extended even to women who seek out sexual pleasure, for while masculine activity was imagined as purposeful, the effect of rational decision-making, women were constructed as incapable of such thought processes and therefore slaves to their whims and desires.[48] The male sodomite, who burns with passions he cannot control, is likewise rendered passive and therefore effeminate. Precluded from rationally motivated action, the best a woman could do was to follow rote instructions laid out for her by those who *did* possess the capacity for ethical deliberation – that is, men.[49] Most of the Knight's exempla portray women who, while passively in thrall to their wayward desires, are nonetheless agential insofar as they pursue those desires. In the Galois community, however, we encounter a different mode of female passivity, one portrayed less as an attribute of female nature than as a deviation from idealized femininity. This mode of female passivity appears in the sinful ordinance of the Galois, which stipulates that adultery be practiced as follows:

> Et . . . estoit ordené entre eulx que dès ce que un des Galois venist la où feust la Galoise, se elle eust mary, il convenist par celle ordenance que il alast faire penser des chevaux au Galoys qui venus feust, et puis s'en partit de son hostel sans revenir tant que le Galoys feust avecques sa femme; et cellui mari estoit aussi Galois et alast veoir s'amie, une autre Galoise, et l'autre feust avecques sa femme, et feust tenu à grant honte et deshonneur se le mary demourast en son hostel, ne commandast ne ordenast riens depuis que le Galois feust venu, et n'y avoit plus de povoir par celle ordenance. (chapter 122, p. 242)

And . . . it was decreed among them that as soon as a Galois man came to there where the Galois woman was, if she was married, it was necessary according to the ordinance that the husband attend to the horses of the Galois who had just arrived, and depart from his home without returning as long as the visiting Galois was with his wife; and if this departing husband was also Galois and went to see

---

[47] Alan of Lille, *Plaint of Nature*, trans. James J. Sheridan (Toronto: Pontifical Institute of Mediaeval Studies, 1980), prose 5, 155–56, 164.
[48] On women, ethics, and rational decision-making in the Middle Ages, see Holly A. Crocker, *The Matter of Virtue* (Philadelphia: University of Pennsylvania Press, 2019), 10–12.
[49] Crocker, *Matter of Virtue*, 11.

his girlfriend, another Galois woman, and she was with her husband, it was considered a great shame and dishonor if that husband remained in his home, he could not give an order or oversee anything while the visiting Galois was there, and the husband no longer had any power, according to this ordinance.

In this description, it is men who undertake the activity of adultery, as they move from one house to another, or vacate their home to accommodate a male visitor; consequently, the ordinance foregrounds *men's* social negotiations, agency, and pleasure. What the Galois women desire appears to be beside the point. The women's lack of desire, however, does not make them any less guilty of sexual transgression, in the Knight's eyes, at least. As a result, this negative exemplum points toward a configuration of virtuous femininity that, while still subordinate to masculinity, nonetheless requires agency.

We find a positive example of this configuration in the Knight's wife, who, immediately following the exemplum of the Galois, engages in a debate with her husband over *fin amor*. By championing marital fidelity, the Lady of the Tower distinguishes herself from adulterous women; by arguing against the Knight, she distinguishes herself from the passive Galoises. For modern readers especially, the Lady's address of the Knight is surprising, both in that she opposes her husband and that she privileges her own opinions and perspectives in doing so: "je vueil debattre contre vous le mien advis, et feablement, selon mon entendement" (I want to present in opposition to you my opinion, and to do so sincerely, according to my understanding [chapter 124, p. 247]). We might be tempted to view the validation of some form – *any* form – of female agency as a boon, a step forward in a Western history that charts progress in terms of liberalism and the lifting of restraints upon the individual's will. In her historical context, however, the Lady's stance looks a bit different. While it would be a mistake to claim that *fin amor* had vanished from the landscape of late medieval France, we can nonetheless identify the Knight's era as one of significant cultural transition and speculate that men like the Knight struggled to commit to marital modernity while maintaining a nostalgic investment in bygone modes of gender and sexuality. If, for our Knight-narrator, *fin amor* is a superseded construction of noble masculinity that he just can't quit, then our backwards-looking Knight himself requires rescue by his more ideologically up to date wife.

This historically contextualized interpretation of the Lady of the Tower is important not just in what it tells us about late medieval Northern Europe, but in the perspective it offers on Western liberalism today. Since the turn of the twenty-first century, progressive, celebratory histories of women and queers have come under increased scrutiny, as has the notion that promoting voluntarism is the panacea for all instances of oppression that women and queers suffer. Feminist and queer philosopher Sara Ahmed has recently devoted attention to what it means to exercise one's will, homing in on the processes by which an individual's will is conditioned and oriented.[50] Insofar as the will functions as "a technique," she argues, "a way of holding a subject to account, it could be understood as *a straightening device*" that does less to promote feminist or queer impulses than to "correct" them.[51] The willful opposition of the Lady of the Tower can be read in these terms: she "straightens" both her daughters and husband in orienting their wills toward marital affection and away from *fin amor*. This reading reveals the powerfully agential woman to be a surrogate for the Knight's perspective as expressed elsewhere in his *Livre* and a means to provide him with a developmental narrative (youth to maturity, *fin amor* to marriage) that is off limits to women, who, should they participate in *fin amor*, are irrevocably tarnished.

Despite this reading of the Lady of the Tower, I want to conclude by suggesting that her agency exceeds the conduct book's didactic program in ways that destabilize the concept of the good wife and might therefore render her queer. As noted above, late medieval wives were expected to exert agency, but to do so within hierarchical structures: the good wife, as Burger notes, willingly submits to her husband.[52] This willing submission results in a mix of active and passive that simultaneously points toward new models of gender and sexuality and disrupts longstanding ones. In her debate with her husband, the Lady of the Tower champions marriage as the institution toward which women should direct their efforts and through which to organize their emotions and ethical decision-making. In orienting herself, and the daughters whom she instructs, toward marriage, the Lady of the Tower ironically pits herself against her husband, who argues in favor of *fin amor*. In their debate, the Lady is less a subordinate helpmeet than a virago-esque saint of hagiographic tradition, a Cecilia or Catherine who rhetorically overpowers her male interlocutor. She nonetheless claims a female perspective, which she pits against the perspectives of both her husband and men more generally, whom she addresses as "vous hommes" (you men [chapter 124, p. 147]). Moreover, the Lady speaks from a position of

---

50 In addition to Freeman's *Time Binds* and Love, *Feeling Backward*, see, for example, Michael Warner, *The Trouble with Normal* (Cambridge: Harvard University Press, 1999); Elizabeth A. Povinelli, *Empire of Love* (Durham: Duke University Press, 2006); Jasbir K. Puar, *Terrorist Assemblages: Homonationalism in Queer Times* (Durham: Duke University Press, 2007); Catherine Rottenberg, "Neoliberal Feminism and the Future of Human Capital," *Signs: Journal of Women in Culture and Society* 42.2 (2017): 329–48; and Amia Srinivasan, "Does Anyone Have the Right to Sex?," *London Reivew of Books* 40. (March 22, 2018): 5–10.
51 Sara Ahmed, *Willful Subjects* (Durham: Duke University Press, 2014), 7.
52 Burger, *Conduct Becoming*, 5.

female experience – she herself was, in youth, the object of *fin amor* overtures – and female vulnerability: the Lady repeatedly notes the penalties a woman must pay for participating in *fin amor*, including the loss of marriage prospects and her good name – penalties which appear not to apply to men. In sum, the activity of the Lady of the Tower renders her a hybrid figure, one whose agency is oriented in multiple directions – to her husband, her daughters, and to women more broadly – and who both upholds and queerly challenges gender dichotomies.

Bibliography

Ahmed, Sara. *Willful Subjects*. Durham: Duke University Press, 2014.
Alan of Lille. *Plaint of Nature*. Translated by James J. Sheridan. Toronto: Pontifical Institute of Mediaeval Studies, 1980.
Bennett, Judith M. *History Matters: Patriarchy and the Challenge of Feminism*. Philadelphia: University of Pennsylvania Press, 2006.
Burger, Glenn D. *Conduct Becoming: Good Wives and Husbands in the Later Middle Ages*. Philadelphia: University of Pennsylvania Press, 2018.
Burgwinkle, William. *Sodomy, Masculinity, and Law in Medieval Literature: France and England, 1050–1230*. Cambridge: Cambridge University Press, 2004.
Chansons du XVe Siècle. Edited by Gaston Paris. Paris: Firmin-Didot et cie, 1875.
Dictionnaire du Moyen Français. http://www.atilf.fr/dmf/.
Crocker, Holly A. *The Matter of Virtue*. Philadelphia: University of Pennsylvania Press, 2019.
Foucault, Michel. *The History of Sexuality*, vol. 1: *An Introduction*. Translated by Robert Hurley. London: Penguin, 1978.
Freeman, Elizabeth. *Time Binds: Queer Temporalities, Queer Histories*. Durham: Duke University Press, 2010.
Geoffrey of Monmouth, *History of the Kings of Britain*. Translated by Lewis Thorpe. London: Penguin Books, 1966.
Godlove, Shannon. "'Engelond' and 'Armorik Briteyne': Reading Brittany in Chaucer's *Franklin's Tale*." *The Chaucer Review* 51 (2016): 269–94.
Grigsby, John L. "*Miroir des bonnes femmes* – a New Fragment of the *Somme le roi* and a *Miroir des bonnes femmes*, a Hitherto Unnoticed Text." *Romania* 82 (1961): 458–89.
Grigsby, John L. "A New Source of the *Livre du Chevalier de la Tour Landry*." *Romania* 84 (1963): 171–208.
Ingham, Patricia Clare. *Sovereign Fantasies: Arthurian Romance and the Making of Britain*. Philadelphia: University of Pennsylvania Press, 2001.
Jones, Michael. *The Creation of Brittany: A Late Medieval State*. London: Hambledon Press, 1988.
Jordan, Mark D. *The Invention of Sodomy in Christian Theology*. Chicago: University of Chicago Press, 1997.
Krueger, Roberta L. "Intergeneric Combination and the Anxiety of Gender in *Le Livre Du Chevalier De La Tour Landry Pour L'Enseignement De Ses Filles*." *L'Esprit Createur* 33 (1993): 61–72.

La Tour Landry, Geoffrey de. *The Book of the Knight of the Tower*. Edited by M. Y. Offord. Translated by William Caxton. Early English Text Society, Supplementary Series 2. Oxford: Oxford University Press, 1971.

La Tour Landry, Geoffrey de. *Le Livre du chevalier de La Tour Landry, pour l'enseignement de ses filles*. Edited by Anatole de Montaiglon. Paris: P. Jannet, 1854. Repr., Nabu Press, 2010.

Lochrie, Karma. *Covert Operations: The Medieval Uses of Secrecy*. Philadelphia: University of Pennsylvania Press, 1999.

Lochrie, Karma. *Heterosyncrasies: Female Sexuality When Normal Wasn't*. Minneapolis: University of Minnesota Press, 2005.

Lochrie, Karma. "Presumptive Sodomy and Its Exclusions." *Textual Practice* 13 (1999): 295–310.

Love, Heather. *Feeling Backward: Loss and the Politics of Queer History*. Cambridge: Harvard University Press, 2007.

Mills, Robert. *Seeing Sodomy in the Middle Ages*. Chicago: University of Chicago Press, 2015.

Povinelli, Elizabeth A. *Empire of Love*. Durham: Duke University Press, 2006.

Puar, Jasbir K. *Terrorist Assemblages: Homonationalism in Queer Times*. Durham: Duke University Press, 2007.

Rottenberg, Catherine. "Neoliberal Feminism and the Future of Human Capital." *Signs: Journal of Women in Culture and Society* 42.2 (2017): 329–48.

Salih, Sarah. "Unpleasures of the Flesh: Medieval Marriage, Masochism, and the History of Heterosexuality." *Studies in the Age of Chaucer* 33 (2011): 125–48.

Srinivasan, Amia. "Does Anyone Have the Right to Sex?," *London Reivew of Books* 40.6 (March 22, 2018): 5–10.

Staley, Lynn. *Languages of Power in the Age of Richard II*. University Park: Pennsylvania State University Press, 2005.

Warner, Michael. *The Trouble with Normal*. Cambridge: Harvard University Press, 1999.

Maud McInerney
Chapter 5
Queer Time for Heroes in the *Roman d'Enés* and the *Roman de Troie*

Romance time, Mikhail Bakhtin argues in *The Dialogic Imagination*, is first and foremost erotic time, characterized by a "random contingency" according to which "initiative is handed over to chance";[1] it is what takes place between the meeting of a pair of young lovers and their eventual marriage. It is thus, explicitly, heterosexual time. Bakhtin, however, limits his consideration to the ancient Greek novels, with a brief gesture to chivalric romance. The *romans d'antiquité*, which initiate the medieval genre, betray a much more ambivalent attitude toward heterosexual relationships, suggesting an alternative temporality, one which is sometimes actually homoerotic, and always fundamentally queer.

The anonymous *Roman d'Enéas* (ca. 1160) and the *Roman de Troie* by Benoît de Sainte-Maure (ca. 1165) both anchor themselves in a particular legendary past, the era of the Trojan War. With its happily-ever-after ending in the wedding of Enéas and Lavine, the *Roman d'Enéas* stands as an early example of the marriage plot, albeit one which already exposes its ideological imperatives. The end of the *Roman de Troie*, however, is inevitably less upbeat. The Horse delivers its treacherous progeny, towers burn, streets run with blood, Pyrrhus slaughters Priam at the altar and Polixena upon the grave of Achilles; the Greeks stone Hecuba to death. Even for the victors, things don't go particularly well. Benoît provides a summary of the homecomings: Agammemnon is murdered by Clytemnestra; Neoptolemus dies mysteriously, perhaps because of his marriage to Helen's daughter; Ulysses is haunted by nightmares and eventually killed by Telegonus, his unrecognized son by Circe. For the heroes of Troy, it turns out, romance time is not all that it's cracked up to be. The return to domesticity and the embrace of family are only a return to death. While the *Roman d'Enéas* works hard to produce a positive and secure vision of the heterosexual bonds of marriage and courtly love, the *Roman de Troie*, ultimately, doesn't bother. Each text, moreover, proposes alternatives to romance time and the imperatives of heteronormativity, even if only to foreclose them. These alternatives take the form of queer characters, united in their belonging not to the world of

---

[1] M. M. Bakhtin, *The Dialogic Imagination: Four Essays*, ed. and trans. Michael Holquist and Caryl Emerson (Austin: University of Texas Press, 1982), 90.

marriage, procreation and genealogy, with its emphasis on a time that continues from the past through the present and on into the future, but instead on a time characterized by stasis, interruption, excess, and death.

In referring to queer characters, I mean those characters who in one way or another live outside of or defy the system of courtly love between men and women which undergirds patriarchal systems of land acquisition and inheritance. A discussion of such characters is part of a larger discussion of queer temporality, for though it may seem obvious, it needs to be said: queer characters and queer time are two different narrative functions which intersect but do not overlap. As Carolyn Dinshaw argues in *How Soon is Now? Medieval Texts, Amateur Readers and the Queerness of Time*, "queerness . . . has a temporal dimension" manifested in "forms of desirous, embodied being that are out of sync with the ordinarily linear measurements of everyday life, that engage heterogenous temporalities, or that precipitate out of time altogether."[2] Jack Halberstam elaborates the linear, genealogical qualities of heterosexual time:

> The time of reproduction is ruled by a biological clock for women and by strict bourgeois rules of respectability and scheduling for married couples . . . wealth, goods and morals are passed through family ties from one generation to the next. It also connects the family to the historical past of the nation and glances ahead to connect the family to the future of both familial and national stability.[3]

The fundamentally gendered quality of many forms of time is buried, Halberstam argues, by the reluctance of philosophers and critics to see difference according to sexuality or gender as anything but a distraction from the real power-engines of history. Halberstam cites David Harvey's *The Condition of Post-Modernity* as an example of an argument that "energetically deconstructs the naturalization of modes of temporality . . . with no awareness of having instituted and presumed a normative framework for his alternative understanding of time."[4] This framework fails to appreciate the degree to which the very concept of "naturalization" is the product of an understanding of the world dependent upon assumptions not just about gender but about sexuality. The subjection of the domestic space to the industrial space does not simply rely upon the subjection of women to men, that is, but also upon the fact that reproductive time, taken for granted as "natural" time, is inevi-

---

[2] Carolyn Dinshaw, *How Soon is Now? Medieval Texts, Amateur Readers and the Queerness of Time* (Durham: Duke University Press, 2012), 4.
[3] J. Halberstam, *In a Queer Time and Place: Transgender Bodies, Subcultural Lives* (New York: New York University Press, 2005), 5.
[4] Halberstam, *In a Queer Time*, 4.

tably imagined as heterosexual.⁵ Living outside of the nuclear family and its attendant logic of the accrual of capital is a choice either made by or imposed upon a great many queer subjects. Halberstam includes drag queens, sex workers, drug-dealers and the unemployed, among others, to whom I would add the mentally ill, families constructed around nuclei other than the married couple, the disabled, and others whose identities exist on the margins of normative, heterosexual society. For Halberstam, the alternative to repro-time, which is quite clearly congruent with romance time, is queer time.

Queer time is associated with death; it "emerges most spectacularly, at the end of the twentieth century, from within those gay communities whose horizons of possibility have been severely diminished by the AIDS epidemic."⁶ But at least queer time seems honestly to admit this, to acknowledge the inevitable truth of individual death, rather than hiding this reality, as both genealogical time and romance time do, behind the promise of immortality in the form of offspring. In a discussion of Michael Cunningham's *The Hours*, a rewriting of Virginia Woolf's *Mrs. Dalloway*, Halberstam points out that the marriage plot is actually a "seemingly inexorable march of narrative time toward marriage (death)."⁷ Queer time, on the other hand, is, even under the shadow of death, "about the *potentiality* of a life unscripted by the conventions of family, inheritance, and child rearing."⁸

The dominant heterosexual temporality of romance, with its emphasis upon the role of women and upon courtly love, clearly belongs to what Halberstam labels reproductive time. Its function in the *Roman d'Enéas* is to establish a dynasty beginning with Enéas and Lavine, and culminating, eons later, in Henry II and Eleanor of Aquitaine (the poem was composed before the fractures in their marriage became evident). Halberstam describes reproductive time, what I call romance time, as a fundamental mode of thinking about time and the human subject in the West:

> In Western cultures, we chart the emergence of the adult from the dangerous and unruly period of adolescence as a desired process of maturation; and we create longevity as the most desirable future. . . . Within the life cycle of the Western human subject, long periods of stability are considered to be desirable, and people who live in rapid bursts (drug addicts, for example) are characterized as immature or even dangerous.⁹

---

5 Halberstam, *In a Queer Time*, 6–8.
6 Halberstam, *In a Queer Time*, 2.
7 Halberstam, *In a Queer Time*, 3.
8 Halberstam, *In a Queer Time*, 2, italics mine.
9 Halberstam, *In a Queer Time*, 4–5.

Halberstam does not explicitly make the point that these values have existed for centuries, even millennia, but this is indeed the case. Cicero's *De Senectute*, a treatise in the voice of Cato the Elder praising the virtues and especially the sobriety of old age, was popular not only in its own time but throughout the Middle Ages and into the Renaissance; writers like Marbod of Rennes (ca. 1035–1123) drew upon Cicero to argue that old age freed the mind from the vices of the body and granted wisdom and peace.[10] As for periods of stability, the very notion of a *pax henrici* coming after the Anarchy of Stephen, suggests a nostalgia for the lost *pax Romana*.[11] Henry's rule, while not exactly peaceful in his French domains, did bring lasting peace to England. The twelfth century also witnessed the emergence of the tournament as a pastime for warriors between wars, one roundly condemned by the Council of Clermont in 1130, which qualified them as "detestable markets or fairs at which knights are accustomed to meet to show off their strength and their boldness and in which the deaths of men and danger to the soul often occur."[12] Similar rhetoric emerges in modern condemnation of night clubs, often associated with gay activity, by the Jehovah's Witnesses ("Youth dance clubs have become very popular in recent years. . . . Moshing often involves jumping up and down, violent head shaking, and mock head butting, as well as crashing into other dancers. Broken limbs and cuts are commonplace, and there have also been spinal and head injuries. Death has even resulted."[13]). I am not suggesting that knights were homosexual, of course, although some certainly were, but simply that the rhetoric against men coming together to commit sin is similar: it focuses on danger to the body as incorporating danger to the soul. While war was a necessary evil in the Middle Ages, and in the case of Crusade even a divine duty, tournaments, which pitched Christian knight against Christian knight for personal glory, for adrenaline, for the fun of it, were clearly "immature or even dangerous," like gay sex in the age of AIDS. Halberstam points out, quoting poet Mark Doty,

---

10 See Bruce C. Barker-Benfield, "A Ninth Century Manuscript from Fleury: Cato de senectute cum Macrobio," in *Medieval Learning and Literature: Essays Presented to Richard William Hunt*, ed. J. J. G. Alexander and M. T. Gibson (Oxford: Clarendon, 1976), 145–65; Juanita Feros Ruys, "Medieval Latin Meditations on Old Age," in *Old Age in the Middle Ages and the Renaissance*, ed. Albrecht Classen (Berlin: De Gruyter, 2007), 180–83.
11 *Anglo Saxon Chronicle*, entry for 1140: "And there was soon so good a peace as never was there before. Then was the king [Stephen] stronger than he ever was before. And the earl [Henry] went over sea; and all people loved him; for he did good justice, and made peace."
12 Richard Barber and Juliet Baker, *Tournaments: Jousts, Chivalry and Pageants in the Middle Ages* (Woodbridge: Boydell, 1989), 17.
13 *The Watchtower*, Watchtower Online Library, http://wol.jw.org/en/wol/d/r1/lp-e/102004290.

that for the first generation of gay men to live under the shadow of AIDS, the generation which was infected before it knew there *was* infection, "while the threat of no future hovers overhead like a storm cloud, the urgency of being also expands the potential of the moment."[14] The same is true for the medieval knight; what, after all, is a warrior, and more particularly a hero, except someone who has chosen to "live in rapid bursts," as Halberstam puts it? Achilles, who chooses early death and eternal fame over a long and happy life without renown, is thus queer in ways that transcend his always ambiguous sexuality. Both the *Roman d'Enéas* and the *Roman de Troie*, invested as they are in war as much as in love, celebrate even as they deny the queer time associated with Nisus and Euryalus, Pallas and Enéas, Patroclus and Achilles by associating them with forms of excess that are both inevitably deadly and aesthetically compelling.[15]

The apparent problem of same-sex love in the *Roman d'Enéas* has been much discussed, particularly in reference to the outburst of the queen (Amata in the *Aeneid*, nameless here) in which she accuses Aeneas in no uncertain terms of preferring sex with boys to sex with women:[16]

> Cil cuivers est de tel nature
> Qu'il n'a de femmes gaire cure.
> Il prise plus le plain mestier,
> il ne veult pas bice chaucier,
> moult par aime char de mallon;
> il prisera mieux son garçon
> que toy ne autre acoler.
> A fumelle ne set voller, (jouer?)

---

14 Halberstam, *In a Queer Time*, 2.
15 The warrior women Camille and Pantesilee also live and die outside of reproductive time, as does the half-human Sagittary; but for reasons of time and space, I shall not treat them in this essay.
16 See, for instance, Simon Gaunt, "From Epic to Romance: Gender and Sexuality in the Roman d'Eneas," *Romanic Review* 83.1 (1992): 1–27 on issues of gender and sexuality in the poem; see also Vincent A. Lankewish, "Assault From Behind: Sodomy, Foreign Invasion and Masculine Identity in Le Roman d'Eneas," in *Text and Territory: Geographical Imagination in the European Middle Ages*, ed. Sylvia Tomasch and Sealy Giles (Philadelphia: University of Pennsylvania Press, 1998), 207–44; Susane Hafner, "Coward, Traitor, Landless Trojan: Aeneas and the Politics of Sodomy," *Essays in Medieval Studies* 19 (2002): 61–69, although Hafner deals primarily with the German *Eneasroman*; Noah D. Guynn, "Eternal Flame: State Formation, Deviant Architecture and the Monumentality of Same-Sex Eroticism in the Roman d'Eneas," *GLQ* 6.2 (2000): 287–319; and William Burgwinkle, "Knighting the Classical Hero: Homo/Hetero Affectivity in *Eneas*," *Exemplaria* 5.1 (1993): 1–43.

ne passera mie au guicet;
moult aime fraise de varlet.¹⁷

That pervert is of such a nature that he doesn't care for women. He much prefers the love of boys. He doesn't like to hunt does, he'd rather have male flesh; he will prefer to embrace his boytoy than you or any other woman. He doesn't know how to play with women; he'll not go through the little gate, he much prefers a boy's bud.

The queen goes on to remind Lavine of Enéas's mistreatment of Didon, and refers to him as a traitor and sodomite; this is a move that may seem counterintuitive to the modern reader, but medievals did not divide the world along the hard lines of hetero- and homosexual. The real point here is treachery, both to the individual and to the genealogical project that underlies romance time:

> De cest sigle seroit tost fin,
> se tuit li home qui i sont
> erent autel par tot 10 mont;
> ja mes feme ne concevroit,
> grant sofraite de gent seroit;
> ran ne feroit ja mes anfanz,
> li siegles faudroit ainz cent anz. (8579–602)

It would be the end of everything if all the men in the world were like him; no woman would ever conceive, there would be great suffering of the people, no one would have children any more, it would be the end of the world.

According to Simon Gaunt, the accusation of homosexuality against Enéas "may reflect contemporary anxieties about homosexuality, but its main effect is to mark Eneas' conformity to a prescribed norm."¹⁸ After all, the reader knows perfectly well that he will, in fact, marry Lavine. For Gaunt, who follows Eve Sedgwick here, homophobia emerges as a result of the conflict between an epic ideology founded on homosocial bonding and a romance ideology in which the status of the hero is measured through his relationship to women – or rather, as courtly lover, to *a* woman – instead of men.¹⁹ In the same vein, William Burgwinkle notes that, in the feudal period and, indeed, in the world of the *chanson de geste*, male–male love, erotic or not, is the norm. For him, the *Enéas* challenges "common assumptions about what distinguishes friends from lovers, men from women in love, and

---

17 *Roman d'Eneas: Edition critique d'après le manuscrit B.N.fr. 60*, ed. and trans. Aimé Petit (Paris: Lettres Gothiques, 1997), ll. 8621–30. All future references are to this edition, by line numbers. Translations are mine.
18 Gaunt, "From Epic to Romance," 23.
19 Gaunt, "From Epic to Romance," 21.

spirituality from sensuality."[20] Burgwinkle further argues that, in the *Enéas*, heterosexual love is associated with land, procreation, and duty, whereas true companionship can only be manifested between warriors; and warriors, as the case of Camille demonstrates, can be female, so long as their military function is masculine: "gender transcends sex."[21] These arguments form a basis from which to consider the creation in the *Enéas* of a kind of queer temporality that is isolated within, even if it does not actively oppose, the heteronormativity of romance time.

The source of the *Enéas*, Vergil's *Aeneid*, also confronts the issue of same-sex love, in the persons of Nisus and Euryalus, a fact noted by both Gaunt and Burgwinkle. Earlier scholars often attempted to banish the "erotic dimensions"[22] of the friendship between Nisus and Euryalus, but in an eloquent and influential essay John F. Makowski argues that the only other place in the poem with so much erotic colour is Book IV and concludes that "it was [Vergil's] genius to suffuse the raw material of Homer with Plato and so to fashion the second greatest love story of the *Aeneid*."[23] The blending of the homosocial and the homoerotic is clearest, perhaps, in the simile describing the death of Euryalus:

> Volvitur Euryalus leto, pulchrosque per artus
> it cruor, inque umeros cervix conlapsa recumbit:
> purpureus veluti cum flos succisus aratro
> languescit ormiens lassove papavera collo
> demisere caput, pluvia cum forte gravantur (Aen. IX 433–37)

> Euryalus in death went reeling down,
> And blood streamed on his handsome length, his neck
> Collapsing let his head fall on his shoulder –
> As a bright flower cut by a passing plow
> Will droop and wither slowly, or a poppy
> Bow its head upon its tired stalk
> When overborne by a passing rain.[24]

Here Vergil melds Homer's image of a young man's death in *Iliad* 8 308–10 with Sappho's of a young woman's virginity as a purple flower trampled on by men – a

---

20 Burgwinkle, "Knighting the Classical Hero," 7.
21 Burgwinkle, "Knighting the Classical Hero," 35.
22 David Meban, "The Nisus and Euryalus Episode and Roman Friendship," *Phoenix* 63.3/4 (2009): 239–59 at 244.
23 John F. Makowski, "Nisus and Euryalus: A Platonic Relationship," *The Classical Journal* 85:1 (1989): 1–15 at 15.
24 Vergil, *Aeneid*, ed. R. A. B. Mynors (Oxford: Oxford University Press, 1969); future references are to this edition by line number.

conflation already made by Catullus in poem 11, where the poet compares his rejected love to a flower on the edge of a meadow, touched by the plow ("velut prati/ ultimi flos, praetereunte postquam/ tactus aratro est").[25] The image, in other words, was ambiguously sexualized already by the time Vergil composed the *Aeneid*. In the next generation, Ovid would make it definitively queer by using it of the death of Hyacinth in *Metamorphoses* X, the book dedicated by Orpheus to the loves of gods and young men. Like Euryalus, the dying Hyacinth is compared to a flower: "ut, siquis violas rigidumve papaver in horto/ liliaque infringat fulvis horrentia linguis,/ . . . sic vultus moriens iacet" (as when in a garden violets/ Or lilies tawny-tongued or poppies proud/ Are bruised and bent . . . so dying lies that face).[26] Apollo then makes the simile literal by transforming his beloved's body into the flower that goes by his name.

What interests me most in the description of Nisus and Euryalus, however, is the authorial encomium pronounced after their deaths, which declares them eternal heroes:

> Fortunati ambo! Siquid mea carmina possunt
> nulla dies umquam memori eximet aevo
> dum domus Aenea Capitoli immobile saxum
> accolet imperiumque pater Romanus habebit. (IX 446–49)

> Fortunate both! If in the least my songs
> Avail, no future day will ever take you
> Out of the record of remembering Time,
> While children of Aeneas make their home
> Around the Capitol's unshaken rock
> And still the Roman Father governs all.

This praise makes it clear that the problem with the love of Nisus and Euryalus is not that it is between men. Rather, it is excessive, and in Vergil's poem excessive passion is always destructive: the desperate love of Dido for Aeneas destroys her and that of Nisus and Euryalus destroys them both, just as the desperate rage of

---

[25] Catullus "11." *Catullus. Tibullus. Pervigilium Veneris*, trans. F. W. Cornish (London: William Heinemann, 1921), 22–24. On the evolution of the image see Don Fowler, "Vergil on Killing Virgins," in *Homo Viator, Classical Essays for John Bramble*, ed. Michael Whitby, Philip R. Hardie, and Mary Whitby (Bristol: Bristol Classical Press, 1987), 188–89.

[26] Ovid, *Metamorphoses* X, ll. 190–95, trans. A. D. Melville, Ovid's Metamorphoses (Oxford: Oxford University Press, 1986). The image retains its queerness in many poems of the First World War, not only the well-known "In Flanders Fields" by John McCrae, but also "Break of Day in the Trenches" by Isaac Rosenberg, "Ancient History" by Siegfried Sassoon, and a host of others. Many of the poets of the trenches had excellent classical educations, and of course quite a few of them, like Sassoon, were gay.

Turnus, paralleling that of *saevus* Achilles in the previous war, will destroy him in turn. Passion is what Aeneas, in order to become the *pius pater* that he is always promised to be, the perfect Roman hero, must sacrifice.[27] As Parry puts it, "the personal emotions of a man [are] never allowed to motivate action . . . [Aeneas] is man himself; not man as the brilliant free agent of Homer's world, but man of a later stage in civilization."[28] Nisus and Euryalus, whose love was too great for the nascent Roman world, live on in words, in the abstract memory of time; Aeneas will live on in the utterly concrete Capitoline Hill and in the race that he, as the original Roman father, will found. Nisus and Euryalus are thus marked as belonging to the Iliadic world of the past that must be left behind, and Aeneas to the new world of emerging history, of Roman futurity, a world in which romance brings only delay, despair, and death.

In the *Roman d'Enéas*, by contrast, passion, so long as it is heterosexual and courtly, is not what hinders the hero's destiny; it is what shapes it, even if it is also, as Burgwinkle argues, "a basically unpleasant initiation experience in which one loses one's 'self' in return for a later reintegration into the larger community."[29] Same-sex love, on the other hand, exists outside of this larger community and the future-oriented concerns with procreation and genealogy that motivate it. In the French poem, the Nisus and Euryalus episode follows the model of the *Aeneid* closely, and the language that characterizes their relationship similarly suggests an erotic dimension: Nisus addresses Eurïalus (5156) as "bels dolz amis" (beautiful sweet friend), a term of affection which, if not explicit, is at least suggestive. As Huguette Legros notes, in the *romans d'antiquité*, the purely homosocial and feudal meaning of *amis* has begun a semantic slide towards courtliness, "contaminated," in her words, by the vocabulary of love;[30] indeed, the very same words will be put by Benoît into the mouth of Briseida, as she addresses Troilus in her first speech in the *Troie*.[31] Nisus's accusation against the killer of Eurïalus has a similarly erotic flavor:

---

[27] This is, of course, why the ending of the poem is so disturbing, since in it a Turnus-like rage overcomes Aeneas, causing him to ignore the advice of Anchises and refusing to spare the conquered.
[28] Adam Parry, "The Two Voices of Virgil's *Aeneid*," *Arion* 2.4 (1963): 66–80 at 79.
[29] Burgwinkle, "Knighting the Classical Hero," 42.
[30] Huguette Legros, "Le vocabulaire de l'amitié, son évolution sémantique au cours du XIIe siècle," *Cahiers de Civilization Médiévale* 29.90 (1980), 135. She suggests an influence from the amorous (and heterosexual) *planhs* of the troubadour South.
[31] Benoît de Sainte-Maure, *Le Roman de Troie*, ed. Léopold Constans, 6 vols. (Paris: Firmin-Didot, 1904–1912), l. 13287. Further references are to this edition by line number.

> Moult a dur cuer qui lui toucha
> quil veult occire onques n'ama
> onques de bonne amor n'ot cure
> qui toucheroit tel creature (5306–9)

Whoever touched him has a very hard heart – he who desires to kill him never loved. No one who knew the goodness of love could touch such a creature.

The image of the falling flower, so poignant in Vergil, is notably absent here; the death of Eurïalus is brutal and unmetaphorized: "Vulcen . . . al damoisel trencha le chief" (Volcens . . . cut off the boy's head). Both the Roman poet's apostrophe and the lament of Euryalus's mother (IX 481–97) are omitted in the medieval author's retelling.[32] Pathos is instead reserved for the death of Pallas, and especially for Enéas's extraordinary lament over the young man's body, which suggests a far more dangerously excessive affection linking the Trojan and the young Arcadian than that between the two acknowledged lovers.

Pallas's queerness does not become apparent until after his death – in fact, as Halberstam might put it, death queers him, and Enéas too, apparently, projecting them into a temporality that is at odds with anything that occurs in Vergil's poem. There is nothing queer at all about their initial meeting; Pallas is the first to greet and challenge the delegation of Trojans approaching Pallantee in search of allies in the fight against Turnus, in a scene quite closely mapped on the *Aeneid*. His father Evandre, who is revealed as an old friend of Anchises, greets Enéas like a long lost relative, and the following morning Enéas participates in the knighting of Pallas, who will return with him to Montauban and the fight against Turnus. The next time we see Pallas, he is first fighting Turnus on the battlefield, and then lying dead at his feet; whatever relationship may have blossomed between the young man and Enéas did so off-stage. The first significant change from the *Aeneid* occurs at this point: Turnus takes a trophy from the young man's body, but instead of a belt-buckle emblazoned with the story of the Danaids, it is a ring, a gift from Enéas.

The change seems slight, but curious. It is possible, of course, that the author feared his audience would not know the story of the fifty Danaids, all but one of whom killed their husbands on their wedding night, thus substituting the blood of murder for that of defloration. Don Fowler argues that in the *Aeneid*, it

---

[32] Christopher Baswell argues that "The female, even the maternal, is thus wholly suppressed at this point in the French version, leaving all the more prominent its focus on male militarism and fidelity." "Men in the *Roman d'Eneas*: The Construction of Empire," in *Medieval Masculinities: Regarding Men in the Middle Ages*, ed. Clare Lees, Thelma Fenster, and Jo Ann McNamara (Minneapolis: University of Minnesota Press, 1994), 151.

is this very association that makes us recognize Pallas himself as a virgin, in spite of his gender.[33] The ring worn by Pallas in the *Enéas*, however, also encodes his sexuality. Its bezel takes the form of a lion-cub, suggesting Pallas's youthful masculinity, carved of *jagonce*. The word *jagonce* is sometimes rendered *jacinthe* in other Old French texts; it is one of the stones used in the walls of the city of Heaven, but in this context another association seems more important: *jacinthe* derives from hyacinth, the name of a flower, but also, as I noted above, the name of Apollo's lover. Thus, the association between dying youth and dying flower, displaced by the French poet from the death of Eurïalus, reemerges here, transformed. Indeed, the language surrounding the dead body of Pallas will, from this point on, oscillate between two linked images: the flower, epitome of fragility, passing time, and lost youth, and the jacinth, eternal, impervious, indestructible, and yet somehow enfolding the fading flower.

Enéas's lament over the young man's body is significantly expanded in the medieval poem, and the register of its language is quite different. Vergil's hero speaks for sixteen lines (XI 42–58); his emphasis is on Evander's loss, and on the loss of a protector for Italy, an ally for Ascanius. The sight of Pallas's face, pale as snow, moves him to tears, but they are dignified tears. Not so the medieval hero, whose lament balloons to fifty-six lines; he begins by kissing the young man's corpse, and then goes on to address him in language that is positively overwrought, both more personal and more eroticized than that of Vergil's poem.

One of the most remarkable features of Enéas's speech over Pallas's body is that it consistently uses the informal *tu* rather than the formal *vous*. By the twelfth century, French had already developed the distinction maintained to this day in modern French,[34] according to which the *vous* form is used as a singular in formal addresses, with the *tu* form reserved for situations marked by distinction in age (a parent addresses a child) or in social class (a lord addresses his vassal); more rarely, given the stratification of courtly society, it is used between equals, either equals in power or equals in affection and intimacy. In Marie de France's *Fresne*, for example, the heroine's mother switches from *vous* to *tu* upon recognizing her long lost daughter[35] Other instances of the use of *tu* in the *Enéas* include Evander's

---

[33] Fowler, "Vergil on Killing Virgins," 185–88. On the problem of male virginity, see Maud Burnett McInerney, "Like a Virgin: The Problem of Male Virginity in the Symphonia," in *Hildegard of Bingen: A Book of Essays*, ed. M. McInerney (New York: Garland, 1998), 133–54.

[34] The modern French of the *héxagone*, in any case; the Québecois distinguish only between singular and plural, not between informal and formal in their use of the second person.

[35] "Kar me dites kil vus bailla!" (Tell me who gave it to you!) (*Fresne* 435); "Tu es ma fille, bele amie!" (You are my daughter, lovely friend!) (*Fresne* 450). *Les Lais de Marie de France*, ed. Jean Rychner (Paris: Champion, 1981).

conversation with Enéas, the son of an old friend, the queen's lectures to her daughter, and Lavine's instructions to the archer, her social inferior, but also, significantly, Eurïalus's plea to accompany Nisus: "Comment remaindrai je sanz toy,/ et tu comment iras sanz moy?" Eurïalus is the younger of the pair, and therefore a different kind of intimacy is being invoked. Heterosexual lovers, constrained by the formalities of the courtly system and the power hierarchies inherent in it, rarely use *tu*; when Marie de France puts a virtually identical sentiment into the mouth of Tristan, he addresses Iseut with the formal pronoun: "Bele amie, si est de nus:/ Ne vus sanz mei, ne jeo sanz vus."[36] Enéas and Lavine, like Enéas and Didon, use *vous*.

Enéas's use of the informal pronoun could, of course, be dismissed as paternal, but it is not the only thing that suggests erotic desire for the dead Pallas, a desire which was never expressed for the living boy. Enéas kisses the body twice (6209, 6274), although neither of Pallas's parents do; he faints upon the body. And, even more significantly, his language is highly eroticized. He addresses Pallas as "flour de jouvente" (flower of youth, 6212), and goes on to develop the floral image some forty lines later:

> moult par est fraille ceste vie;
> tant estiez bel hier matin
> soz ciel n'avoit plus bel meschin;
> en poy d'eure te voy müé,
> palli et tout descouloré:
> ta blanchour est toute nercie,
> et ta rouvours toute persie.
> Clere faiture, gentil chose,
> si com soleil flastrit la rose,
> si t'a la mort moult tost plessié,
> et tout flastri et tout changié! (6249–59)

This life is very fragile; you were so handsome yesterday morning, there was no more beautiful young man beneath the sky and now in a few hours I see you changed, pale and all discoloured. Your whiteness is all blackened and your rosiness is all bluish. Brilliant creature, noble being, just as the sun wilts the rose, so death has left you withered and faded and entirely changed.

The image of the falling flower, omitted from the death of Eurïalus, blossoms fully here, and if the sentiment seems familiar, it is because it is. The author exploits the *carpe diem* topos according to which youthful beauty is linked to the ephemerality of flowers, and especially roses; the temporal markers fall thick

---

36 Marie de France, *Chievrefoil*, ll. 77–78.

and fast as Enéas invokes yesterday morning, the turning sky, the rays of the sun. Perhaps most familiar from Ronsard's poem ("Mignonne, allons voir si la rose/ qui ce matin avait desclose") the topos of the fading rose goes back to Horace (where it is homoerotic) and even to Anacreon, although it was probably best known in the early Middle Ages from a poem ascribed to the fourth-century Gallo-Roman poet, Ausonius, which ends with the oft-quoted line "collige virgo, rosas dum flos novus et nova pubes/ et memor esto aevum sic properare tuum" (So, girl, gather roses while their bloom and your youth are fresh, and be mindful that your time too hastens away).[37] In the Middle Ages, the poem was believed to be by Vergil, and so it may have seemed a reasonable way to expand on the brief image of fading flowers that occur (in the narrator's voice, not the hero's) in the *Aeneid*. When Pallas is loaded onto his bier, he is like a flower picked by a young girl, a soft violet or drooping hyacinth ("qualem virgineo demessum pollice florem/ seu mollis violae seu languentis hyacinthi," XI 68–69).

It is not only the language of flowers, and particularly of the hyacinth, that casts Pallas as the object of erotic love, however. The phrase "cler faiture, gentil chose" also resonates with the language of courtly love. *Faiture* can simply mean creation or person, and indeed some of the uses cited in Godefroy are religious. At least as common, however, are the erotic uses of the term. The lady in Marie de France's *Equitan* is possessed of "gent cors . . . et bele faiture," as well as a complexion "colur de rose";[38] Chrétien, a few decades later, will describe Perceval's beloved as "biaux de corps et de faiture," and the heroine of *Amadas et Idoine*, written shortly after 1200, is simply called a "bele faiture." *Cler*, too, crops up regularly with an erotic meaning, as in *Flor et Blancheflor* (like the *Lais* de Marie, dated to around 1160), "une pucele/ Clere come rose nouvele." *Gentil chose*, perhaps, is neutral – and yet, in this context, it cannot help but recall the Wife of Bath's sly reference to her "bele chose," some two hundred years later.

The real threat of all this excessive emotion to the heteronormative, genealogical purpose of the poem is encapsulated precisely and briefly when Enéas laments that, when he had won, he would have shared the whole country with Pallas: "quant eüsse le tout conquis,/ je te partisse le pays" (6232). Such a partition would have made nonsense of the grand imperial project according to which the sons of Enéas and Lavine and only the sons of Enéas and Lavine (Ascanius will be supplanted) must inherit Italy and become Romans, and

---

[37] The poem, now believed to be anonymous, is included in the appendix to the *Works of Ausonius*, ed. Hugh G. Evelyn White, Loeb Classical Library, vol. 2 (London: Heineman, 1921), 280.
[38] Marie de France, *Equitan*, ll. 33, 39.

eventually Angevins.[39] The text shuts off this possibility in the past subjunctive realm of what might have been, just as it will shut up Pallas's disturbingly desirable dead body in his tomb, and frees Enéas to move into the future by marrying Lavine.

In *The Cultural Politics of Emotion*, Sara Ahmed underscores the way in which "the coupling of man and woman becomes a kind of 'birthing,' a giving birth not only to new life but to ways of living that are already recognizable as forms of civilization."[40] Queer lives thus "become readable as the failure to reproduce, and as a threat to the social ordering of life itself."[41] Thus, in the *Roman d'Enéas*, characters such as Nisus and Eurïalus and Pallas are evoked only to be disavowed, relegated to stasis, death, and the past. They are flies in amber, contained so that they may not hinder the forward progress of genealogical time. The *Roman de Troie*, on the other hand, is not about the birth of a new civilization, but about the death of an old one. It refuses to value the romance time upon which the *Roman d'Enéas* is founded, and also refuses to cordon off queer characters as its predecessor does. Instead, it multiplies not only deviant characters but forms of deviance, no longer simply defined by sexuality; the temporality of its narrative, existing as it does entirely under the shadow of death, always already part of a futureless past, is thus fundamentally queer; as Lee Edelman puts it, echoing Halberstam's insistence on the deadly and deluded quality of reproductive time, "[queer subjects] aren't, in fact, subjects of history constrained by the death-in-life of futurism and its illusion of productivity. We're subjects, instead, of the real, of the encounter with futurism's emptiness, with negativity's life-in-death."[42] Heterosexual couplings in the poem prove inevitably destructive rather than generative, leading both to the death of individuals (in the case of the love-affair between Troilus and Briseida) and of Troy itself (in the case of Paris and Helen).[43] The world of the poem is one of heterosexual failure, futurelessness and queer grief, multiplied across major and minor characters but all embodied most powerfully in the figure of Achilles.

---

[39] The lesson against partition is one Henry II was slow to learn; his insistence on dividing his realm (co-kingship for Henry, the Young King, Aquitaine for Richard, Brittany for Geoffrey) caused nothing but trouble.
[40] Sara Ahmed, *The Cultural Politics of Emotion* (Edinburgh: University of Edinburgh Press, 2014), 144.
[41] Ahmed, *Cultural Politics*, 145.
[42] Carolyn Dinshaw et al., "Theorizing Queer Temporalities: A Roundtable Discussion," *GLQ* 13.2–3 (2007): 177–95 at 181.
[43] The fact that women in the *Troie* are more likely to survive heterosexuality than men is a topic for another day.

One of the structural curiosities of the *Troie* is the series of character descriptions provided from ll. 5093–582. These are derived, for the most part, from Benoît's source, the late antique "eyewitness" account of the Trojan War by pseudo-Dares; in their expansions upon Dares's bald text, however, they form an index to Benoît's method of translation through expansion. Where Dares gives a list, proper name in the accusative, followed by a flat list of adjectives, like "Podalirium crassum valentem superbum tristum,"[44] Benoit elaborates:

> Polidarius iert si gras
> Que a grant peine alot le pas
> En plusors choses iert vaillanz
> Mais toz jors iert tristes dolanz
> Ainz le cerchast par mainte terre
> Qui plus ergoillos vousist querre. (5257–62)

Polidarius was so fat that he could scarcely walk. He was worthy in several ways, but always sad and mournful. You could search the world over and never find a more arrogant man.

No longer merely "heavy, worthy, arrogant, and sad," Polidarius is now both obese and severely depressed. Similarly, Hecuba, who in Dares had a manlike mind (*mente virili*), actually looks like a man: "De cors senblot home bien pres/ N'aveit pas femenin talant" (Her body seemed like that of a man. She lacked feminine gifts) (5514–15). Memnon the Ethiopian, who does not appear in Dares (and is not given a physical description in Dictys), is not explicitly described as Black in this passage (although he will be later in the poem) but has dark blond frizzy hair and yellow eyes, suggesting a stereotypical description of a biracial man. And finally, the description of Patroclus is significantly altered. Dares tells us that Achilles's friend is "pulchro corpore, oculis vividis et magnis, verecundum, rectum, prudentem, dapsilem" (beautiful of body, with big bright eyes, modest, upright and generous). Benoit develops as follows:

> Patroclus ot le cors mout gent
> E mout fu de grant escïent.
> Blans fu e blois e dreiz e granz
> E chevaliers mout avananz.
> Les oilz ot vairs, n'ot pas grant ire
> Biaus fu mout, ce puet hon bien dire,
> Larges, d'ovraigne merveillos,
> Mais mout par esteit vergoindos. (5171–78)

---

44 Dares Phrygius, *De Excidio Troiae Historia*, ed. Ferdinand Meister (Leipzig: Benedictus Gotthelf Teubner, 1873), 17.

Patroclus had a noble body and he was extremely wise. He was white-skinned and blond and stood tall and large, he was a most appealing knight. His eyes were grey and not wrathful, he was extremely handsome, it must be said, generous, wonderful in his actions, but also extremely shameful.

Vergoindos is etymologically descended from *verecundus*, but over the centuries the meaning of the word slipped from "modest, shy, easily ashamed" to include also "shameful" or "dishonorable."[45] The other details that Benoît adds (grey eyes, white skin, blond hair) could easily describe a courtly lady; in fact, *blanc et blois* is what Tarchon calls Camille in the *Enéas*. Even in these rapid descriptive sketches, Benoît creates, from Dares's much straighter (and more tedious) narration, a gallery of oddities: obese depressives, viragos, racial others, queers.

While medieval writers generally represent Achilles as heterosexual and the nature of his bond with Patroclus as non-erotic, Benoît's depiction of the hero is much more ambiguous. As in the *Enéas*, there is from an enemy an accusation of sodomy. Hector taunts Achilles with the loss of his companion in terms that are less explicit than those of Lavine's mother, but that nonetheless are clear:

> L'ire grant que vostre cuers a
> Porriez vengier . . .
> E la dolor del cumpaignon
> Dont j'ai fet la desevreison,
> Que tante nuit avez sentu
> Entre vos braz tot nu a nu.
> Icist jués est vils e hontos,
> Dont li plusor sunt haïnos
> As deus, quin prenent la venjance
> Par la lor devine puissance. (13178–88)

You will be able to avenge the great wrath your heart feels, and the grief for that companion I separated from you, whom you have held naked in your arms so many nights. Such games are vile and shameful, and hateful to the gods who punish them with their divine power.

Hector is no courtly lover, as his brutal treatment of his wife makes clear (ll 15329–54); still, he speaks here for the reproductive, patriarchal order, invoking the gods as vengeful guarantors. Baumgartner notes that, in the Milan

---

[45] In their translation (which became available too late to be used more generally for this essay) Burgess and Kelly render this as "had very shameful ways"; they note that both Constans and Baumgartner also interpret the word as implying shame. *The Roman de Troie by Benoît de Sainte-Maure*, trans. Glyn S. Burgess and Douglas Kelly (Woodbridge: Boydell and Brewer, 2017), 104 n.45.

manuscript, these lines are highlighted by a pointing finger in the margin, emphasizing (presumably) their shocking character.[46] Katherine Callen King notes that Benoît is one of the few medieval authors to "resurrect" the notion of Achilles as homosexual, but she restricts her discussion to this passage, thus leaving open the question of whether Achilles and Patroclus actually are lovers, or whether Hector is merely repeating gossip.[47] Achilles's lament over the body of Patroclus, however, suggests a more than "Platonic" friendship, especially when read in the context of the *Roman d'Enéas*. Initially, it echoes that of Nisus over Euryalus: "Ne fis pas bien, biaus chiers amis,/ Quant je sans moi vos i tramis" (I did the wrong thing, beautiful dear friend, when I let you go without me) (10335–36); it goes on to emphasize Patroclus's physical attributes, his beauty and his body, before promising to mourn for him forever:

> En vois estoit mes cuers trestoz,
> Quar mout esteiez biaus e proz . . .
> Amis, por quei vos ai perdu?
> Vostre gent cors, tant mare fu!
> Quar je ere vostrë e vos miens.
> A plors, a lermes vos plaindrai
> A toz les jours mais que vivrai.

My heart was entirely yours, for you were so beautiful and brave . . . Friend, why have I lost you? Your sweet body, what has become of it? For I was yours and you were mine. With tears and weeping I will mourn you all the days of my life.

The emphasis here is on desirability, not, as might be expected, on courage or loyalty. Finally, Achilles faints on the body, moved by what the narrator calls *estrange duel*, strange or extraordinary or even queer grief.

In a discussion of queer grief centered primarily on the queer victims of 9/11 and the AIDS crisis, Ahmed argues that

> the failure to recognise queer loss as loss is also a failure to recognise queer relationships as significant bonds, or that queer lives are lives worth living, or that queers are more than failed heterosexuals, heterosexuals who have failed "to be". Given that queer becomes read as a form of "non-life"–with the death implied by being seen as non-reproductive – then queers are perhaps even already dead and cannot die.[48]

---

[46] Baumgartner, *Roman de Troie*, note p. 275; she points out too that the same marginalia are found at two other places in the MS, in different contexts.
[47] See Katherine Callen King, *Achilles: Paradigms of the War Hero from Homer to the Middle Ages* (Berkeley: University of California Press, 1987), 172–73.
[48] Ahmed, *Cultural Politics*, 156.

Hector's taunting of Achilles performs exactly this kind of denial of the value of queer lives and queer relationships and indeed echoes the rhetoric of those evangelicals who see AIDS as divine punishment for homosexuality. Even more tellingly, perhaps, the death of Patroclus makes all the other deaths in the poem, especially that of Achilles himself, inevitable.

In the *Enéas*, the hero's passion for Pallas was essentially a stage he had to get over before being fully initiated into the heterosexual world of heirs and descendants. The *Roman de Troie*, as I have noted, is much less sanguine than its predecessor about courtly love and the whole concept of dynastic, reproductive, romance time. Like Enéas, Achilles will fall in love with a perfect woman, beautiful, virgin, royal, the potential solution to prolonged war. Like Patroclus, Polixena is blonde and has grey eyes. Achilles's first glimpse of her, however, occurs as she weeps at Hector's tomb, and is immediately associated with death:

> Veüe i a Polixenein
> Apertement en mi la chiere:
> C'est l'achaison e la maniere
> Par qu'il sera gitez de vie
> E l'ame de son cors partie. (ll.17540–44)

He saw Polixena he saw her face clearly, and it will be the cause and the manner of his departure from life, of the separation of his soul and body.

It is tempting to read yet another separation into this moment, the final separation of Achilles from his previous lover, since in falling in love with Polixena he allows himself to forget his promise to mourn Patroclus every day of his life.

Even as he declares his love for Polixena his language is shadowed by death and by forbidden forms of desire:

> Cum est Amors seisiz de mei!
> Ne puis aveir por rien confort,
> Car mis cuers me pramet la mort. (17670–72)

How love has laid ahold of me! There is no comfort for me, my heart forebodes my death.

All courtly lovers claim that they will die of their affliction, but few first glimpse the beloved weeping over the perfectly embalmed body of her recently deceased brother. And, of course, Achilles is right: loving Polixena will be the immediate cause of his death, as her mother Hecuba baits a trap for him with the body of her youngest daughter, and sets Paris to murder Achilles when he comes to the promised betrothal. Oddly, though, Achilles also invokes the example of Narcissus to describe the emotional condition in which he finds himself upon first beholding the Trojan princess:

> Narcisus sui, ce sai e vei,
> Qui tant ama l'umbre de sei
> Qu'il en morut sor la funteine.
> Iceste angoisse, iceste peine
> Sai que je sent. Je raim mon onbre,
> Je aim ma mort e mon encombre.
> Ne plus qu il la puet baillier
> Ne acoler ne enbracier,
> Car riens nen est ne riens ne fu,
> Ne qui ne pot estre sentu,
> Plus ne puis je aveir leisor
> De li aveir ne de s'amor. (ll. 17691–702)

I am Narcissus, I know it for certain, who so loved the shadow of himself that he died at the fountain. I know that I feel the same anguish, the same pain. I love my shadow, I love my death and my suffering. No more than he could grasp it or take it in his arms, embrace it, for it is nothing, was nothing, no more than he could feel it, no more will I be able to have her or her love.

In associating himself with the beautiful but self-absorbed young man from *Metamorphoses* III, Achilles invites identification with the epitome of queer desire: Narcissus's obsession with his own reflection is not only queer in the sense of same sex (the reflection that he adores is that of a beautiful young man), but queerer in that it takes him entirely outside of the norms of desire, either hetero- or homo-, since he desires not an other but himself. Such desire is inevitably deadly, and, like his equally queer counterpart, Hyacinth, Narcissus loses his human form, becoming a flower.

What does it mean for Achilles to define his love for Polixena as love for his own reflection? Alfred Adler notes the "affinity between narcissism and homosexuality . . . implied in the character sketch of Achilles,"[49] but this does not go quite far enough. There would have been a logic to comparing Achilles's love for Patroclus to that of Narcissus for himself, but that the comparison should arise when Achilles experiences (for the first time?) heterosexual love with all its courtly trappings suggests something more complicated. It establishes Achilles's love for Polixena as a phenomenon quite distinct from the Trojan princess herself; this new love, courtly love, is as deceptive

---

[49] Alfred Adler, "Militia et amor in the *Roman de Troie*," *Romanische Forschengen* 72 (1960): 14–29 at 22.

and deadly as Narcissus's reflection, and it is *out of time*: "riens nen est ne riens ne fu" (it is nothing and it was nothing). It has no existence, either in the present, or in the past.

Perhaps what the image of Narcissus reflects from within Achilles's self is precisely his own inescapable impulse toward death. That is, in allowing himself to fall in love with Polixena, not only does Achilles betray his promise to love Patroclus forever, but he also moves not toward heterosexual marriage and the possibility of a future dynasty – toward reproductive time, in Halberstam's phrase – but rather toward the ultimate queerness of death itself, of the end of personal, individual time. He fails to heterosexualize himself as Enéas does; where Enéas was "saved" by the love of a good woman, Achilles is damned by it. The *Roman de Troie*, indeed, proves to be a Romance in which romance, the heterosexual system of courtly love with its promise of creating and maintaining patriarchal structures down through the ages, fails. Romance time, and particularly its ethos of heterosexual courtly love, is instead revealed as a tyrannical and ultimately tragic temporality.

Bibliography

Adler, Alfred. "Militia et amor in the *Roman de Troie*." *Romanische Forschengen* 72 (1960): 14–29

Ahmed, Sara. *The Cultural Politics of Emotion*. Edinburgh: University of Edinburgh Press, 2014.

Bakhtin, M. M. *The Dialogic Imagination: Four Essays*. Edited and translated by Michael Holquist and Caryl Emerson. Austin: University of Texas Press, 1982.

Barber, Richard and Juliet Baker. *Tournaments: Jousts, Chivalry and Pageants in the Middle Ages*. Woodbridge: Boydell, 1989.

Barker-Benfield, Bruce C. "A Ninth Century Manuscript from Fleury: Cato de senectute cum Macrobio." In *Medieval Learning and Literature: Essays Presented to Richard William Hunt*, edited by J. J. G. Alexander and M. T. Gibson, 145–65. Oxford: Clarendon, 1976.

Baswell, Christopher. "Men in the *Roman d'Eneas*: The Construction of Empire." In *Medieval Masculinities: Regarding Men in the Middle Ages*, edited by Clare Lees, Thelma Fenster, and Jo Ann McNamara, 149–68. Minneapolis: University of Minnesota Press, 1994.

Benoît de Sainte-Maure. *Le Roman de Troie*. Translated by Emmanuèle Baumgartner. Paris: Librairie Générale Française, 1987.

Benoît de Sainte-Maure. *Le Roman de Troie*. Edited by Léopold Constans. 6 vols. Paris: Firmin-Didot, 1904–1912.

Burgwinkle, William. "Knighting the Classical Hero: Homo/Hetero Affectivity in *Eneas*." *Exemplaria* 5.1 (1993): 1–43.

Catullus. "11." *Catullus. Tibullus. Pervigilium Veneris*. Translated by F. W. Cornish. London: William Heinemann, 1921.

Dares Phrygius. *De Excidio Troiae Historia*. Edited by Ferdinand Meister. Leipzig: Benedictus Gotthelf Teubner, 1873.

Dinshaw, Carolyn. *How Soon is Now? Medieval Texts, Amateur Readers and the Queerness of Time*. Durham: Duke University Press, 2012.
Dinshaw, Carolyn and Lee Edelman, Roderick A. Ferguson, Carla Freccero, Elizabeth Freeman, J. Halberstam, Annamarie Jagose, Christopher S. Nealon, and Tan Hoang Nguyen."Theorizing Queer Temporalities: A Roundtable Discussion." *GLQ* 13.2–3 (2007): 177–95.
Fowler, Don. "Vergil on Killing Virgins." In *Homo Viator, Classical Essays for John Bramble*, edited by Michael Whitby, Philip R. Hardie, and Mary Whitby, 185–98. Bristol: Bristol Classical Press, 1987.
Gaunt, Simon. "From Epic to Romance: Gender and Sexuality in the Roman d'Eneas." *Romanic Review* 83.1 (1992): 1–27.
Guynn, Noah D. "Eternal Flame: State Formation, Deviant Architecture and the Monumentality of Same-Sex Eroticism in the *Roman d'Eneas*." *GLQ* 6.2 (2000): 287–319.
Hafner, Susane. "Coward, Traitor, Landless Trojan: Aeneas and the Politics of Sodomy." *Essays in Medieval Studies* 19 (2002): 61–69.
Halberstam, J. *In a Queer Time and Place: Transgender Bodies, Subcultural Lives*. New York: New York University Press, 2005.
King, Katherine Callen. *Achilles: Paradigms of the War Hero from Homer to the Middle Ages*. Berkeley: University of California Press, 1987.
Lankewish, Vincent A. "Assault From Behind: Sodomy, Foreign Invasion and Masculine Identity in *Le Roman d'Eneas*." In *Text and Territory: Geographical Imagination in the European Middle Ages*, edited by Sylvia Tomasch and Sealy Giles, 207–44. Philadelphia: University of Pennsylvania Press, 1998.
Legros, Huguette. "Le vocabulaire de l'amitié, son évolution sémantique au cours du XIIe siècle." *Cahiers de Civilization Médiévale* 29.90 (1980): 131–39.
Les Lais de Marie de France. Edited by Jean Rychner. Paris: Champion, 1981.
Makowski, John F. "Nisus and Euryalus: A Platonic Relationship." *The Classical Journal* 85.1 (1989): 1–15.
McInerney, Maud Burnett. "Like a Virgin: The Problem of Male Virginity in the Symphonia." In *Hildegard of Bingen: A Book of Essays*, edited by M. McInerney, 133–54. New York: Garland, 1998.
Meban, David. "The Nisus and Euryalus Episode and Roman Friendship." *Phoenix* 63.3/4 (2009): 239–59.
Ovid. *Metamorphoses* X. Translated by A. D. Melville. Oxford: Oxford University Press, 1986.
Parry, Adam. "The Two Voices of Virgil's *Aeneid*." *Arion* 2.4 (1963): 66–80.
The Roman de Troie by Benoît de Sainte-Maure. Translated by Glyn S. Burgess and Douglas Kelly Woodbridge: Boydell and Brewer, 2017.
Roman d'Eneas: Edition critique d'après le manuscrit B.N.fr. 60. Edited and translated by Aimé Petit. Paris: Lettres Gothiques, 1997.
Ruys, Juanita Feros. "Medieval Latin Meditations on Old Age." In *Old Age in the Middle Ages and the Renaissance*, edited by Albrecht Classen, 171–200. Berlin: De Gruyter, 2007.
Vergil. *Aeneid*. Edited by R. A. B. Mynors. Oxford: Oxford University Press, 1969.
The Watchtower. Watchtower Online Library. http://wol.jw.org/en/wol/d/r1/lp-e/102004290.
Works of Ausonius. Edited by Hugh G. Evelyn White. Loeb Classical Library, vol. 2. London: Heineman, 1921.

Part III: **Insular Queerness: English and the Nonnormative**

Margaret Cotter-Lynch
Chapter 6
The Gender Genealogy of St. Mary of Egypt

Diane Watt and Clare Lees have suggested that we can productively see St. Mary of Egypt, as represented within the Old English *Life of St. Mary of Egypt*, as genderqueer, transcending gender boundaries by simultaneously embodying both male and female identities.[1] This claim surprisingly places Mary of Egypt into a category with saints such as Pelagia and Thecla, who tradition tells us (miraculously) dressed as men in order to pursue a religious life not ordinarily open to women, and who contemporary critical conversations suggest should be considered through transgender theory. M. W. Bychowski has productively outlined parameters for discussing transgender saints, specifically saints who have historically been understood to transcend conventional and putatively essential gender boundaries.[2] I see here the convergence of two ideas: one, the gender fluidity in miraculous saints' narratives, always located in the distant past, even for their medieval audiences; and two, emerging contemporary understandings of gender as non-binary. This essay examines the ways in which grammatical and semantic gender markers are deployed in the Old English version of the story of St. Mary of Egypt and the Latin version that was likely its source, in order to demonstrate the genealogical relationship between texts and elucidate the ambiguities and complexities that cluster around the gendered representation of the saint. I argue that the multiple possibilities for configuring and representing gender offered by these medieval texts expand our modern possibilities for imagining the relationship between sanctity, sexuality, and gender. As Blake Gutt reminds us, "the theorization and discussion of non-normative gender is in evidence throughout recorded history."[3] We might learn about future possibilities for understanding gender in our current world by

---

[1] Diane Watt and Clare A. Lees, "Age and Desire in the Old English Life of St. Mary of Egypt: A Queerer Time and Place?," in *Middle-Aged Women in the Middle Ages*, ed. Sue Niebrzydowski (Cambridge: D. S. Brewer, 2011), 53–68.
[2] M. W. Bychowski, "The Authentic Lives of Transgender Saints: *Imago Dei* and *Imitatio Christi* in the *Life* of Saint Marinos the Monk," in *Trans and Genderqueer Subjects in Medieval Hagiography*, ed. Alicia Spencer-Hall and Blake Gutt (Amsterdam: Amsterdam University Press, forthcoming 2020). I wish to thank the author for sharing this article with me before its publication.
[3] Blake Gutt, "Transgender Genealogy in *Tristan de Nanteuil*," *Exemplaria* 30.2 (2018): 129–46. M. W. Bychowski, "Were there Transgender People in the Middle Ages?," *The Public Medievalist* (blog), November 1, 2018, https://www.publicmedievalist.com/transgender-middle-ages/.

https://doi.org/10.1515/9781501513701-007

reexamining articulations of gender from the past, since, upon reflection, these articulations don't function as we might have been trained to expect.

Mary of Egypt was one of the most popular saints of the medieval period, and her hagiography survives in multiple versions and languages. The Old English *Life of St. Mary of Egypt* is preserved in three eleventh-century manuscripts, only one of which, Cotton Julius E. vii, is complete (or nearly so, with two small lacunae). This manuscript contains the only extant full version of Aelfric's *Lives of the Saints*, but modern scholars agree that Mary of Egypt's *Life* was not translated by Aelfric, nor included by him in his collection, nor, quite likely, approved of by him. The Old English version of Mary's story is based upon a ninth-century Latin version by Paul of Naples, itself a translation of the sixth-century Greek version (controversially) attributed to Sophronius of Jerusalem.[4] A historical person called Mary of Egypt almost certainly did not exist; there is no evidence of a cult, and the *vita* in all of its versions bears the hallmarks of a compilation of popular hagiographic tropes, rather than an account derived from historical events. Nevertheless, the story of St. Mary of Egypt was quite popular across Europe in the Middle Ages, and it was translated into a number of vernacular languages.[5] The diffusion of her *vita* in various forms and translations thus provides an exemplary case of the ways in which hagiographies were written, rewritten, translated, and adapted to particular needs in particular times and places. In the case of the Latin and Old English texts, we see a subtle transformation in the ways gender is represented, even as the overarching stories are largely similar.

---

[4] Original Greek in Sophronios, "The Life of Mary of Egypt, the Former Harlot who in Blessed Manner Became an Ascetic in the Desert of the River Jordan," trans. Marie Kouli, in *Holy Women of Byzantium: Ten Saints' Lives in English Translation*, ed. Alice-Mary Talbot (Washington, DC: Dumbarton Oaks, 1996). For a thorough account of the manuscript tradition for the Old English text, see the introduction to Hugh Magennis, *The Old English Life of Saint Mary of Egypt* (Exeter: University of Exeter Press, 2002). Magennis's edition includes both the Old English text and the CCLLatin source text. All quotations are taken from Magennis's edition of the Old English and Latin texts; modern English translations, except where noted, are his.

[5] Old and Middle French versions are collected in Peter F. Dembowski, *La Vie De Sainte Marie L'égyptienne: Versions en ancien et en Moyen Français* (Geneva: Droz, 1977). Latin and Spanish poetic versions can be found translated in Ronald E. Pepin and Hugh Feiss, *Saint Mary of Egypt: Three Medieval Lives in Verse* (Kalamazoo: Cistercian Publications, 2005). A Portuguese version is discussed in Ana Maria Machado, "Memory, Identity, and Women's Representation in the Portuguese Reception of *Vitae Patrum*: Winning a Name," in *Reading Memory and Identity in the Texts of Medieval European Holy Women*, ed. Margaret Cotter-Lynch and Brad Herzog (New York: Palgrave Macmillan, 2012), 135–64.

The extant Latin version of the *vita* that most closely resembles the probable source text for the Old English translation is found in the Cotton-Corpus Legendary (CCL).⁶ This collection of saints' lives was likely compiled in late ninth- or early tenth-century Flanders, and made its way to England by the late tenth century, where it apparently enjoyed quite wide popularity and liturgical use. The CCL was the primary source for Aelfric's *Lives of the Saints* – although, while Mary of Egypt is present in the CCL, her *Life* is notably absent from Aelfric's collection. The CCL contains the Latin version of Mary's *Life* attributed to Paul of Naples, but with perhaps some textual variants from the exact source text for the Old English version.⁷ It is ultimately impossible to know, however, from the extant evidence, how much of the variation between the Old English and CCL versions of the hagiography can be attributed to a putative now-lost Latin source-text for the Old English, versus the innovation of the Old English translator. Regardless of exact source, however, it is useful to note the clear differences in the designation of gender in the extant Latin and Old English texts. As my argument will show, some of these variations, I believe, are intrinsic in the different possibilities for gendered representation in the two languages, and therefore likely point toward differences between the Old English and original Latin source-texts.

Part of this adaptation between languages, then, also involves the refiguration of gender: where it is designated, where it is not, in what ways, and why. In the extant ninth- and tenth-century versions of her *vita*, the gender and sexuality of St. Mary of Egypt are continuously refigured in ways that challenge modern binary categorizations. Gender simultaneity – the simultaneous embodiment of both male and female characteristics and identities – provides a useful framework for considering the distinctions made around sexuality, gender, and embodiment as represented in the Latin and Old English stories. In addition, examining the figuration of gender in these texts also helps to elucidate the relationships between the texts themselves, telling us something of textual as well as gender genealogies.

To clarify what I mean when I call Mary of Egypt genderqueer, and how that is situated in relationship to a variety of ways of talking about gender in both the medieval and modern worlds, I will start with some distinctions. I am not referring to the concept of teleological gender change between binary poles, as when

---

6 Magennis, *Life of Saint Mary*, 13, 30–35.
7 As Magennis notes, "What is striking about the evidence of the Old English version is that where it contrasts with existing copies of C-C, or indeed with C, it generally preserves what must have been original readings." Magennis, *Life of Saint Mary*, 35.

particularly holy women are referred to as "becoming male."[8] Nor, indeed, am I talking about genderlessness, as when Joyce Salisbury calls St. Pelagia "an asexual eunuch for Christ."[9] I also make a distinction between Mary's version of genderqueer and what many have termed the ecclesiastical "third gender," defined by chastity for both sexes.[10] Rather, I posit a reformulation and recombination of traditional gender categories, not toward teleological gender transformation, or eradication, but rather a syncretic conceptualization of gender that embraces simultaneity. I am not claiming that Mary ceases to be female and becomes male – thus switching positions in a still-intact binary hierarchical sex/gender system – but rather positing a both–and position that calls into question the very categories of male and female, mixing them up without eradicating genderedness. Mary of Egypt's status as genderqueer is thus in close conversation with Jack Halberstam's assertion that we understand trans* in the inclusive sense, "organized around but not confined to forms of gender variance."[11] Mary is, I argue, simultaneously male and female, and as such instantiates an apophasis of gender, in which the truth of God, beyond all human understanding, incorporates a reconceptualization of gender categories beyond what we can know in this world.

Catherine Keller's apophatic conception of gender, as traced through reference to later medieval mystical texts, is useful here in explaining Mary's status as genderqueer. Keller posits that the innate unspeakability of God – the inability, that is, of human language or understanding to fully encompass God in any form, including the incarnation of Christ – means that every human expression of gender, being simultaneously incarnate and spoken, is itself incomplete in its expression of the divine. Gender as we understand and express it is a human and bodily category, and thus necessarily insufficient, in theological terms.

---

8 The scholarly literature on this common patristic trope is vast. See, for instance, L. Stephanie Cobb, *Dying to Be Men: Gender and Language in Early Christian Martyr Texts* (New York: Columbia University Press, 2008); Kerstin Aspegren, *The Male Woman: A Feminine Ideal in the Early Church* (Stockholm: Almquist & Wiksell, 1990); Barbara Newman, *From Virile Woman to Womanchrist: Studies in Medieval Religion and Literature* (Philadelphia: University of Pennsylvania Press, 1995); Jane Tibbetts Schulenburg, *Forgetful of Their Sex: Female Sanctity and Society, Ca. 500–1100* (Chicago: University of Chicago Press, 1998).
9 Joyce E. Salisbury, *Church Fathers, Independent Virgins* (London and New York: Verso, 1992), 103.
10 Jo Ann McNamara, "Chastity as a Third Gender in the History and Hagiography of Gregory of Tours," in *The World of Gregory of Tours*, ed. Kathleen Mitchell and Ian Wood (Leiden: Brill, 2002), 199–209.
11 Jack Halberstam, *Trans*: A Quick and Quirky Account of Gender Variability* (Oakland: University of California Press, 2018), 4.

Therefore, she claims, "What is at stake is ultimately irreducible to the shape of gender or to the rights of those gendered or ungendered or transgendered in one way or another. And yet in all of those contours of embodiment, all those carnalities in which the incarnation lives in the body of Christ, we have walked the edge of the unspeakable."[12] Similarly, Brian McGrath Davis claims, "Translated for a specific analysis of gender, I am suggesting that an apophatic sensibility shows us that we must always be recreating what we mean by gender, always theoretically and practically working to undo the genders we perform, never accepting any form of bodily signification as either accurate or complete."[13] Mary of Egypt's gender, then, as expressed in the Old English *vita*, might be read as indicative of a theology of gender that undermines any number of established binaries. As Victoria Blud writes in her introduction to a book that includes discussion of the Old English *Life of Saint Mary of Egypt*, "The unspeakable is a mode that queers the apophatic, the divine and transcendent, that recalls and even foregrounds their relation to the flesh."[14] Queerness, in its essence, is about moving beyond binary systems. Thus, as we will see with the Old English *Life of St. Mary of Egypt*, the undoing of gender is intimately connected to the undoing of a network of distinctions and hierarchies, among them whore/saint, age/youth, religious/lay, now/then. As Jack Halberstam has explored, the ways in which human conceptions of time have historically been constructed around reproduction and generations mean that queerness also disrupts linear temporality.[15] This, too, is evident in Mary's *Life*, as cyclical liturgical time and linear chronological time, linked to human capability (for instance, the time it takes Zosimas, as opposed to Mary, to walk a physical distance) are likewise repeatedly disrupted.

---

12 Catherine Keller, "The Apophasis of Gender: A Fourfold Unsaying of Feminist Theology," *Journal of the American Academy of Religion* 76.4 (2008): 905–33 at 912.
13 Brian McGrath Davis, "Apophatic Theology and Masculinities," *CrossCurrents* 61.4 (2011): 502–14 at 511.
14 Victoria Blud, *The Unspeakable, Gender, and Sexuality in Medieval Literature, 1000–1400* (Cambridge: D. S. Brewer, 2017), 11. For a discussion of the relationship between the apophatic and "transsexual" bodies, see Sigridur Gudmarsdottir, "Feminist Theology and the Sensible Unsaying of Mysticism," in *Apophatic Bodies: Negative Theology, Incarnation, and Relationality*, ed. Chris Boesel and Catherine Keller (New York: Fordham University Press, 2009), 273–85.
15 Jack Halberstam, *In a Queer Time and Place: Transgender Bodies, Subcultural Lives* (New York: New York University Press, 2005). For an application of these ideas to specifically medieval examples, see Blake Gutt, "Transgender Genealogy." The relationship between transgender and history/chronology is also explored in *TSQ: Transgender Studies Quarterly* special issue on *Trans*historicities*, ed. Leah DeVun and Zeb Tortorici. 5.4 (November, 2018).

I am far from the first to consider Mary of Egypt's story from the perspective of gender.[16] I will therefore limit my intervention here to a consideration of how and why we might consider Mary of Egypt as genderqueer, and what it might tell us not only about Mary but also about gender and queerness, to think about the story in this way. To accomplish this, we will compare the representation of Mary's gender identity in the Old English version of the text and the ninth-century Latin version believed to be its source. In so doing, I draw a distinction between the representation of Mary's sexuality (central to discussions of her as a "holy harlot") and her gender, which is variously figured as ambiguous, problematic, and/or irrelevant in Zosimas's interactions with her. I perceive four different possibilities for the gendered representation of Mary's transformation over her years in the desert: her aged body, as encountered by Zosimas, can be figured as gendered female, gendered male, genderless, or genderqueer. Thinking through early medieval figurations of these categories can then shed light on future possibilities for our modern notions of sexuality and gender.

In both the Latin and Old English versions of Mary's *vita*, the outline of the story is as follows: Zosimas, an exemplary monk who has been cloistered since boyhood, goes into the desert for forty days in observance of a Lenten ritual. While there, he encounters a figure of indeterminate gender, who turns out to be St. Mary of Egypt. After repeated urging by Zosimas, Mary recounts her story of sin and repentance. At the age of twelve, she tells us, she ran away from her family to Alexandria, where she lived for seventeen years as what Ana Maria Machado has called "an insatiable instrument of public debauchery."[17] The Old English version of her life specifies that she was even worse than a prostitute, since

> Ne forleas ic na minne fæmnhad for æniges mannes gyfum oþþe ic witodlice ahtes onfenge fram ænigum þe me aht gyfan woldon, ac ic wæs swiðe onæled mid þære hatheortnysse þæs synlustes, þæt ic gewilnode butan ceape þæt hi me þe mænigfealdlicor to geurnon, to þy þæt ic þe eð mihte gefyllan þa scyldfullan gewilnunga mines forligeres.

Nor did I lose my maidenhood at all in exchange for gifts from anyone or in fact that I might receive anything from any people who wished to give me anything,

---

16 Lynda L. Coon, *Sacred Fictions: Holy Women and Hagiography in Late Antiquity* (Philadelphia: University of Pennsylvania Press, 1997); Benedicta Ward, *Harlots of the Desert: A Study of Repentance in Early Monastic Sources*, vol. 106, (Kalamazoo: Cistercian Publications, 1987); Paticia Cox Miller, "Is There a Harlot in This Text? Hagiography and the Grotesque," *Journal of Medieval and Early Modern Studies* 33.3 (2003): 419–35; Virginia Burrus, *The Sex Lives of Saints: An Erotics of Ancient Hagiography*, ed. Daniel Boyarin, Virginia Burrus, Charlotte Fonrobert, and Robert Gregg (Philadelphia: University of Pennsylvania Press, 2004); Robin Norris, "*Vitas Matrum*: Mary of Egypt as Female Confessor," *Old English Newletter Subsidia* 33 (2005): 79–109.
17 Machado, "Memory, Identity," 155.

but I was very much on fire with the passion of desire for sin, so that I desired that they might rush to me the more numerously without payment, my purpose being to satisfy the more easily the disgraceful desires of my sexual depravity.[18]

After describing at length the debaucheries that occupied her teens and twenties, Mary tells us that she traded sexual favors for passage to Jerusalem on a ship of pilgrims – motivated by curiosity and a desire for adventure, rather than piety. Once in the Holy Land, Mary attempts to follow the pilgrims to church for the celebration of the exaltation of the cross, but miraculously encounters an invisible barrier to her entrance. She then, in the courtyard, earnestly prays, is overcome by divine revelation of her sin, and finds an image of the Virgin Mary, to whom she prays. Mary of Egypt is thereby converted – without human intervention – and promises to live out her life in penance. She enters the church, prays before the holy cross, and later baptizes herself in the Jordan before receiving communion in the church of St. John the Baptist. She then crosses the Jordan and begins her solitary sojourn in the desert, where she is miraculously sustained by God for the intervening forty-seven years before meeting Zosimas.

After recounting this story to Zosimas, Mary asks that he return to her in a year, and at that time administer the Eucharist to her (a sacrament which she had theretofore only experienced once). He obliges, and when he returns the next year he observes her walking on water to cross the Jordan to meet him. Another year passes, and this time Zosimas finds Mary's dead body, neatly arranged, with a note in the sand explaining that she had died one hour after their previous meeting. He then buries her with the aid of a tame lion, who miraculously appears.

Perhaps the key moment for the consideration of Mary's gender in the Old English and Latin texts comes when Zosimas first perceives the figure of Mary of Egypt in the desert. Both the Latin and Old English texts imbue this moment with gender ambiguity, but in slightly different ways. In Paul's Latin text, we are told that Zosimas sees "umbram quasi humani corporis apparentem"; Magennis translates this as "a shadow appearing of what seemed to be a human body."[19] A close examination of the Latin grammar here demonstrates the gendered indeterminacy of this formulation. More literally, in Latin Zosimas says that he sees "an appearing shadow as if of a body of a human." Both "humani" and "corporis" are in the genitive case. Grammatical gender in Latin takes three possible forms: masculine, feminine, and neuter. As a noun, "corpus, corporis" is gendered masculine, regardless

---

18 Magennis, *Life of Saint Mary*, 82–83.
19 Magennis, *Life of Saint Mary*, 157; chapter 7 of Paul's text.

of the gender of the body in question. "Humanum, humani," meanwhile, is gendered neuter – it is specifically a word to designate a human being without designating that human's gender. Here, then, we have the body of a human whose gender is indeterminate or not yet designated. Zosimas's first perception of Mary's bodily form is thus explicitly designated as gender-neutral.

In the next two sentences, we then get further indeterminacy in the gender identification of the still-apparitional Mary: "uidit aliquem in ueritate properantem ad partem occidentis. Mulier autem erat quod uidebatur" (he saw that there really was someone hastening in a westerly direction. It was a woman that he saw).[20] The *humani corporis* of the last sentence is now designated as "aliquem," a pronoun meaning "someone." *Aliquem* is the accusative masculine and feminine form of the pronoun, as distinct from the neuter "aliquid." So now the text specifies that this human exists in a gendered system of male and female, but has not yet been designated as one or the other. Finally, in the second sentence, Mary is designated as "mulier," a woman. The syntax of this last sentence in the Latin, with "mulier" as the first word, draws attention to the revelation of the apparition's gender. Thus, the moment of Mary's first appearance is marked by both uncertainty about and ultimately emphasis upon her gender, as first she is a human apart from gender designation, then a gendered being whose gender is not yet revealed, and finally a woman.

The Old English version of this first encounter is similarly marked by gender ambiguity, but slightly differently. There is a lacuna in the Old English text at Zosimas's first perception of Mary, so the grammar of the entire sentence is not clear, but the object of Zosimas's perception is "on mennisce gelicnysse," "in manly likeness," or, as translated by Magennis, "in human physical form." Magennis is of course correct that we might take "mennisce," and later "man," to be accurately translated as "human," but this translation choice elides the gendered nature of the word in Old English.[21] In Latin, remember, "humanum" is grammatically neuter, and semantically separate from a word for adult male human, for instance "vir": human and man are different words in Latin. In Old English, however, like in the modern English of the twentieth century, "man" can mean both an adult human gendered male, and a human, generally. I argue that this semantic difference between the two languages becomes important in how the two texts represent the gender of Mary.

---

[20] Magennis, *Life of Saint Mary*, 156–57; chapter 7 of Paul's text.
[21] Several previous scholars have also noted the implications of gender oscillation in this passage. See, for instance, Blud, *The Unspeakable, Gender, and Sexuality*, 31; Gillian R. Overing and Clare A. Lees, *Double Agents: Women and Clerical Culture in Anglo-Saxon England*. (Cardiff: University of Wales Press, 2010), 141.

As we continue to the elaboration of Zosimas's investigation of the appearance or likeness in the Old English version, we find that he "þær soðlice man geseah," which Magennis renders as "really saw there a human being." We are thus moving toward more specificity in what Zosimas perceives – from likeness of a human, to certainly a human – but again we repeat the slippage inherent in the word "man." The next clause, then, gives either a further specification, or a correction, to this perception: "and witodlice þæt wæs wifman þæt þær gesewen wæs," "and it was actually a woman that appeared there." We move from "man" to "wifman"; the form of "wifman" demonstrates that a woman is a kind of man – we thought it was a man, now we know it is a wo-man. The semantic gender categories in the Old English are much more slippery than in the Latin: while Latin has clearly separate words for designating adult male ("vir"), adult female ("mulier"), and general human ("humanum"), in Old English the word "man" designates either human regardless of gender, or adult male, while "wifman" designates a (hu)man who is female. In other words, Latin posits human as a category within which male and female are separate sub-categories. Old English posits (hu)man as a category within which some are also (wo)man – every woman, then, is by definition also a man. Linguistically, this is further underlined by the fact that, in Old English, the word "wifman" is grammatically gendered male, a fact that often befuddles modern students of Old English.

Watt and Lees translate this same Old English passage a bit differently from Magennis, underlining the gender shift: "Truly he [Zosimas] saw there a man hastening westwards in the desert, and really it was a woman who was there seen."[22] Both of these translations, of course, are correct: the "man" in Old English means both man and human, as the etymology of our modern English words man, human, and woman imply. The crux of my argument here is not that one translation is better than the other, but rather that the simultaneous correctness of them both tells us something about the differing ways in which Latin and Old English categorize and designate gender. The Latin text and the Old English text represent gender differently because the two languages provide different opportunities for and constraints upon how Mary's (always ambiguous) gender is designated, particularly at a moment where expected ecclesiastical gender categories are subverted, and the relationship between gender, sexuality, and sanctity is problematized.

Throughout the Old English text, gender, authority, and ecclesiastical prestige are constantly questioned and reconfigured in ways that can be designated as queer. The initially competing, but in the end complementary, positions of

---

[22] Watt and Lees, "Age and Desire," 53.

authority for Mary and Zosimas provide a clear example. Upon their first meeting in the desert, each prostrates him/herself to the other: "He þa sona on þa eorðan hine astrehte and hire bletsunga bæd. Heo ongean hi astrehte and his bletsunga bæd" (He then immediately prostrated himself on the ground and asked for her blessing. She in turn prostrated herself and asked for his blessing).[23] This competitive prostration apparently lasts for hours, with Mary arguing to Zosimas that his priestly authority should be honored, while Zosimas asserts that Mary is "soðlice Godes þinen" (truly God's handmaid). After further back and forth, we are told that Mary eventually acquiesces to give her blessing to Zosimas, and the two get up off the ground to continue their conversation. This episode is echoed later, when Zosimas attempts to kneel to Mary, but she "him ne geþafode fulfremodlice on þaeorðan astreccan" (did not let him prostrate himself fully on the ground).[24] She then proceeds to demonstrate her miraculous knowledge of the (imperfect) practices of Zosimas's monastery, on which she corrects him, and orders him to return next year and bring her the Eucharist. Here, Mary and Zosimas both physically and verbally perform an ambiguous, hybrid, and queer relationship to authority, as Mary refuses Zosimas's subjection to her, then commands him, but commands him to demonstrate his own ecclesiastical superiority in priestly administration of the sacrament.

In fact, the text's representation of the administration of sacraments repeatedly queers hierarchical ecclesiastical authority. Mary's initial conversion simultaneously confirms the importance of ecclesiastical sacraments while reconfiguring traditional roles of authority. As Mary recounts the story, she was physically, yet invisibly, barred entrance from the church of the Holy Cross, which the other pilgrims were able to enter. After repeated physical struggle against this invisible divine force, Mary tells us:

> Ða gewat ic witodlice þanone, and me ana gestod on sumum hwomme þæs cafertunes and on minum mode geornlice þohte and smeade for hwilcum intigum me wære forwyrned þæs liffæstan treowes ansyn. Þa onhran soðlice min mod and þa eagan minre heortan hælo andgit, mid me sylfre þencende þæt me þone ingang belucen þa unfeormeganda minra misdæda.

So then I went away from there, and I stood alone in a particular corner of the courtyard, and in my mind I earnestly pondered and considered for what reason it was that the sight of the life-giving tree was being denied me. Then truly

---

[23] Magennis, *Life of Saint Mary*, 74–77.
[24] Magennis, *Life of Saint Mary*, 88.

knowledge of salvation touched my mind and the eyes of my heart, when I reflected that the inexpiable circumstances of my misdeeds had closed the entrance against me.²⁵

While entry into the church is clearly Mary's goal, demonstrating the importance of the Church and the holy relics, Mary's conversion happens only after she removes herself from the doorway of the church and the crowds of pilgrims. It is then, alone, that she comes to the revelation of her prior misdeeds; true knowledge touches her mind and her heart only after individual contemplation, without interference from other Christians or clergy. Conversion, then, is between only Mary and her God, not a function of the Church.

After this epiphany, Mary of Egypt finds an icon of the Virgin Mary in the courtyard of the church, and enters into conversation directly with the Mother of God. Mary of Egypt recounts to Zosimas her lengthy prayer to the Virgin, culminating with a command and a promise:

> Ac hat nu, þu wuldorfæste hlæfdige, me unmedemre for þære godcundan rode gretinge þa duru beon untynede, and ic me þe bebeode and to mundbyrdnysse geceose wið þin agen bearn.

But command now, O glorious lady, the door to be unfastened for me in my unworthiness to greet the divine cross, and I will commit myself to you and choose you as my advocate against your Son.²⁶

The disrupted hierarchies here are striking, as Mary of Egypt commands the Mother of God to be her ally not only in opening the doors of the church (and, implicitly, Church), but also in interceding *against* her son. The word "bearn," furthermore, denotes not only son, but more generally, child – designating age, not necessarily biological relation. This places additional weight on the disruption of hierarchies in this prayer – the sinner commands the Virgin Mother, who will (and does) advocate for the sinner against Christ, figured as a child. All of this is done to gain Mary of Egypt admittance to the Church.

The hierarchical disruptions of Mary's miraculous conversion continue after she leaves the church of the Holy Cross and makes her way to the river Jordan, where, it would seem, she baptizes herself:

> and ic me þyder inn eode and me þær gebæd, and sona in Iordane þa ea astah and of þam halgan wætere mine handa and ansynu þwoh, and me þær gemænsumode þam unbesmitenum gerynum ures Drihtnes Hælendes Cristes on þære ylcan cyrcan þæs halgan forryneles and fulluhteres Iohannes.

---

25 Magennis, *Life of Saint Mary*, 88–91.
26 Magennis, *Life of Saint Mary*, 90–91.

And I went in there and prayed, and, immediately after, I descended into the Jordan and washed my hands and face with the holy water, and I partook in the life-giving and undefiled sacrament of our Lord the Saviour Christ in that same church of the holy Precursor and Baptist John.[27]

The baptism is strongly implied not only by her washing in the holy water of the Jordan, but also by the fact that she partakes of the Eucharist only after this ablution, even though this is, apparently, her third time in a church that day (once in the church of the Holy Cross, and twice in the church of St. John, once before and once after her apparent baptism). Again, we see the simultaneous confirmation and reorientation of ecclesiastical authority. The story of Mary's miraculous conversion makes very clear that church entry, holy relics, and the Eucharist are all essential, even while conversion and baptism happen without priestly intervention. Simultaneously, the power of the Virgin Mary is confirmed, as, paradoxically, is Christ's – were Mary of Egypt not deeply concerned by Christ's forgiveness, there would be no need to solicit – or command – the Virgin Mary's intercession. In addition, throughout these episodes Mary of Egypt depicts herself as abject and subservient: weeping and throwing herself upon the mercy of both the Virgin Mary and anonymous strangers who give her money, bread, and direction. She makes very clear that she is deeply aware of her own sinfulness and unworthiness, even as she exhibits primary agency in her conversion and attendant actions.

These episodes repeatedly reconfigure systems of gendered and ecclesiastical authority, as Mary of Egypt is converted by women (herself and the Virgin) and baptized by a woman (herself) while consistently still recognizing the authority and importance of Christ and the Church. As in the episodes of competing and ultimately unsuccessful prostrations, hierarchical gender systems are consistently disrupted. But the resolution is not reversal – that is, the holy woman is not figured as unequivocally above the monk, nor the Virgin above Christ. Rather, these instances reveal the inappropriateness and insufficiency of such binary categorizations and hierarchical symbolism – prostration itself, whether Zosimas to Mary or Mary to Zosimas – is rendered inappropriate and even ridiculous. As Victoria Blud observes,

> In the symbiosis that flowers in the desert, between pious and penitent, cenobitic and eremitic, learned and unlettered, cloistered and outcast – Mary and Zosimas are constantly occupying the same spaces. They are both repenting, both advising: the territories that might have found a natural allotment in accordance with their respective professions and lifestyles are, instead, overlapping – a common ground.[28]

---

27 Magennis, *Life of Saint Mary*, 94–97.
28 Blud, *The Unspeakable, Gender, and Sexuality*, 32.

Chapter 6 The Gender Genealogy of St. Mary of Egypt — 143

In the story of Mary and Zosimas, binaries are repeatedly collapsed as the two protagonists are represented as both–and. Sacraments – whether baptism or the Eucharist – are essential and sin is abhorrent, but the navigation of sin and redemption is complex and involves multiple actors of multiple genders. Conversion, salvation, and sanctity are more complex than binaries and hierarchies will allow or describe. What we see represented instead is not only Mary's queer gender, but the queering of social and ecclesiastical relationships.

The final episode of the Old English *Life* recounts Zosimas burying the body of Mary with the help of a lion, and again gender simultaneity characterizes the encounter. This time, however, it is the genders of the lion and Zosimas that are queered. One year exactly after Zosimas administers the Eucharist to Mary, he returns to the desert again for the monastery's Lenten ritual, and again seeks to find Mary. After twenty days' walk, he arrives at the dry streambed of their first encounter, and finds, there, Mary's intact dead body. Next to the body he finds writing in the sand, seemingly composed by the illiterate Mary, explaining that she died in this spot one year prior, the same day that she had received communion. There are a number of miraculous aspects to this discovery by Zosimas. The writing, apparently composed by a woman who professed to be illiterate, has been preserved undisturbed, like the body itself, for a full year. Furthermore, Mary had apparently reached this location the same day as she had received the Eucharist, in spite of the fact that traveling the distance between the two locations took Zosimas twenty days' walking. And then, in a desert where Mary professed to have seen no living animal or human for forty-seven years, a tame lion appears to help Zosimas bury Mary's body – indeed, it is the lion who enables the burial, as the elderly Zosimas, without tools, is unable to dig an effective grave in the hard desert ground. The lion digs Mary's grave with its claws, after which Zosimas washes Mary's feet with his tears, and buries her body in the grave while praying "Þæt heo for eallum Þingode" (that she would intercede for all).[29]

This episode inscribes queerness on multiple levels. As Watt and Lees have noted, the scene is notable for the gender fluidity of the lion. As the lion is referred to over the course of the passage, it is first gendered male, then female, then male, then female again.[30] Strikingly, this gender alternation is an innovation of the Old English text, as the Latin version of the *Life* is consistent in gendering the lion male.[31] Onnaca Heron has discussed this passage in detail,

---

29 Magennis, *Life of Saint Mary*, 119.
30 Watt and Lees, "Age and Desire," 64.
31 Watt and Lees suggest that it may be relevant that the episode seems to be borrowed from St. Jerome's *Life of Paul of Thebes* (chapter 16), which contains two lions rather than the one in Mary's *vita*. However, Jerome's text refers to the lions only collectively, in the plural male form

explicating the gendered grammatical functions of the Old English text in comparison to the Latin and Greek, amply demonstrating the gender shifting apparent in this passage. Heron cites this shift as evidence of her claim that the Old English text "immasculates" Mary of Egypt, viewing Mary's gender as accomplishing a linear trajectory from female to male over the course of her life, and the text.[32] However, I concur with Irina Dumitrescu's assertion that Heron's "examples in support of the claim that Mary is a 'manly woman' do not demonstrate Mary's manliness as much as they do the general indeterminacy of Mary's character, gender, and body."[33] Certainly, the lion's gender oscillation in the Old English text is non-linear, and ultimately lands on female, undermining claims of teleological gender transformation while highlighting the possibility of gender mutability. In addition to the ambiguous gendering of the lion, we also see Zosimas here clearly elided with the woman in the Gospels who washes Jesus's feet with her tears.[34] Mary, meanwhile, is elided with Christ, as she is referred to as the "halgan lichaman" (literally "holy body") whose feet are washed.[35] This episode, then, echoes the gender syncretism of the text as whole; in this final moment, gender is simultaneous and unstable, as the lion(ess) oscillates gender while the male body performs the biblical sinful woman and the female body performs the male Christ.

(which could, of course, designate either two male lions, or a male and a female), and so does not provide a textual source for reference to a female lion. Similarly, the entry for Paul the Hermit on January 10 of the *Old English Martyrology* refers to two lions collectively without indicating their individual genders. Christine Rauer, *The Old English Martyrology: Edition, Translation and Commentary* (Woodbridge: Boydell and Brewer, 2013), 46.
32 Onnaca Heron, "The Lioness in the Text: Mary of Egypt as Immasculated Female Saint," *Quidditas* 21 (2000): 23–44.
33 Irina Dumitrescu, *The Experience of Education in Anglo-Saxon Literature* (New York: Cambridge University Press, 2018), 196. Dumitrescu's examination of the Old English *Life of Saint Mary of Egypt*, while focused primarily on representations of pedagogy and the student–teacher relationship, also emphasizes the continual complication of binaries within the story. Most important, of course, is the fact that the sinful Mary is represented as teacher, and the monk Zosimas as student. Additionally, Mary is represented as an "ambivalent mentor" (130), and conventional categorizations of body/spirit, outward/inward are drawn into question. Dumitrescu writes: "The result is two instructional encounters between Zosimas and Mary characterized by oscillation between sanctity and temptation, curiosity and coercion, holy desire for learning and lust for the teacher's body. This wavering is intensified in the Old English version" in comparison to the Latin (132).
34 Luke 7:38.
35 Magennis, *Life of Saint Mary*, 118. Magennis translates "halgan lichaman" as "saint." While this is clearly in keeping with the overall meaning of the passage, the more literal rendering of "holy body" makes clearer the connection with Christ.

In their argument for seeing Mary of Egypt in the Old English recension as genderqueer, Watt and Lees claim that: "Mary is, in short, represented as going beyond, or transcending both her womanliness and physicality, even as the *Life* insists on both. And in transcending gender and sex, she is, or becomes, transgendered or genderqueer."[36] Watt and Lees productively explain this thesis through an examination of the roles played by age and desire in Mary's *vita*; the aged Mary, they claim, is outside of or beyond a gender system defined through sexual desire, even as she and Zosimas reconfigure expected relationships based upon desire. I, on the other hand, want to lean more on what it means to claim that Mary transcends gender. The claim of "transcending gender" can take multiple forms. Perhaps the most well known is the "virile woman" trope, in which exceptionally holy women were seen to "become male." This conception is well documented among patristic writers, including Saints Ambrose and Augustine, and has been well explored by a variety of feminist scholars.[37] Alternatively, the idea of a "third gender," instantiated by those vowed to religious chastity, is documented in medieval rhetoric and has garnered attention in recent scholarship.[38] The connection between chastity and a third gender, however, necessarily links to a system of gender defined by sexuality; a refusal to participate in a heterosexual system of desire removes one from the binary gender categories upon which such a system depends. Being asexual, however, is not the same as being genderqueer; I argue here that Mary (and perhaps also Zosimas, and the lion(ess)) does not reject gender categories so much as refigure them toward inclusivity, allowing one individual to be simultaneously male and female.

Victoria Blud addresses this rejection/reconfiguration of categories, gendered and otherwise, in Mary's *Life* in terms of the unspeakable. She draws an explicit connection between the unspeakable, queerness, and the apophatic, as noted above.[39] Blud's analysis centers on gender indeterminacy or ambiguity in the Old English *vita*, citing the ancient and medieval theory of bodily humors to demonstrate how Mary and Zosimas invert expected medicalized gender categories; she also highlights the movement of the text between the physical and the spoken word. As Blud points out, the body is in fact necessary for speech – and

---

36 Watt and Lees, "Age and Desire," 59.
37 As seen above, Onnaca Heron, "The Lioness in the Text," has made specifically this claim about Mary of Egypt. I explore St. Augustine's development of this trope through his discussions of St. Perpetua in Margaret Cotter-Lynch, *St. Perpetua Across the Middle Ages: Mother, Gladiator, Saint* (New York: Palgrave Macmillan, 2016). Other major works addressing this trope include Cobb, *Dying to Be Men* and Newman, *From Virile Woman*.
38 See, for instance, McNamara, "Chastity as a Third Gender."
39 Blud, *The Unspeakable, Gender, and Sexuality*, 11.

so rather than body and word being opposed, they are in fact interdependent. At the end of the text, both the Eucharist and the burial of the dead body of Mary play primary roles, demonstrating the continued importance of the body, even as Mary herself moves from a physical person to a story to be told. As Blud further asserts, "Mary is a decidedly liminal character . . . repeatedly cast in suspension between extremes."[40] In describing Mary as genderqueer, I claim that this in-betweenness is inclusive of, rather than apart from, the designated extremes. She is simultaneously sinner and saint, teacher and student, male and female.

Several previous scholars have discussed Mary of Egypt alongside transvestite or cross-dressing saints, despite the fact that Mary engages in no intentional sartorial disguise.[41] Watt and Lees, meanwhile, claim that Mary of Egypt can usefully be categorized with Saints Euphrosyne and Eugenia, whom they classify as transgender.[42] Ana Maria Machado has discussed a similar dynamic in the Portuguese tradition of Mary of Egypt and Pelagia, in which "The change in name and gender can be read as an allegory for the brutal change sinners must go through in order to attain sanctity," leading to an emphasis on gender hybridity in the *vitae* of these saints.[43] All of these scholars, in offering reclassifications of Mary of Egypt, ask us to look at a "holy harlot" alongside "holy transvestites," and therefore to reconsider the possible gender configurations for the saints in these stories.

Here, the work of M. W. Bychowski is helpful, as she refigures previous discussions around "transvestite" saints, particularly St. Marinos, to instead talk about transgender saints in terms of authenticity and artifice. Bychowski coins the terms "*imago transvesti*" and "*imitatio transvesti*" to discuss transgender saints in terms of medieval conceptions of *imago dei* and *imitatio Christi*, which she identifies with an authenticity of the soul, in contrast to the artifice entailed in "*imagines mundi*," "the socially assigned images of the self which contrast with those made by God."[44] For St. Marinos, Bychowski asserts, transitioning to live as a male monk functions as an authentic movement of the soul toward living out his existence as *imago dei*, and the public revelation of his gender transition after his death serves as an inspiration to others toward *imitatio Christi*. As such, the earliest *vita* of St. Marinos posits the disruption of socially

---

[40] Blud, *The Unspeakable, Gender, and Sexuality*, 30.
[41] Sandra Lowerre, *The Cross-Dressing Female Saints in Wynkyn De Worde's 1495 Edition of the Vitas Patrum: A Study and Edition of the Lives of Saints Pelage, Maryne, Eufrosyne, Eugene, and Mary of Egypt* (Bern: Peter Lang, 2006).
[42] Watt and Lees, "Age and Desire," 60–61.
[43] Machado, "Memory, Identity," 153, 157–58.
[44] Bychowski, "Authentic Lives," n. p.

constructed gender categories as integral to the saintly life. Bychowski views "the transition of the saint as an act of salvation that embodies the creative, transformational, and reforming image of the Creator."[45] We might see a similar movement in the Old English *Life* of Mary, where the elderly Mary in the desert is represented as an authentic *imago dei*, in contrast to Zosimas's expectations, which are based upon *imagines mundi*. As Blud describes, "Zosimas, desiring a male counsellor, stumbles across a woman (indeed, a naked woman), but is initially able to 'see' a masculine figure; Mary, whose object of desire is the very personification of feminine sanctity [the Virgin Mary], finds the role of her Marian guide supplied by a man."[46] In Bychowski's reading of transgender saints, we see an echo of Keller's theological assertions drawn from late medieval mystics. By transcending earthly categories of gender, albeit in different ways, both St. Marinos and St. Mary of Egypt embody the divine.

Watt and Lees discuss the ways in which Mary, in the Old English *Life*, is explicitly depicted as a Christ figure. In both the Latin and Old English texts, Zosimas observes Mary levitating in prayer and walking on water. Zosimas's original quest, when leaving the monastery to spend forty days in the desert for Lent, structurally and liturgically parallels Christ's forty days in the desert, but Zosimas himself frames his quest as one to find Christ – or a "holy father" who is like Christ – in a double mimetic relationship. Instead of a desert father, he finds a desert mother, in Mary, but the depiction of this desert/holy mother/father explicitly undermines Zosimas's (and potentially the reader's) expected categories as defined through binaries and hierarchy. Perhaps Zosimas does not look for a father and find a mother, but instead looks for a holy person who is defined by gender whom he can emulate, and instead finds that the holy person, Mary, while clearly Christ-like, recombines and transcends gender categories in ways that can most readily be described as queer. As Watt and Lees assert,

> There is something ineffable and transcendental about this transgendered Mary, who is harlot and virgin, penitent and Christ, woman and monk. In offering a model of female asceticism in the desert that is a model for male asceticism – the desert father is a desert mother – Mary empowers other religious to explore desires that reside, perhaps, across and within genders and across age and mortality too.[47]

---

45 M. W. Bychowski, "Transgender Saints: The Imago Dei of St. Marinos the Monk," *Things Transform* (blog) August 19, 2016, http://www.thingstransform.com/2016/08/transgender-saints-imago-dei-of-st.html.
46 Blud, *The Unspeakable, Gender, and Sexuality*, 33.
47 Watt and Lees, "Age and Desire," 64.

If we follow the implications of Bychowski, and the assertions of Watt and Lees, in labeling Mary as transgender, I suggest that we read "trans" in the inclusive, expansive sense of the Latin preposition: trans means across, through, and beyond, in a cluster of simultaneous meanings that at once draw together and elide distinctions.[48] This, I claim, is what the Old English figuration of Mary of Egypt does: eradicate binary categories of gender without eradicating gender itself, as Mary is across, through, and beyond both male and female.

This also places the Old English depiction of Mary of Egypt within a matrix of medieval texts in which gender is represented as variously queered. Tison Pugh, addressing queer masculinity in several Middle English texts, writes that "consisting both of sexual acts and breaches of normativity, queerness comprises sexual, amatory, and gendered practices that ostensibly depart from prevailing cultural norms."[49] Robert Mills considers the various gendered representations of St. Eugenia in visual art.[50] Most notably, a special issue of *Medieval Feminist Forum: A Journal of Gender and Sexuality* in October 2019 demonstrates the application of transgender theory to a range of texts from across the Middle Ages.[51]

Fashioning Mary as genderqueer in the Old English *Life* destabilizes a femininity defined by and based upon heteronormative desire; when we cease to define women by means of male desire and reproductive function, the gender binary dissolves. This dissolution allows us a rereading of the implicit dangers of Mary's promiscuous youth: she has sex but not for money, and never reproduces; she defines her own desire, rather than being defined by men's desires. Thus, even when presented as putatively female, Mary positions herself outside of a heteronormative gender system that would categorize, or control, her agency and desire. What is striking about her Alexandrine youth is her brazenness, her aggressiveness, her agency. Mary is, throughout the text, whether harlot or holy woman, the author of her own life. This is reflected in the structure of the Latin and Old English versions of her *vita*, where her story is written as reported speech: Mary tells her story in her own words to Zosimas, which are then written down in the *vita*. She frames her own story. This is different from

---

[48] For the inclusive definition of trans*, see, most recently, Halberstam, *Trans**. For one account of the history of the development of the term, see David Valentine, *Imagining Transgender: An Ethnography of a Category* (Durham: Duke University Press, 2007). See also Susan Stryker, *Transgender History: The Roots of Today's Revolution*, revised edition (New York: Seal Press, 2017).

[49] Tison Pugh, *Sexuality and its Queer Discontents in Middle English Literature* (New York: Palgrave, 2008), 3.

[50] Robert Mills, "Visibly Trans? Picturing St. Eugenia in Medieval Art," *TSQ: Transgender Studies Quarterly* 5.4 (November 2018): 540–64.

[51] *Medieval Feminist Forum: A Journal of Gender and Sexuality*, guest editors M. W. Bychowski and Dorothy Kim, Vol 55.1 (October, 2019).

some other versions of her *vita*, in which the story is told chronologically from the point of view of an unnamed omniscient narrator who reports on Mary's life.[52]

We see Mary's agency asserted throughout the text, perhaps most strikingly in her conversion without human intervention – based only upon the invisible force barring her entry to the church, and her prayerful conversation with the image ("anlicnysse")[53] of the Virgin Mary – and her apparent self-baptism in the river Jordan before entering the church of St. John the Baptist to receive her first communion.[54] As we have seen, she does not wholly reject the structures, sacraments, and authority of the Church. Sacraments are still sacraments, after all – as Mary makes clear, Eucharist and church entry and monastic practice are important. However, she selects when, where, and how to utilize the Church in service of her own sanctity. Like desire, gender, and authority, she does not reject the Church but queers it, recombining aspects of both ecclesiastical authority and charismatic inspiration to fashion a paradoxically inclusive Christian community. If Mary can simultaneously be defined by her sexuality and her genderqueerness, we must think of her not as beyond gender, or apart from gender, but embodying a syncretic gender identity which is both–and, a gender which is separate from, without denying the existence of, her sexuality, and which posits ways of thinking gender which are perhaps new to us but also a thousand years old.

Bibliography

Aspegren, Kerstin. *The Male Woman: A Feminine Ideal in the Early Church*. Stockholm: Almquist & Wiksell, 1990.
Blud, Victoria. *The Unspeakable, Gender, and Sexuality in Medieval* Literature, *1000–1400*. Cambridge: D. S. Brewer, 2017.
Burrus, Virginia. *The Sex Lives of Saints: An Erotics of Ancient Hagiography*. Divinations: Rereading Late Ancient Religion. Edited by Daniel Boyarin, Virginia Burrus, Charlotte Fonrobert, and Robert Gregg. Philadelphia: University of Pennsylvania Press, 2004.
Bychowski, M. W. "The Authentic Lives of Transgender Saints: *Imago Dei* and *Imitatio Christi* in the *Life* of Saint Marinos the Monk." In *Trans and Genderqueer Subjects in Medieval Hagiography*, edited by Alicia Spencer-Hall and Blake Gutt. Amsterdam: Amsterdam University Press, forthcoming 2020.

---

52 See, for example, the twelfth-century *Vie de Sainte Marie l'Egyptienne* in Dembowski, *Vie De Sainte Marie*.
53 Magennis, *Life of Saint Mary*, 90.
54 Magennis, *Life of Saint Mary*, 94.

Bychowski, M. W. "Transgender Saints: The Imago Dei of St. Marinos the Monk." *Things Transform* (blog), August 19, 2016. http://www.thingstransform.com/2016/08/transgender-saints-imago-dei-of-st.html.

Bychowski, M. W. "Were there Transgender People in the Middle Ages?" *The Public Medievalist* (blog), November 1, 2018. https://www.publicmedievalist.com/transgender-middle-ages/.

Cobb, L. Stephanie. *Dying to Be Men: Gender and Language in Early Christian Martyr Texts*. New York: Columbia University Press, 2008.

Coon, Lynda L. *Sacred Fictions: Holy Women and Hagiography in Late Antiquity*. Philadelphia: University of Pennsylvania Press, 1997.

Cotter-Lynch, Margaret. *St. Perpetua Across the Middle Ages: Mother, Gladiator, Saint*. New York: Palgrave Macmillan, 2016.

Davis, Brian McGrath. "Apophatic Theology and Masculinities." *CrossCurrents* 61.4 (2011): 502–14.

Dembowski, Peter F. *La Vie De Sainte Marie L'égyptienne: Versions en ancien et en Moyen Français*. Geneva: Droz, 1977.

Dumitrescu, Irina. *The Experience of Education in Anglo-Saxon Literature*. New York: Cambridge University Press, 2018.

Gudmarsdottir, Sigridur. "Feminist Theology and the Sensible Unsaying of Mysticism." In *Apophatic Bodies: Negative Theology, Incarnation, and Relationality*, edited by Chris Boesel and Catherine Keller, 283–75 (New York: Fordham University Press, 2009).

Gutt, Blake. "Transgender Genealogy in *Tristan de Nanteuil*." *Exemplaria* 30.2 (2018): 129–46.

Halberstam, J. *In a Queer Time and Place: Transgender Bodies, Subcultural Lives*. New York and London: New York University Press, 2005.

Halberstam, J. *Trans*: A Quick and Quirky Account of Gender Variability*. Oakland: University of California Press, 2018.

Heron, Onnaca. "The Lioness in the Text: Mary of Egypt as Immasculated Female Saint." *Quidditas* 21 (2000): 23–44.

Keller, Catherine. "The Apophasis of Gender: A Fourfold Unsaying of Feminist Theology." *Journal of the American Academy of Religion* 76.4 (December, 2008): 905–33.

Lowerre, Sandra. *The Cross-Dressing Female Saints in Wynkyn De Worde's 1495 Edition of the Vitas Patrum: A Study and Edition of the Lives of Saints Pelage, Maryne, Eufrosyne, Eugene, and Mary of Egypt*. Bern: Peter Lang, 2006.

Machado, Ana Maria. "Memory, Identity, and Women's Representation in the Portuguese Reception of *Vitae Patrum*: Winning a Name." In *Reading Memory and Identity in the Texts of Medieval European Holy Women*, edited by Margaret Cotter-Lynch and Brad Herzog, 135–64. New York: Palgrave Macmillan, 2012.

Magennis, Hugh. *The Old English Life of Saint Mary of Egypt*. Exeter: University of Exeter Press, 2002.

McNamara, Jo Ann. "Chastity as a Third Gender in the History and Hagiography of Gregory of Tours." In *The World of Gregory of Tours*, edited by Kathleen Mitchell and Ian Wood, 199–209. Leiden: Brill, 2002.

Medieval Feminist Forum: A Journal of Gender and Sexuality. Guest editors M. W. Bychowski and Dorothy Kim. 55.1 (October, 2019).

Miller, Paticia Cox. "Is There a Harlot in This Text? Hagiography and the Grotesque." *Journal of Medieval and Early Modern Studies* 33.3 (Fall, 2003): 419–35.

Mills, Robert. "Visibly Trans? Picturing St. Eugenia in Medieval Art." *TSQ: Transgender Studies Quarterly* 5.4 (November, 2018): 540–64.
Newman, Barbara. *From Virile Woman to Womanchrist: Studies in Medieval Religion and Literature*. Middle Ages Series. Philadelphia: University of Pennsylvania Press, 1995.
Norris, Robin. "*Vitas Matrum*: Mary of Egypt as Female Confessor." *Old English Newletter Subsidia* 33 (2005): 79–109.
Overing, Gillian R. and Clare A. Lees. *Double Agents: Women and Clerical Culture in Anglo-Saxon England*. Cardiff: University of Wales Press, 2010.
Pepin, Ronald E. and Hugh Feiss. *Saint Mary of Egypt: Three Medieval Lives in Verse*. Kalamazoo: Cistercian Publications, 2005.
Pugh, Tison. *Sexuality and its Queer Discontents in Middle English Literature*. New York: Palgrave, 2008.
Rauer, Christine. *The Old English Martyrology: Edition, Translation and Commentary*. Woodbridge: Boydell and Brewer, 2013.
Salisbury, Joyce E. *Church Fathers, Independent Virgins*. London and New York: Verso, 1992.
Schulenburg, Jane Tibbetts. *Forgetful of Their Sex: Female Sanctity and Society, Ca. 500–1100*. Chicago: University of Chicago Press, 1998.
Sophronios. "The Life of Mary of Egypt, the Former Harlot who in Blessed Manner Became an Ascetic in the Desert of the River Jordan." Translated by Marie Kouli. In *Holy Women of Byzantium: Ten Saints' Lives in English Translation*. Edited by Alice-Mary Talbot. Washington, DC: Dumbarton Oaks.
Stryker, Susan. *Transgender History: The Roots of Today's Revolution*. Revised edition. New York: Seal Press, 2017.
Valentine, David. *Imagining Transgender: An Ethnography of a Category*. Durham: Duke University Press, 2007.
Ward, Benedicta. *Harlots of the Desert: A Study of Repentance in Early Monastic Sources*. Cistercian Studies. Vol. 106. Kalamazoo: Cistercian Publications, 1987.
Watt, Diane and Clare A. Lees. "Age and Desire in the Old English Life of St. Mary of Egypt: A Queerer Time and Place?" In *Middle-Aged Women in the Middle Ages*, edited by Sue Niebrzydowski, 53–68. Cambridge: D. S. Brewer, 2011.

Micah Goodrich
Chapter 7
"Ycrammed ful of cloutes and of bones": Chaucer's Queer Cavities

Dum tua bursa sonat, comitum te turba coronat:
exausto sonitu comes incipis esse tibi tu.

As long as your purse jingles, a crowd of friends makes a fuss over you.
When the sound is gone, you become your own friend.[1]

The Pardoner, the famous extortionist of the *Canterbury Tales*, carries with him objects that promise transformation and reward. Robyn Malo has shown that when Chaucer introduces the Pardoner in the *General Prologue* he "makes it clear that we should pay special attention to the Pardoner's relics."[2] Where, though, does the Pardoner contain all of these fraudulent treasures? This essay locates the object of the "purs" as a queer cavity, a hollow orifice that hoards, swallows, and transforms all that enters its circuit. In addition to its pedestrian use as a money-sack, the image of the purse stands in as a descriptor of reproductive genitalia.[3] The economic and erotic registers of Middle English words for purse – "purs," "bagge," "male," "walet" – articulate the ideological association between production and procreation.[4] As such, the pecuniary and sexually inflected object of the purse challenges intersecting modes of social organization based on class, gender, and sexuality. For instance, the Wife of Bath's admission

---

[1] *Dum tua bursa sonat* in *Medieval Latin Poems of Male Love and Friendship*, trans. Thomas Stehling (New York: Garland Publishing, 1984), 94–95.
[2] Robyn Malo, "The Pardoner's Relics (and Why They Matter Most)," *The Chaucer Review* 43 (2008): 82–102 at 82.
[3] Carolyn Dinshaw, *Chaucer's Sexual Poetics* (Madison: University of Wisconsin Press, 1989), 164; and Robert S. Sturges, *Chaucer's Pardoner and Gender Theory: Bodies of Discourse* (New York: St. Martin's Press, 2000), 15–17, 68–69. See also David Rollo, *Kiss My Relics: Hermaphroditic Fictions of the Middle Ages* (Chicago: University of Chicago Press, 2011), specifically chapter 9.
[4] See various entries in *Middle English Dictionary*, ed. Hans Kurath, 13 vols. (Ann Arbor: University of Michigan Press, 1952–2001), s. v. "purs(e," "bagge," "mal(e, (n.(2))," and "walet."

Note: I wish to thank the editors of this volume, Will Rogers and Christopher Michael Roman, and the anonymous readers for their support and feedback on this essay. I am grateful to Glenn Burger for his response to an early draft of this essay at the 43rd Annual Sewanee Medieval Colloquium.

https://doi.org/10.1515/9781501513701-008

that she picks her husbands based on their "nether purs and of here cheste" (l. 44b) equivocates purses and genitalia with accumulation – it is her husbands that multiply, not her progeny.[5] Similarly, *The Complaint of Chaucer to His Purse* despairs over empty purses as sites of both economic and sexual depletion.[6] Death is the outcome for the speaker if the purse does not become "hevy ageyn" (ll. 7, 14, 21). At the close of the poem the *Lenvoy de Chaucer* emphasizes the king's authority "by lyne" (l. 23); the king is in a position to fill the speaker's purse through patronage. Money, pleasure, and power materially collapse in the image of the "purse" (l. 1). In this way purses as cavities must be "hevy," filled and stored with pleasures, to have value.

Cavities, apertures, and openings threaten to engulf the pilgrimage – and the audience – in the Canterbury project. The purses, bags, sacks, and wallets that the Pardoner bears transform their owner into a Charybdian cavity. This essay looks to the purse as a queer hole, an opening that refuses socially prescribed models of production: that is, the purse as queer cavity swallows and repurposes all that enters its domain. Purses as cavities cache what enters them, removing contents from social, economic, sexual, and spiritual circulation.[7] Chaucer uses the image of the purse to critique models of transactional productivity. As the image of the purse shifts between its valences as sacks of money and reproductive genitalia, Chaucer asks how the items and ideologies the purse contains are exchanged and exploited by the pilgrimage on the route to Canterbury.

This project locates the "purs" as a gendered, sexualized, and economized site of social exchange. Meg Wesling's articulation of queer value joins together psychic desire and material accumulation that establishes value through social hierarchies based on exchange, commodification, and production.[8] By recognizing queerness in value we see that desire – socially categorized by sexuality and gender – is oriented by the dominance of materialized capital.[9] Asking

---

[5] All references to Chaucer's works are cited in *The Riverside Chaucer*, ed. Larry D. Benson, 3rd ed. (Boston: Houghton Mifflin Company, 1987).

[6] For a discussion of the kaleidoscopic nature of gender in *The Complaint of Chaucer to His Purse*, see Sturges, *Chaucer's Pardoner and Gender Theory*, 15–17.

[7] I use the term "cache" throughout the essay in its sense of a hole or concave space used to hide objects as well as a phenomenon of enveloping something to obscure it from view. See the noun and verb forms of "cache" in the *Oxford English Dictionary*. The economic valence of caching – storing goods for later reward – makes the term a potential pun with "cashing." *Oxford English Dictionary*, 2nd edition, ed. John Simpson and Edmund Weiner (Oxford: Clarendon Press, 1989).

[8] Meg Wesling, "Queer Value," *GLQ* 18.1 (2011): 107–25.

[9] Wesling, "Queer Value," 122–23. See Rosemary Hennessey, *Profit and Pleasure: Sexual Identities in Late Capitalism* (New York: Routledge, 2000); and Gayatri Chakravorty Spivak, "Scattered

how value is queer, Wesling remarks that this enables us to "think about the labor of sexuality and gender identity beyond what is recognizably queer."[10] In the case of the *Canterbury Tales*, and the figure of the Pardoner in particular, the purses, bags, sacks, and wallets that the Pardoner carries and comments upon speak perhaps more overtly to his queerness than readings of his potentially castrated body attend to. The Pardoner is a self-sufficient unit and he carries his false relics, brimming bags, and compartmentalized body along for the pilgrimage to act as a site of exchange: a traveling marketplace of material, spiritual, and sexual transaction.

The Pardoner's purse is his site of queer (re)production, the location where objects generate and transform. Purses act as self-sustained cavities that swallow and hoard the items that move beyond the threshold of the opening. Cavities have capacity to eliminate items from social, sexual, or spiritual circulation. These cavities have the ability to absorb something and transform items into something new. In this way cavities are autarkic systems that operate in a self-sufficient, closed method of (re)production. If something cannot be circulated it cannot be critiqued or obstructed, enjoyed by or benefit a larger social collective. The cavity-as-purse stands in as an antisocial, closed creative outlet that produces and reproduces without aid. Beyond its role of production, the purse also connotes excess because of its capacity to withhold things from social circulation, often to the benefit of the possessor.

Physically, the makeup of the purse-as-cavity is a "middling" phenomenon where transformative possibility happens in the middle. Glenn Burger has suggested in *Chaucer's Queer Nation* that Chaucer's pilgrimage to Canterbury is more a process of becoming and suggests itself through the trans-ness of travel, of telling and giving an account, of a fusion of various groups within medieval society who all repurpose, process, and produce in the "middle" of the journey to Canterbury.[11] To borrow Burger's image of processing in the "middle," we might look to the "purs" as a middling site, one that engulfs and extinguishes the tales and tellers in the Canterbury project. The materiality of the Pardoner's position as an ecclesiastical official, a member of the pilgrimage, and a queer subject extends to the fellowship through the object of the purse. His desire to

---

Speculations on the Question of Value," in *In Other Worlds: Essays in Cultural Politics* (New York: Routledge, 1988), 154–75. On orientation, value, and Marx's model of "commodity fetishism" see Sara Ahmed, *Queer Phenomenology: Orientations, Objects, Others* (Durham: Duke University Press, 2006), 42–43.

10 Wesling, "Queer Value," 122.
11 Glenn Burger, *Chaucer's Queer Nation* (Minneapolis: University of Minnesota Press, 2003), xiii and chapter 5.

proffer his relics and open his purse to the pilgrims is both a method to profit and a mode of social seduction. Burger writes that the Pardoner's desire consumes "both the material resources of the communities he 'ministers' to and the symbolic capital that has accumulated within the church."[12] In a similar vein, Will Stockton measures the Pardoner's economic activity as profiteering, stating that the "Pardoner must exploit his audience's will to misperception if he wishes to profit financially from the spiritual economy – an economy that must trade in material objects, that must make something out of nothing."[13] The Pardoner and his purse appeal to the power of the Church and operate outside of its authority. His acknowledgement of his own fraudulence shows that the Pardoner understands the ideological "impoverishment"[14] of his purse and all that it represents.

This essay will first discuss how Chaucer's queer cavities operate by looking at the General Prologue portraits of the Pardoner and his riding companion, the Summoner. Reading the bodies of the pilgrims not just for purses but *as* purses articulates the social threat and personal possibilities that queer cavities afford. Building on the Pardoner's affiliation with purses and sacks, the second section will take on the transformative qualities of cavities as objects of exchange value. The final section asks how queer cavities are cached, enveloped, and unbuckled as forms of social and economic control. Chaucer uses the image of the cavity to consider the panic of hidden things, whether objects or abstractions. The anxiety surrounding these cavities reveals a disjunction between the Canterbury collective and the objects that initiate exchange between pilgrims. In this way, purses, cavities, and holes in the *Canterbury Tales* construct queerness through objects and the way that people relate to each other through modes of exchange. By mapping a few of Chaucer's many cavities in the Canterbury project we begin to uncover how the medieval queer is assembled, reassembled, and interchanged among a social collective.

Into the Hollow

We meet the Pardoner in pieces. Chaucer's presentation of the Pardoner's fragmented body directs the fellowship to interact with the Pardoner's cavities. The

---

[12] Burger, *Chaucer's Queer Nation*, 157.
[13] Will Stockton, "Cynicism and the Anal Erotics of Chaucer's Pardoner," *Exemplaria* 20 (2008): 143–64 at 148.
[14] Stockton, "Cynicism," 143.

Chapter 7 "Ycrammed ful of cloutes and of bones": Chaucer's Queer Cavities — 157

Pardoner's debut as a cavity begins with his mouth which opens "ful loude" (l. 672); he sings "Com hider, love, to me!" (l. 672). His song beckons the pilgrimage to approach him, and his open mouth threatens to swallow those who come. At work, the Pardoner sings offertories while collecting alms. He "wel affile his tonge,/ to wynne silver" (ll. 712–13), and sings "murierly and loude" (l. 714). His mouth acts as a cajoling orifice.[15] Outward from the vortex of his mouth, we learn of his smooth, yellow hair that hangs like flax over his shoulders, a sign that many scholars read as a mark of his queerness.[16] We are able to imagine the Pardoner's locks because the Pardoner decidedly does not wear his hood, a cavity and container for his abundance of hair. Instead the hood is "trussed up" (l. 681) in his "walet" (ll. 681, 686) – he does this for "jolitee" (l. 680) – that lay in his lap while riding. The "walet" of the Pardoner, brimming, "bretful" (l. 687), with pardons, shows the operation of the Pardoner's productive mode through an economically inflected object.

Imagining the Pardoner's aesthetic as economy, the narrator measures and weighs his body into fragments.[17] The Pardoner's hair hangs like "a strike of flex" (l. 676) and it dangles "by ounces" (l. 677). His flaxen hair is so long that it envelops his shoulders, but it covers his body like cut pieces, "by colpons oon and oon" (l. 679). The Pardoner is on display and for sale. These mercantile analogies are undergirded by the narrator's perception of the Pardoner: that he thought himself to be riding in "al of the newe jet" (l. 682). The Pardoner is a newfangled object, a novel curiosity that threatens the pilgrimage with his gadgetry. The Middle English word "jet" has the meaning of "fashion" and "new custom" as well as signifying a contrivance or device.[18] In the *Canon's Yeoman's Tale*, for instance, when the devious canon prepares the crucible to dupe the priest, the "crosselet" (l. 1276) is referred to as a "false jet" (l. 1277). It is significant that the

---

15 On the Pardoner and the Orphean tradition see Michael A. Calabrese, "'Make a Mark That Shows': Orphean Song, Orphean Sexuality, and the Exile of Chaucer's Pardoner," *Viator* 24 (1993): 269–86; and see Sturges, *Chaucer's Pardoner and Gender Theory*, 107–22.
16 For an overview of scholarship on the Pardoner's sexuality and gender, see Sturges, *Chaucer's Pardoner and Gender Theory*, 21–62. Scholarship that explicitly takes on the Pardoner's sexual and gendered identity: Glenn Burger, "Kissing the Pardoner," *PMLA* 107.5 (1992): 1143–56 and *Chaucer's Queer Nation*, specifically chapters 4 and 5; Dinshaw, *Chaucer's Sexual Poetics*, Madison: University of Wisconsin Press (1989): 156–84.
17 Sturges sees fragmentation as the Pardoner's "defining attribute," *Chaucer's Pardoner and Gender Theory*, 124. He grounds this fragmentation in the Pardoner's potentially castrated body (see chapter 6, specifically). I am disinterested in determining the Pardoner's genitalia; it is the objects that the Pardoner carries on his body which convey his embodiment in a social collective.
18 See *Middle English Dictionary*, s. v. "get."

Pardoner, wearing "al of the newe jet" (l. 682), is decked out with devices; his purse, hood, hair, vernicle, and song all convey his reliance on newness. What the narrator perceives of the Pardoner, that the Pardoner thought himself "newe," characterizes this pilgrim as a locus of curiosity. Patricia Ingham's work on medieval constructions of newness considers how debates on novelty engage questions about value and profit, invention and creation.[19] Ingham notes that, unlike late capitalism, the "new" in medieval culture did not carry with it a progress narrative. Rather, new things "served as a means to adjudicate the ethics of invention and eventual change, leveraging thorny problems of fate, creativity, and desire."[20] When the Pardoner has finished his tale and asks the pilgrims to receive his pardon, he styles the act as "newe":

> Al newe and fressh at every miles ende –
> So that ye offren, alwey newe and newe,
> Nobles or pens, whiche that be goode and trewe. (ll. 928–30)

That the Pardoner equivocates exchanging money for pardons with newness reinforces the link between the pecuniary purses and cavities as contraptions. The "nobles" and "pens" are deposited into the Pardoner's cavities, and these offers – in exchange for pardons – are "alwey newe and newe," always changing. The Pardoner, then, is this site of newness, or, to use a favorite word of Chaucer's, "newfanglednesse" – his body a locus for Chaucer to question the slippage between innovation and machination.[21]

We might imagine the Pardoner wearing a fourteenth-century peddler's coat, high on his horse stealthily opening his coat to show his body covered in illicit items for sale. The gadgets and instruments that the Pardoner carries on his person reinforce his own body as a contraption: his cavities are his contrivances. The Pardoner has loosened two cavities: his mouth in song and his hood to unleash a growth of hair while packing another cavity, his purse, that is overflowing with pardons, false relics, his hood, and money. That the brimming purse lay "in his lappe" (l. 686) on his groin marks the Pardoner's overproductive eroticism. When describing what his brimming purse contains, the narrator switches to "male" (l. 694), a term for a sack that emphasizes its

---

[19] Patricia Clare Ingham, *The Medieval New: Ambivalence in the Age of Innovation* (Philadelphia: University of Pennsylvania Press, 2015).
[20] Ingham, *Medieval New*, 4.
[21] The fifteenth-century *Promptorium parvulorum*, a bilingual English and Latin dictionary, glosses "get" and "gyn" for the Latin "machina." *The Promptorium Parvulorum: The First English–Latin Dictionary*, ed. A. L. Mayhew. EETS 102 (London, 1908).

anatomical and testicular qualities. The Pardoner's "male" is a fourteenth-century Mary Poppins bag: it contains a "pilwe-beer" (l. 694), a pillow-case, a cavity within a cavity, that he flaunts as the Virgin Mary's veil; a "gobet" (l. 696), a fragment, of a sail that St. Peter used when he traveled to see Christ. In his "male" he also carries a brass cross "ful of stones" (l. 699) and a glass container stocked with the bones of pigs. This image that asks us to read the Pardoner's anatomy and the contents of his "male" as teeming follows the narrator's uncertainty of how to interpret his body:

> No berd hadde he, ne nevere sholde have;
> As smothe it was as it were late shave.
> I trowe he were a geldyng or a mare. (ll. 689–91)

The narrator's inability or, more likely, refusal to read the Pardoner as a legible body is undone by his initial up close and personal reading of the Pardoner. We first learn more about what the Pardoner looks like than we learn of his practices. The narrator is certain – expressed in the verb "trouen" – of his inability to interpret the Pardoner.[22]

Efforts to read the Pardoner as a castrated eunuch or an effeminate queer dandy are often held in contrast to the futile and transphobic attempts to redeem the Pardoner of his masculine ethos through over-inscribing a cisgender male embodiment onto his character.[23] Forcing the Pardoner to have or not have a phallus betrays his queerest articulation: his purse. Scholars have looked to the line "I trowe he were a geldyng or a mare" to debate the Pardoner's sexual, erotic, and gendered identity, and this discussion constantly focuses on the possibility of the

---

[22] See *Middle English Dictionary*, s. v. "trouen."
[23] For an inclusive and respectful article on the Pardoner's gender identity see Kim Zarins, "Intersex and the Pardoner's Body," *Accessus: A Journal of Premodern Literature and New Media* 4 (2018): 1–63. For other scholarship that has engaged the question of the Pardoner's sexuality, gender, or both, see variously: Richard Firth Green, "The Pardoner's Pants (And Why They Matter)," *Studies in the Age of Chaucer* 15 (1993): 131–45; Stephen F. Kruger, "Claiming the Pardoner: Toward a Gay Reading of Chaucer's *Pardoner's Tale*," *Exemplaria* 6 (1994): 115–39; Monica McAlpine, "The Pardoner's Homosexuality and How It Matters," *PMLA* 95 (1980): 8–22; and Robert P. Miller, "Chaucer's Pardoner, the Scriptural Eunuch, and the *Pardoner's Tale*," in *Chaucer Criticism: The Canterbury Tales*, ed. Richard Shoeck and Jerome Taylor (South Bend: University of Notre Dame Press, 1960), 221–44. Elspeth Whitney falls into a diagnostic of the Pardoner's body, explaining away his queerness against medieval humoral theory: "What's Wrong with the Pardoner? Complexion Theory, the Phlegmatic Man, and Effeminacy," *The Chaucer Review* 45 (2011): 357–89. Other scholars attempt to heterosexualize and cisnormativize the Pardoner: see Richard Firth Green, "The Sexuality Normality of Chaucer's Pardoner," *Mediaevalia* 8 (1982): 351–58; and C. David Benson, "Chaucer's Pardoner: His Sexuality and Modern Critics," *Mediaevalia* 8 (1982): 337–49.

Pardoner's dismembered genitals. Robert S. Sturges sees the Pardoner's obsession with dismemberment as a destruction of form that results in the Pardoner's "imaginary union of male and female, masculine and feminine, in one body – the longing for a state in which the sexes and genders are not differentiated."[24] Sturges, who works to reassemble the Pardoner's body, suggests that the Pardoner hopes to achieve this bodily union by appealing to the divine in order to restore "wholeness and phallic authority,"[25] a unity that the Pardoner never receives. This tidy solution to the Pardoner's possible dismemberment shifts focus from the way the Pardoner presents himself through the assorted appendages that he bears on his body. Unification is not on the Pardoner's mind, but rather transformations and (re)productions.

Chaucer writes the Pardoner as a corporeal and spiritual contortionist, and his movements stir and pulse in the objects that he carries, wears, and becomes. If the body of the Pardoner behaves like a cavity, then his riding companion, the Summoner, is linked into the Pardoner's network of concavity. The Summoner famously supports the Pardoner's singing with a "stif burdoun" (l. 673), often cited as a phallic pun but which may also be a pun on a woman's *burden* to pregnancy or the marital debt.[26] With his "trompe" (l. 674), the Summoner assists in the Pardoner's siren-song to incite the pilgrims to come look at his cavities. Together the Summoner and the Pardoner act as an over-productive unit in the pilgrimage, but their production is one of "fruitless expenditure."[27]

Although the Summoner does not carry a purse, we might consider that the Pardoner himself acts as the Summoner's "male" – both as his male counterpart and as his accompanying purse. Because both the Summoner and the Pardoner work in offices prone to corruption, their association with pecuniary extortion is unsurprising.[28] In the *Friar's Tale*, for instance, the Friar typecasts a summoner as the evil protagonist who loves to turn a profit. For the Friar, the summoner of his *Tale* is a "false theef" (l. 1338) like Judas:

> He took hymself a greet profit therby;
> His maister knew nat alwey what he wan.
> Withouten mandement a lewed man
> He koude somne, on peyne of Cristes curs,

---

24 Sturges, *Chaucer's Pardoner and Gender Theory*, 138.
25 Sturges, *Chaucer's Pardoner and Gender Theory*, 138.
26 Stockton, "Cynicism," 149.
27 Stockton, "Cynicism," 149.
28 On the portraits of the Summoner and the Pardoner see Jill Mann, *Chaucer and Medieval Estates Satire* (Cambridge: Cambridge University Press, 1973), 137–51.

> And they were glade for to fille his purs
> And make hym grete feestes atte nale.
> And right as Judas hadde purses smale,
> And was a theef, right swich a theef was he;
> His maister hadde but half his duetee. (ll. 1344–52)

This unfavorable portrait linking summoners to Judas locates the role of the purse in a salvific history of betrayal and duplicitousness.[29] This duplicity underscores the Summoner in his role as an ecclesiastical court official accustomed to taking bribes – "ful prively a fynch eek koude he pulle" (l. 652).

Even though the description in the *Friar's Tale* typifies summoners as avaricious thieves, the Summoner's own sentiment on purses in his General Prologue portrait seems largely disavowing. The Summoner figures the "purs" as a site of retribution, one that can and should be monetarily and physically abused. The Summoner's introduction to the pilgrimage defines him in terms of his corruptive office. His drunkenness animates his tongue to Latinate legal pronouncements – both the Pardoner and the Summoner expel words that hurt and entice – and he excuses misdemeanors with one exception:

> But if a mannes soule were in his purs;
> For in his purs he sholde ypunysshed be.
> "Purs is the ercedekenes helle," seyde he. (ll. 656–58)

For the Summoner, the "purs" is open to legal and religious punishment. Equated with the archdeacon's hell, the purse stands in and epitomizes the bottomless depth of Satan's territory. The Summoner further associates hell as a cavity in his *Prologue*, a response to the Friar's tale. He explains a vision of an Angel who leads a friar to Satan's hell. The Angel commands Satan to hold his tail in the air and show his anus to the friar. Satan releases his tail and the friar sees a "nest of freres" (l. 1691) that swarm out of Satan's cavity like bees swarming out from a hive. The anal whiplash of the friars swarming "al aboute" (l. 1696), "on a route" (l. 1695) all "thurghout helle" (l. 1696), accelerates as they "comen agayn as faste as they may gon" (l. 1697). The rapidity of their swarming is truncated by their leisurely creeping back into Satan's cavity: "And in his ers they crepten everychon"

---

29 John 12:6, "Dixit autem hoc non quia de egenis pertinebat ad eum sed quia fur erat et loculos habens ea quae mittebantur portabat" (Now he said this not because he cared for the poor; but because he was a thief, and, having the purse, carried the things that were put therein). Latin in *Bibla sacra iuxta vulgatam versionem,* 5th edition, ed. Robert Weber (Stuttgart: Deutsche Bibelgesellschaft, 2007), the translation in *The Holy Bible: Translated from the Latin Vulgate* (New York: The Douay Bible House, 1941), 106. See also *Riverside Chaucer*, n. to ll. 135051, 875.

(l. 1698). Once all the friars have wriggled inside of Satan's anus, he violently shuts his tail to seal his anal opening. The verb "clappen," used to signal the sealing of Satan's cavity, has a primary meaning of pulsating and throbbing as well as closing by thrusting, such as a window or door.[30] Once Satan has "clapte" (l. 1699) his tail shut, he ceases to move – he "lay ful stille" (l. 1699). The Summoner's anatomical lesson of Satan's ass cinching calls attention not simply to the condemnation of "freres and feendes" (l. 1674), but rather to the precarity of cavities. The friars are only ever able to swarm free around hell when Satan chooses to unleash them from his own body. Cavities act as swallowing machines that eject what they consume at their own discretion.

The comeuppance that the Summoner advocates in his *Prologue* suggests that the purse-as-cavity acts as a site of punishment. In this way, one who puts his soul "in his purs" (l. 656) is punished in the same place. Effectively, the more productive a purse, the greater the punishment. Purses might well be the corporate symbol of the sins of *luxuria* and *avaritia*, the physical site where desire and greed convene. The Summoner uses the space of his *Tale* to punish the Friar's ornery depiction of summoners as thievish devils. In his *Tale*, the Summoner recounts the story of a greedy friar who nags an ill man named Thomas for money. The friar tells Thomas that a "ferthyng" (l. 1967) is worth nothing when divided into twelve parts. At the end of the *Summoner's Tale* Thomas finally assents to give money to the friar and says "in me shal be no lak" (l. 2139), a visualization that anticipates Thomas's anus as an endless cavity. Thomas explains the directions to the friar that he must fish for the money with his own hands:

> "Now thanne, put in thyn hand doun by my bak,"
> Seyde this man, "and grope wel bihynde.
> Bynethe my buttok there shaltow fynde
> A thyng that I have hyd in pryvetee." (ll. 2140–44)

Thomas's direction that the friar grope "doun" into his backside, "bynethe" his buttocks to find what he has "hid" renders his anal cavity as a hoard. The indescribable "thyng" – what the friar assumes is money – is cached "in pryvetee," highlighting the site of hoarding as a bodily orifice as well as a socially unspeakable phenomenon. In this exchange the obscured cavity presents the panic of hidden things and the problematic desire to uncover, expose, and possess the contents.

Hoarding and hiding an object – "a thyng" (l. 2144) – removes that object from social circulation until, of course, the hoarder chooses to distribute the

---

30 See *Middle English Dictionary*, s. v. "clappen."

object.³¹ Satan expels the friars from his anus when he wishes, and the Pardoner's wallet is visually brimming in his lap. Thomas's hidden "thyng," however, must be sought out, and this mode of seeking illustrates the desirability of the cavity. Without hesitation the friar "launcheth to the clifte" (l. 2145) of Thomas's backside and reaches his hand further down to find the money that Thomas has hidden. Like the Summoner's description of Satan's anal cavity, Thomas designs the terms and controls the contents of his cavity. In a ventricular magic trick, Thomas can feel the friar's hand groping "aboute his tuwel" (l. 2148). It is precisely when he feels the friar's hand "amydde" (l. 2149) his anus that he lets out a fart from his anal cavity.

The act that takes place in the middle of the cavity is the transformative zone of production: the friar learns that his gift is paid out to him in a fart and that the hidden cavity is an anus.³² The unknowability of Thomas's "thyng" inspires the friar to enter into the hollow and determine if the hidden "thyng" is indeed what he desires it to be. Of the *Summoner's Tale*, Tiffany Beechy has argued that excess of desire and greed does not merely limit production, but also has the power to turn "the desired object itself into shit."³³ Crucially, the friar tells Thomas that he will "abye this fart" (l. 2155), joining the economic, scatological, and erotic registers of Thomas's rectum.³⁴

Determined to figure out how to divvy up his gaseous gift, the friar gets a lesson from a "lordes squier" (l. 2243) in "ars-metrike" (l. 2222) on how to "karf" (l. 2243) up a fart. Using a cartwheel to demonstrate the distribution of gas, the squire explains that noses of twelve friars will sit at the ends of twelve spokes on a cartwheel, ready to take in the stench from a fart centered at the hub.³⁵ Centralizing the fart at the center of the circular cartwheel plays on the image of enclosure and circling that the cavity encourages. These examples of cavity punishment by the Summoner suggest that these hollow sites – purses, anuses,

---

31 On hoarding and collecting as a perverse activity see Jean Baudrillard, *The System of Objects*, trans. James Benedict (London: Verso, 1996), 85–105.
32 On money in the *Summoner's Tale* see Robert Epstein, "Sacred Commerce: Chaucer, Friars, and the Spirit of Money," in *Sacred and Profane in Chaucer and Late Medieval Literature: Essays in Honour of John V. Fleming*, ed. Robert Epstein (Toronto: University of Toronto Press, 2010), 129–45.
33 Tiffany Beechy, "Devil Takes the Hindmost: Chaucer, John Gay, and the Pecuniary Anus," *The Chaucer Review* 41 (2006): 71–85 at 73.
34 See *Middle English Dictionary*, s. v. "abien," as well as a potential pun with "abeien," which means to "bend down."
35 For a scientific and scholastic understanding of the twelve-spoked cartwheel see Robert J. Hasenfratz, "The Science of Flatulence: Possible Sources for the *Summoner's Tale*," *The Chaucer Review* 30 (1996): 241–61.

hell, or otherwise – are instruments of desire. The queer value assigned to cavities orients the realm of desire with the operation of material exchange: the friar goes into the hollow desiring to find a hidden "thyng." The fart that he receives in exchange for his desirous groping resignifies the production of the cavity and reorients the value that the friar assigned to it in the first place.[36]

Pledges of Transformation

Punishment is not the only outcome when interacting with cavities. In fact, the Pardoner is a sort of "purs" representative in that he publicizes the value that his many cavities can offer. The Pardoner is a conduit for the pilgrimage to access his cavities, but the value of cavities is in their self-sustaining quality. Queer cavities act as autarkic systems because they are self-sufficient and able to thrive and survive without external aid. The Pardoner and his self-sufficient "purs" challenge the political project of the *Canterbury Tales* that promotes community-building and interdependence. In particular, the Pardoner's "purs" protests the burden of exchange between pilgrims – of tale-telling, of the potential for winning the game and eating a free supper at the *expense* of the community that each pilgrim is embedded within. Purses, then, are the symbol of loss in the Canterbury project because these objects, when opened, lose contents at the expense of another's gain.

Community-building in the *Canterbury Tales* relies on larger fourteenth-century ideas of "commune profit," a model of collective labor that works to ensure the salvific future of a community.[37] How does a body share in the "commune profit" when that social community rejects the body to begin with? The Pardoner acknowledges the system that betrays him, and yet he is adamant on exchanging, sharing, and communing with a pilgrimage contingent that refuses his tale –

---

[36] I have in mind Leo Bersani's essay "Is the Rectum a Grave?," in *Reclaiming Sodom*, ed. Jonathan Goldberg (New York: Routledge, 1994): 249–64: "It may, finally, be in the gay man's rectum that he demolishes his own perhaps otherwise uncontrollable identification with a murderous judgment against him" (262).

[37] For work on fourteenth-century conceptions of the *commune profit* see variously: Mark W. Ormod, "The Good Parliament of 1376: Commons, *communes*, and 'Common Profit' in Fourteenth-Century English Politics," in *Comparative Perspectives on History and Historians: Essays in Memory of Bryce Lyon (1920–2007)*, ed. David Nicholas, Bernard Bachrach, and James M. Murray (Kalamazoo: Medieval Institute Publications, 2012), 169–88; Kellie Robertson, "Common Language and Common Profit," in *The Postcolonial Middle Ages*, ed. Jeffrey Jerome Cohen (Basingstoke: Macmillan, 2000), 209–28; and Yasunari Takada, "*Commune Profit* and Libidinal Dissemination in Chaucer," in *The Body and the Soul in Medieval Literature*, ed. Piero Boitani and Anna Torti (Cambridge: D. S. Brewer, 1999), 107–21.

Chapter 7 "Ycrammed ful of cloutes and of bones": Chaucer's Queer Cavities —— **165**

"But right anon thise gentils gonne to crye,/ Nay, lat hym telle us of no ribaudye!" (ll. 323–24). Models of obligatory community-making and world-building have come under scrutiny in queer theory discussions of the "antirelational turn."[38] Theories of queer antisociality, inaugurated by Leo Bersani's *Homos*,[39] have asked if the queer subject has any obligation to uphold sociality and community-building. Antirelationality figures the queer subject as anti-productive, antisocial, anti-future, anti-family.[40] Advocates of the queer antirelational turn, Lee Edelman and Jack Halberstam, have followed Bersani's critique, linking the heteronormative future-orientation to capitalist ideologies of social productivity.[41] In *The Queer Art of Failure*, for instance, Halberstam writes, "capitalist logic casts the homosexual as inauthentic and unreal, as incapable of proper love and unable to make the appropriate connections between sociality, relationality, family, sex, desire, and consumption."[42] Under a capitalist model, queer bodies are failed subjects, bodies that cannot "embody the connections between production and reproduction."[43] Chaucer's Pardoner, of course, lives outside of modern conceptions of capitalism, and yet, through the image of the "purs," the Canterbury project questions how words are valued, judged, and exchanged among communities. The "purs" lives outside of community, in that it swallows and absorbs

---

38 See the MLA Forum publication on "The Antisocial Thesis in Queer Theory: MLA Annual Convention, 27 December 2005, Washington, D.C." *MLA* 121.3 (2006): 819–27. This includes responses from the panel by Robert L. Caserio, Lee Edelman, J. Halberstam, José Esteban Muñoz, and Tim Dean.
39 Leo Bersani, *Homos* (Cambridge: Harvard University Press, 1996).
40 This position has been importantly criticized by José Esteban Muñoz in his *Cruising Utopia: The Then and There of Queer Futurity* (New York: New York University Press, 2009), where he instead focuses on queer potential, possibility, and utopia. Muñoz rejects Edelman's conception of the queer death drive, the desire to have "no future" and no responsibility to a future as this position is available to a white, cisgender, queer male subject. Halberstam, too, has condemned Edelman's ideation as an "excessively small archive," that is, the "gay male archive" (824). Instead, Halberstam asks where the space exists for "dyke anger, anticolonial despair, racial rage, counterhegemonic violence, punk pugilism," (824) since Edelman's polemic does not account for these anti-futures. See J. Halberstam, "The Politics of Negativity in Recent Queer Theory," in "The Antisocial Thesis in Queer Theory: MLA Annual Convention, 27 December 2005, Washington, D.C." *MLA* 121.3 (2006): 823–25.
41 Lee Edelman, *No Future: Queer Theory and the Death Drive* (Durham: Duke University Press, 2004); and J. Halberstam, *The Queer Art of Failure* (Durham: Duke University Press, 2011). On the relationship between queer identity and capitalist-nationalist projects see John D'Emilio, "Capitalism and Gay Identity," in *Making Trouble: Essays on Gay History, Politics, and the University* (New York: Routledge, 1992), 3–16; and Jasbir K. Puar, *Terrorist Assemblages: Homonationalism in Queer Times* (Durham: Duke University Press, 2007).
42 Halberstam, *Queer Art of Failure*, 95.
43 Halberstam, *Queer Art of Failure*, 95.

what enters it, and yet the "purs" also opens and beckons for interactive investment. The meaning of the Pardoner's purse – and all his accoutrements like it – figures his identity in the pilgrimage far more industriously than questions of his sexuality or gender, all of which boils down to repealing or redeeming his genitalia. Purses are production machines for the Pardoner, and his ability to reproduce their contents is totalized in his role to exchange pardons for payment.

Self-sufficient cavities threaten models of social production that require exchange of labor to operate. The pilgrimage sees the Pardoner's cavities as hazardous because they are self-sustaining units of production. The Pardoner, his purse, and his various other cavity-systems do not need the pilgrimage to be fruitful – he arrives at the tavern already with pardons from "Rome al hoot" (l. 687). At the same time, the Pardoner invites the fellowship to share in his cavities with the promise that what he carries inside of those cavities has the power to transform.

The Pardoner's reliance on cavity-systems frames his portrait as a pilgrim and informs how he tells his tales, both as a preacher and a tale-teller. He uses the space of his *Prologue* to think "upon som honeste thyng" (l. 328) while he drinks. His mouth takes in liquid and transforms his thinking so that he may tell a moral tale: "Now have I dronke a draghte of corny ale,/ By God, I hope I shal yow telle a thyng/ That shal by reson been at youre likyng!" (ll. 456–58). The act of ingestion provides the Pardoner with the words he needs to tell his *Tale*, and his *Prologue* acts as the cauldron. Like the Summoner, the Pardoner explains that he uses Latin like saffron to pepper his preaching and "stire" (l. 346) people to devotion. He conducts his mouth like a vessel as it cooks up a linguistic feast to deliver to the pilgrimage. These culinary allusions attest to the transformative possibilities that cavities have on community-making. The Pardoner says that it pains him to have "an hauteyn speche" (l. 330), and to ring out as loudly as a church bell in his sermons. Yet, because the pilgrims know of his predilection for singing, the Pardoner becomes a factotum of cavitary speech.

As the Pardoner speaks, then, his *Prologue* becomes a Charybdian text. Throughout his pseudo-autobiographical *Prologue*, the Pardoner figuratively proffers several of his cavities to the pilgrims, with the promise that these items have a transformative quality. While his portrait in the General Prologue already mentions his false relics, it is in his *Prologue* that he recounts how he auctions his goods at the church:

> Thanne shewe I forth my longe cristal stones,
> Ycrammed ful of cloutes and of bones –
> Relikes been they, as wenen they echoon.
> Thanne have I in latoun a sholder-boon,
> Which that was of an hooly Jewes sheep. (ll. 347–51)

The image of the Pardoner in his peddler's coat works all too well here since he becomes an exhibition of illicit materials that he owns – "my longe cristal stones." Like his purse "bretful of pardoun" (l. 690), the Pardoner's long crystal stones are "ycrammed" full of fragmented pieces of cloth and bone. The verb "crammen" illustrates the relic-cavity as packed to capacity, but also the act of stuffing it in the first place: a space can be crammed and packed full, but one can also cram things into cavities. These possibilities make the cavity as vulnerable as the carrier. This is to say that the Pardoner's cavities are insatiable because they are always already brimming, always already begging for more material exchange.

Further delivering the selling points, the Pardoner explains that the shoulder bone contained in a "latoun," a brass container, if submerged into water in a "welle" (l. 353), will have the property to heal sick livestock. By licking, drinking, or tonguing the bone-touched water, the farm animals are promised to "be hool" (ll. 357, 359) and rehabilitated from disease. From one cavity, the "latoun," into another, the well, the bone has the power to imbue and transform the water. This water then can be transferred into another cavity, the mouth of the livestock, in order to cure the animals and make them "hool" (ll. 357, 359). Equally playful and threatening, the Pardoner's ability to make something "hool" is both remedial and hollowing. Sturges remarks of this passage that "wholeness is paradoxically to be achieved through fragmentation; or fragmentation is to give way to an idealized wholeness."[44] Cavities betray and resist ideas of wholeness. For the Pardoner, the ideation of wholeness is to embrace being a hole: to become "hool" is to become a cavity. Becoming a cavity is the Pardoner's pledge of transformation.

Curative fantasies of restoration through reproduction decorate the Pardoner's sales pitch. Beyond healing diseases, the bone-touched well water can help livestock reproduce. If a householder has his animals drink from water from the well each week, "his beestes and his stoor shal multiplie" (l. 365). The Pardoner's fragmented bones and false relics not only can restore wholeness but also duplicate bodies through multiplying. Further, the Pardoner pledges that this bone-touched well water can heal "jalousie" (l. 366) between a husband and wife. Consuming soup made with the water ensures that the husband trusts his wife, even though he knows the truth "of hir defaute" (l. 370). Here the Pardoner's remedy circumvents sin: the wife may still sin but the husband will not dwell on it in jealousy.

The transformative promise becoming "hool" requires that one engage with hollow things: the "latoun," the "welle," mouths, and bodily orifices. In the

---

44 Sturges, *Chaucer's Pardoner and Gender Theory*, 125.

Pardoner's recreated preaching pitch, he holds up his final cavity, a mitten, to speak of its transformative value:

> Heere is a miteyn eek, that ye may se.
> He that his hand wol putte in this mitayn,
> He shal have multiplying of his grayn,
> Whan he hath sowen, be it whete or otes,
> So that he offre pens, or elles grotes. (ll. 372–76)

In order to benefit from the cavity, one must go inside of it. The Pardoner optically entices the audience, just as he showed his "longe cristal stones." The catch is that the audience must want to put, "wol putte," a hand inside the mitten. The verb "willen" suggests that the act of putting a hand inside a cavity is one of volition.[45] The cavity will ensure that his fields will yield and then multiply the grain that he has planted. The mitten-as-cavity is only effective if a person "offre pens, or elles grotes"; the cavity's transformative function only works in exchange for money. Crucially, the Pardoner's suggestion that grain will multiply by engaging with the mitten-hole privileges the reproductive work of cavities over cisnormative models of procreation.

The transformative capacity of cavities cements in the Pardoner's moralizing tale. The *Pardoner's Tale* undermines the role of exchange in community-building through the image of the cavity. The three rioters, who swear a fraternal vow to each other, seek out Death in an attempt to kill him.[46] As the tale goes, the three brothers encounter an Old Man who instructs them on Death's location. It is not Death that they find under a tree but rather gold florins, which they decide to divvy up equally among themselves. When one brother goes to town to acquire food and drink, the other two brothers conspire to kill him upon his return. The third brother, likewise, prepares his brothers' drinks with poison. All die, and only gold is left behind.

The collective fratricide of the three rioters is made possible because of cavity-systems. At the beginning of his tale, the Pardoner draws our attention to bodily cavities as the culprits of "lechery" (l. 481), "glotonye" (l. 482), and "excesse" (l. 514). Citing the false swearing of Jews, the drunkenness of Lot and Herod, and the corruption of Adam and Eve, the Pardoner bewails the act of ingestion, of entertaining a beckoning cavity. He explains that the "shorte

---

45 See *Middle English Dictionary*, s. v. "willen."
46 Tison Pugh notes that it is interesting that the Pardoner satirizes brotherhood as he himself rides in the pilgrimage with his "freend" and "compeer," the Summoner. See Tison Pugh, *Chaucer's (Anti-) Eroticisms and the Queer Middle Ages* (Columbus: Ohio State University Press, 2014), 91.

throte" and "the tendre mouth" (l. 517) is the site on the body that makes "men to swynke" (l. 519) and require food and water to sustain labor. Providing more evidence, the Pardoner paraphrases Paul's epistle to the Philippians, suggesting that the enemies of Christ have one end in death because "wombe is hir god" (l. 533).[47] The Pardoner exclaims,

> O wombe! O bely! O stynkyng cod,
> Fulfilled of dong and of corrupcioun!
> At either ende of thee foul is the soun.
> How greet labour and cost is thee to fynde! (ll. 534–37)

Physically leading the pilgrimage from the throat to the "wombe," the Pardoner effectively swallows the pilgrimage whole with his tale. Consumption moves from the throat to the belly, where the corruption of gluttony transforms a man's throat into a latrine: "his throte he maketh his pryvee" (l. 527). Before telling a tale on the annihilation of avarice, the Pardoner's emphasis on gluttony warns the pilgrimage that the body-as-cavity has the capacity to corporeally transform. By making one's throat into a privy, the body becomes spiritually and physically "fulfilled of dong" (l. 535). These bodily cavities are "deed" (l. 548) while they live.

Bodies are cavities in life and the Pardoner shows this paradox in the figure of the Old Man who, held captive in his life-body – he is literally "forwrapped" (l. 718) – cannot seem to die. He asks his deceased mother if he may join her underground, begging to leave one cavity (his body) for another (the grave): "Leeve mooder, leet me in!" (l. 731). The Old Man tries to exchange with his mother, one cavity for another:

> Allas, whan shul my bones been at reste?
> Mooder, with yow wolde I chaunge my cheste
> That in my chambre longe tyme hath be,
> Ye, for an heyre clowt to wrappe me! (ll. 733–36)

The Old Man knows that cavities operate networks of exchange. He desires to exchange a chest in a chamber for a cloth to be wrapped in and placed underground. Yet, death is beyond the reach of exchange: these items have no value to the mother underground; the transaction cannot take place. The Old Man, "forwrapped" (l. 718) with a desire to be further wrapped and enveloped by a hair cloth, begs to prepare for his final subterranean cavity. Seeta Chaganti reads the Old Man's description of the enclosure of death as "instrumental to

---

[47] *Riverside Chaucer*, 908, n. ll. 529–35.

acts of transformation."⁴⁸ She argues that the Pardoner's relics and the objects within his *Tale* "reveal the material realities of death and ask the viewer to envision a process of symbolic and literal transformation through their enclosure."⁴⁹ The *Pardoner's Tale* teaches that transformation happens through the exchange of cavities. The Old Man's longing to be enveloped speaks to the affinity between cavities and enclosure and the exchange necessary to seal a cavity. Yet, the potential for a cavity-enclosure to open and engulf is what the pilgrimage sees as a threat from the Pardoner and his purses.

Enveloping, Unbuckling, Shrining

Our Pardoner operates between two modes of concavity. His purse acts like Satan's anus that has the power to contain and seal items from circulation. At the same time, the Pardoner's "male" threatens to be a Pandora's Box, a cavity that unleashes objects and information without election. The Pardoner's body, too, moves between registers of containment and expulsion. His body is like an accordion: it absorbs its exterior environment in order to contain it but has the capacity to expel what it contains in order to transmit a new form. In this way the body of the Pardoner becomes both extremely porous and sealed tightly shut, and the boundaries of the Pardoner's body are contingent on the interaction between these two modalities. The Pardoner's purse, filled as it is with haphazard and fraudulent material, unfastens for those who come into the Pardoner's circuit.

The opening of the Pardoner's cavities is nowhere more pregnant than in his exchange with the Host at the close of his *Tale*. His initial reflection of his preaching technique in his *Prologue* takes form when he invites the pilgrims into his purse:

> But, sires, o word forgat I in my tale:
> I have relikes and pardoun in my male,
> As faire as any man in Engelond,
> Whiche were me yeven by the popes hond. (ll. 919–22)

---

48 Seeta Chaganti, *The Medieval Poetics of the Reliquary: Enshrinement, Inscription, Performance* (New York: Palgrave Macmillan, 2008), 137; see the larger chapter for a reading of reliquary enclosure in the *Pardoner's Tale*.
49 Chaganti, *Medieval Poetics of the Reliquary*, 133.

Filled with relics and pardons for the taking, the Pardoner's contents in his "male" are likened to "faire" men in England. That the Pardoner's "male" is as fair as any man in England is his selling point. Granted by hand by the pope and hand-delivered to the pilgrimage by the Pardoner, the brimming "male" serves as the Pardoner's attempt to authorize the queer cavities that he carries. He articulates that his presence as a "suffisant" (l. 932) pardoner, one who was able to deliver a moral tale, ensures that he is a "seuretee" (l. 937) to the fellowship. Still, the Pardoner recognizes and openly admits and commits to a fraudulent and faulty ideological system.[50] The Pardoner's insistence that he can pardon the sins of the pilgrimage requires that he open his "male" to the community, to let his fellowship touch his relics and to swallow monetary reward in return. The Pardoner must participate in a system that has already failed him.

In the Pardoner's mind, what he failed to state in his *Tale* through forgetting he is able to recover with his purse. His purse stands in as the material answer for the "o word" he "forgat" to tell the pilgrims. As Beryl Rowland has observed, poets used the image of the wallet to envisage mental storage systems for memory recall.[51] Rowland cites Stephen Hawes's use of the "male" as a storage site in his sixteenth-century allegorical poem *The Passetyme of Pleasure*. In the text Hawes presents Dame Rhetoric explaining the art of memory to poets, where she associates tale-telling and oratory with looking inward to access images in a purse:

> Yf to the orature many a sundry tale
> One after other treatably be tolde
> Than sundry ymages in his closed male
> Eache for a mater he doth than well holde
> Lyke to the tale he doth than so beholde. (ll. 1247–51)[52]

Unbuckling a purse, in this instance, is associated with unlocking one's memory treasury.[53] Chaucer scatters the command to unbuckle one's purse three

---

50 Stockton, "Cynicism," 143–64.
51 Beryl Rowland, "Bishop Bradwardine, the Artificial Memory, and the *House of Fame*," in *Chaucer at Albany*, ed. Rossell Hope Robbins (New York: Burt Franklin, 1975), 46–47.
52 Cited in Rowland, "Bishop Bradwardine, " 47. See also *The Pastime of Pleasure*, ed. William Edward Mead. EETS 173 (London, 1927), 52.
53 Unbuckling one's purse to tell tales is similar to the Old English trope of unlocking one's word-hoard in *Beowulf*: "Him se yldesta ondswarode, werodes wisa, wordhord onleac" (The eldest answered him, leader of the band, unlocked his word-hoard" (ll. 258–59) in *Klaeber's Beowulf*, 4th edition, ed. R. D. Fulk, Robert E. Bjork, and John D. Niles (Toronto: University of Toronto Press, 2009). This also occurs in the opening to *Widsith*: "Widsið maðolade, wordhord onleac" (Widsith spoke, unlocked his word-hoard) (l. 1) in *The Exeter Book*, The Anglo-Saxon

times throughout the *Canterbury Tales*, and two are spoken by the Host.[54] In response to the Knight's finished tale, the Host explains that his story was worth recalling from "memorye" (l. 3112):

> That he ne seyde it was a noble storie
> And worthy for to drawen to memorie,
> And namely the gentils everichon.
> Oure Hooste lough and swoor, "So moot I gon,
> This gooth aright; unbokeled is the male.
> Lat se now who shal telle another tale;
> For trewely the game is wel bigonne." (ll. 3111–17)

Opening the "male" of memory allows the speaker to recall images that make tale-telling possible. The first tale-teller, the Knight, must draw his tale out from his memory just as one might extract an item from a purse. But the purse must be open for that extraction to take place.

The Canterbury project is framed by the unbuckling of purses. In the Parson's *Prologue* the Host encourages the Parson to open his "male" for the pilgrims so that he may not "breke" (l. 24) the "pley" (l. 24) of tale-telling:

> Unbokele and shewe us what is in thy male,
> For trewely, me thynketh by thy cheere
> Thou sholdest knytte up wel a greet mateere.
> Telle us a fable anon, for cokkes bones! (ll. 26–29)

If the Parson refuses to "unbokele" his purse and "shewe" the pilgrims what it contains, he will fissure the activity of the game. The Host's request that the Parson first unbuckle his purse is tamed by his follow-up suggestion that the Parson can "knytte up" a good tale from the contents of his "male" – a purse should never stay open too long. Harry Bailly commands the Parson to "beth fructuous" in "litel space" (l. 71), conveying that the Parson's unlocking of his purse should be efficient in its multiplicity of words.[55] That the Host comments

---

Poetic Records III, ed. George Philip Krapp and Elliott van Kirk Dobbie (New York: Columbia University Press, 1936). See Martin Stevens, "The Structure of *Beowulf*: From Gold-Hoard to Word-Hoard," *Modern Language Quarterly* 39 (1978): 219–38.

54 The Host's request to unbuckle a purse occurs in the *Miller's Tale*, l. 3115 and the Parson's *Prologue*, l. 26. The other two occurrences are voiced by the Pardoner in his *Tale*, l. 945 (discussed below). There is a fourth reference to unbuckling a "galoche," shoe, in the *Squire's Tale*, l. 555: "Ne were worthy unbokelen his galoche."

55 John Plummer, "'Beth fructuous and that litel space': The Engendering of Harry Bailly," in *New Readings of Chaucer's Poetry*, ed. Robert G. Benson and Susan J. Ridyard (Cambridge: D. S. Brewer, 2003), 107–18.

at the beginning of the pilgrimage that the "male" has been opened, and here at the close of the pilgrimage he must encourage the Parson to show the pilgrims what his "male" contains, envelops and circles the *Canterbury Tales*.

For the Host, the breaking of the game results in social and economic panic. The Host's stake in unbuckling purses is one of investment: the game of tale-telling to and from Canterbury is a supper at the cost of the collective – "at oure aller cost" (l. 799). Twice the Host explains that those who refuse his judgment will "paye al that we spenden by the weye" (l. 806) and "whoso be rebel to my juggement/ Shal paye for al that by the wey is spent" (ll. 833–34). These two economic modes of exchange – that all pay for one tale-teller, or one rebellious loser pay for all – is in itself a game of caching the pilgrims: hoarding the value of stories in purses. The Host sets the price of the supper and rules over the pilgrims "at his devys" (l. 816) and the Host himself rides along with the pilgrims as their guide at his "owene cost" (l. 804).

The spending habits of the pilgrimage – the payment, the cost – are contingent on the Host's valuation of the tale-teller with the "best sentence" and "moost solaas" (l. 798). For the Host, then, the image of the purse represents his own social and economic control over the Canterbury group. He encourages the pilgrims to unbuckle their purses and tell their tales, ensuring that the Host's terms of the game will operate as he desires. The Pardoner's overt affinity with purses, and his place in the center of the tale-tellers,[56] acts as a maelstrom of speechmaking and opening of cavities. Purses may act as vaults for memory, but the Pardoner's association with purses relies on this rhetorical activity to ask those in the pilgrimage to face what their purses may contain.

Since the Host's association between unbuckling purses and telling tales centers on the economic crisis of the game, that is, paying for what is spent "by the wey" (ll. 806, 834), the fracas with the Pardoner at the end of his tale is the Host's attempt to reauthorize the terms of the pilgrimage. As Tison Pugh has aptly noted, the Host's construction of his own authoritative masculinity is built into the design of the tale-telling game.[57] After the Host assumes his role over the pilgrimage, the narrator reports that the Host "roos" up and was "oure aller cok,/

---

[56] Glenn Burger writes that Fragment VI is "apparently uniquely isolated within the Canterbury project and curiously alienated from (or by) its ordering principles" (*Chaucer's Queer Nation*, 119). Burger cites Donald Howard's *The Idea of the Canterbury Tales* where Howard states that "You can put the fragment in any of the gaps in the existing structure . . . and manufacture a literary or thematic relationship, but none asserts itself" (*Chaucer's Queer Nation*, 334).

[57] Tison Pugh, "Queering Harry Bailly: Gendered Carnival, Social Ideologies, and Masculinity Under Duress in the *Canterbury Tales*," *The Chaucer Review* 41 (2006): 39–69.

And gadred us togidre in a flok" (ll. 823–24). The phrase "oure aller cok" complements the Host's request that the winner will have supper at "oure aller cost" (l. 799) where "cok" and "cost" become nearly synonymous. Although the *Oxford English Dictionary* lists the first use of "cock" as phallus in 1618 and the *Middle English Dictionary* does not have the sense of "cok" as phallus listed in the entries, this description of the Host assuming control over the pilgrimage, gathering the company as a flock, reinforces a masculinist approach to community-building. With or without the phallic pun, the centering of male authority is crucial in this slippage between "cost" and "cok."[58] Harry Bailly has assembled himself as the political and economic center of the pilgrimage as well as a ridiculous, rising phallic pillar of the community flock. The Pardoner's predilection for cavities inverts the Host's necessity for cisnormative phallic governance.

The Pardoner refuses the Host's sovereignty and terms of rule when he upends the Host's role as guide and commands that the Host unbuckle his own "male." If unbuckling a purse figures the act of telling a tale, then the Pardoner's command that the Host open his purse is a request for payment from the Host to the pilgrimage. He seeks to equalize the terms of the community, ousting the Host's position of "masculine and bourgeois"[59] control. The Pardoner wants the Host to pay up to the pilgrimage, to offer something in return than simply ruling over the community and paying his own way. Framing this request, the Pardoner offers to pardon those in the fellowship beginning with the Host because he is "moost enveluped in synne" (l. 942). Asking the Host to come forth first and kiss his relics, he requests payment – "for a grote" (l. 945). Then, the Pardoner commands that the Host unbuckle his purse:

> I rede that oure Hooste here shal bigynne,
> For he is moost enveluped in synne.
> Com forth, sire Hoost, and offre first anon,
> And thou shalt kisse the relikes everychon,
> Ye, for a grote! Unbokele anon thy purs. (ll. 941–45)

Reading the purse as a queer cache reframes the Pardoner's demand that the Host unbuckle his purse. Instead of a joke that centers queer panic, the interaction between the two pilgrims suggests a more complicated exchange that involves the violent exposure of a cavity and its hidden contents. It is in this scene that we see the Host's body being read like the Pardoner's image. The Host's unbuckling of his purse is linked to his envelopment of sin. Envelopment in this instance figuratively wraps and encases the Host in immorality; that he is "moost

---

58 See the entry for "cock" n.1 in the *Oxford English Dictionary*.
59 Pugh, "Queering Harry Bailly," 56.

enveluped" in sin approximates the act of enclosure that the purse-as-cavity conveys. In a move to wrest control from the Host's game, the Pardoner requests that the Host now make a payment to the pilgrimage. In requesting that the Host unbuckle his purse, the Pardoner is asking the Host to contribute something to the community: coin, tale, or favor.

By suggesting that the Host should unbuckle his purse the Pardoner teases the boundaries of sin that engulf the Host. Not only is the Host's purse vulnerable to opening his cavities but also, in order for the Pardoner to access his purse, the Host's veil of sin must be punctured. The Host's angry refusal to the Pardoner is not simply because he has asked him to kiss all of his relics, but rather that the Pardoner has overturned the Host's power over the pilgrimage by threatening the Host's own cavity. The Host exclaims that he will not unbuckle his purse because if he does he will have "Cristes curs" (l. 946). In this way, the Canterbury project shows that the Host's request of opening purses is part of the play and rules of the game, but the Pardoner's attempt to seize control results in spiritual damnation. The Host replies:

> Thow woldest make me kisse thyn olde breech,
> And swere it were a relyk of a seint,
> Thogh it were with thy fundement depeint!
> But, by the croys which that Seint Eleyne fond,
> I wolde I hadde thy coillons in myn hond
> In stide of relikes or of seintuarie.
> Lat kutte hem of, I wol thee helpe hem carie;
> They shul be shryned in an hogges toord! (ll. 948–55)

If the Host is to kiss the Pardoner's relics, purse, fundament, or breeches, the Host must, as Stockton writes "come face-to-face with the solid material foundation of the spiritual economy of the pilgrimage."[60] That spiritual economy is contained within the queer cavities that the pilgrims embody and carry with them. In the Host's pursuit to hold and carry the Pardoner's "coillons" in his hand, the Host attempts to withdraw the Pardoner's aberrant objects from his purse in order to reveal what he himself believes the objects to be. The problem is that the purse itself stands in as a space that has the power to alter objects which, even if withdrawn, reforms the object into something entirely different. In effect, the Pardoner's rightful provocation of the Host's authority incites the Host to cache him in response. Enraged by the Pardoner's request, the enveloped Host censures the Pardoner by verbally caching and enveloping his items and body. By construing his fraudulent relics as smeared with "fundement,"

---

60 Stockton, "Cynicism," 151.

the Host conceptually removes the relics from the Pardoner's cavity to expose not just that the relics are products of his cavity, but *how* they are transformed within it. As the Host verbally uncovers the tainted relics, his scatological panic inflames him to quickly envelop the Pardoner again through shrining. Because the Host is uncertain which cavity to control, the Host's anger at the Pardoner splits direction between the Pardoner's purse and his testicles. Exchanging one purse for another, the Host violently asserts his desire to cut off the Pardoner's "coillons," in order to enshrine them as relics within hog shit.[61]

Marijane Obsorn's work on this passage uses the poetic *integumentum*, "a covering, cloak, disguise,"[62] to discuss Chaucer's shifting discourses, that is, how his language acts as a shroud, enclosing and caching the meaning and translatability of words. Chaucer, then, uses envelopment as a literary-poetic tool of queer caching. As the Host and Pardoner attempt to cache the other, they both obscure and disclose the meanings that they seek to control. Once the Host has threatened the Pardoner with enshrinement, the spiral of governance over the game is reinstituted by the Host when he silences the Pardoner – "This Pardoner answerde nat a word;/ So wrooth he was, no word ne wolde he seye" (ll. 956–57). Formerly, the Host's remarks on the Knight's tale-telling suggested an initiation of opening of purses, of speaking and exchanging tales in a community. Now, in silencing the Pardoner at the close of his tale, the Host metaphorically seals the Pardoner's purse and revises the terms of the game. He brings the Knight back into the fold to reinstitute his authority since the Knight's tale-telling unbuckled the purse of the pilgrimage, authorizing the exchange of speech between pilgrims. Harry Bailly commands that the Pardoner's newly closed mouth kiss the "worthy" (l. 960) Knight.[63] The kiss between the Knight and the Pardoner seals their mouths together in a promise to make all hollow orifices cooperate for the duration of the pilgrimage.

Chaucer's queer cavities punctuate the pilgrimage as sites of concavity scattered on and among the pilgrims, modeled in the stories they share. Purses highlight the possibilities and limits of the erotic economic exchange between bodies where caching is the process of making one into a cavity. The pilgrimage is formed by queer cavities as the Host beckons the pilgrims to unbuckle their purses and mouths in exchange of stories. Tale-telling becomes currency as the

---

[61] For an excellent reading of these lines against the *Roman de la Rose* see Marijane Osborn, "Transgressive Word and Image in Chaucer's Enshrined *Coillons* Passage," *The Chaucer Review* 37 (2003): 365–84, specifically 370–72.

[62] Osborn cites Dolores Warwick Fresne, *An Ars Legendi for Chaucer's* Canterbury Tales: *Re-Constructive Reading* (Gainsville: University of Florida Press, 1991), 236.

[63] See Burger, "Kissing the Pardoner," 1143–56 and Burger, *Chaucer's Queer Nation*, 140–56.

fellowship will all pay out for the one who can unbuckle their purse the best. It is the figure of the Pardoner and his purse that demonstrate the pecuniary and sexualized stakes of the queer cavity in a social collective. As the pilgrim most affiliated with orifices and openings, the Pardoner's pursuit in transforming the authority of the pilgrimage through his cavity-systems fails as the Host violently seals all cavities tightly shut. Chaucer's queer cavities epitomize the fraudulence of a socioeconomic system that refuses to regard nonnormative bodies as productive and withdraws all reward, salvific, social, sexual, or economic. Possibilities of community-making, transformative politics, connectivity, and reciprocal exchange are hidden and remain within the Pardoner's purse.

Bibliography

Ahmed, Sara. *Queer Phenomenology: Orientations, Objects, Others*. Durham: Duke University Press, 2006.
Baudrillard, Jean. *The System of Objects*. Translated by James Benedict. London: Verso, 1996.
Beechy, Tiffany. "Devil Takes the Hindmost: Chaucer, John Gay, and the Pecuniary Anus." *The Chaucer Review* 41 (2006): 71–85.
Benson, C. David. "Chaucer's Pardoner: His Sexuality and Modern Critics." *Mediaevalia* 8 (1982): 337–49.
Bersani, Leo. *Homos*. Cambridge: Harvard University Press, 1996.
Bersani, Leo. "Is the Rectum a Grave?" In *Reclaiming Sodom*, edited by Jonathan Goldberg, 249–64. New York: Routledge, 1994.
Bibla sacra iuxta vulgatam versionem. Edited by Robert Weber. 5th edition. Stuttgart: Deutsche Bibelgesellschaft, 2007.
Burger, Glenn. *Chaucer's Queer Nation*. Minneapolis: University of Minnesota Press, 2003.
Burger, Glenn. "Kissing the Pardoner." *PMLA* 107.5 (1992): 1143–56.
Calabrese, Michael A. "'Make a Mark That Shows': Orphean Song, Orphean Sexuality, and the Exile of Chaucer's Pardoner." *Viator* 24 (1993): 269–86.
Casiero, Robert L., Lee Edelman, J. Halberstam, José Esteban Muñoz, and Tim Dean. "The Antisocial Thesis in Queer Theory: MLA Annual Convention, 27 December 2005, Washington, D.C." *MLA* 121.3 (2006): 819–27.
Chaganti, Seeta. *The Medieval Poetics of the Reliquary: Enshrinement, Inscription, Performance*. New York: Palgrave Macmillan, 2008.
D'Emilio, John. "Capitalism and Gay Identity." In *Making Trouble: Essays on Gay History, Politics, and the University*, 3–16. New York: Routledge, 1992.
Dinshaw, Carolyn. *Chaucer's Sexual Poetics*. Madison: University of Wisconsin Press, 1989.
Edelman, Lee. *No Future: Queer Theory and the Death Drive*. Durham: Duke University Press, 2004.
Epstein, Robert. "Sacred Commerce: Chaucer, Friars, and the Spirit of Money." In *Sacred and Profane in Chaucer and Late Medieval Literature: Essays in Honour of John V. Fleming*, edited by Robert Epstein, 129–45. Toronto: University of Toronto Press, 2010.

The Exeter Book. The Anglo-Saxon Poetic Records, III. Edited by George Philip Krapp and Elliott van Kirk Dobbie. New York: Columbia University Press, 1936.

Fresne, Dolores Warwick. *An Ars Legendi for Chaucer's* Canterbury Tales: *Re-Constructive Reading*. Gainsville: University of Florida Press, 1991.

Green, Richard Firth. "The Pardoner's Pants (And Why They Matter)." *Studies in the Age of Chaucer* 15 (1993): 131–45.

Green, Richard Firth. "The Sexuality Normality of Chaucer's Pardoner." *Mediaevalia* 8 (1982): 351–58.

Halberstam, Jack. *The Queer Art of Failure*. Durham: Duke University Press, 2011.

Hasenfratz, Robert J. "The Science of Flatulence: Possible Sources for the *Summoner's Tale*." *The Chaucer Review* 30 (1996): 241–61.

Hennessey, Rosemary. *Profit and Pleasure: Sexual Identities in Late Capitalism*. New York: Routledge, 2000. The Holy Bible: Translated from the Latin Vulgate. New York: The Douay Bible House, 1941.

Ingham, Patricia Clare. *The Medieval New: Ambivalence in the Age of Innovation*. Philadelphia: University of Pennsylvania Press, 2015.

Klaeber's Beowulf. Edited by R. D. Fulk, Robert E. Bjork, and John D. Niles. 4th edition. Toronto: University of Toronto Press, 2009.

Kruger, Stephen F. "Claiming the Pardoner: Toward a Gay Reading of Chaucer's *Pardoner's Tale*." *Exemplaria* 6 (1994): 115–39.

Malo, Robyn. "The Pardoner's Relics (and Why They Matter Most)." *The Chaucer Review* 43 (2008): 82–102.

Mann, Jill. *Chaucer and Medieval Estates Satire*. Cambridge: Cambridge University Press, 1973.

McAlpine, Monica. "The Pardoner's Homosexuality and How It Matters." *PMLA* 95 (1980): 8–22.

Medieval Latin Poems of Male Love and Friendship. Translated by Thomas Stehling. New York: Garland Publishing, 1984.

Middle English Dictionary. Edited by Hans Kurath, 13 vols. Ann Arbor: University of Michigan Press, 1952–2001.

Miller, Robert P. "Chaucer's Pardoner, the Scriptural Eunuch, and the *Pardoner's Tale*." In *Chaucer Criticism: The Canterbury Tales*, edited by Richard Shoeck and Jerome Taylor, 221–44. South Bend: University of Notre Dame Press, 1960.

Muñoz, José Esteban. *Cruising Utopia: The Then and There of Queer Futurity*. New York: New York University Press, 2009.

Ormod, Mark W. "The Good Parliament of 1376: Commons, *communes*, and 'Common Profit' in Fourteenth-Century English Politics." In *Comparative Perspectives on History and Historians: Essays in Memory of Bryce Lyon (1920–2007)*, edited by David Nicholas, Bernard Bachrach, and James M. Murray, 169–88. Kalamazoo: Medieval Institute Publications, 2012.

Osborn, Marijane. "Transgressive Word and Image in Chaucer's Enshrined *Coillons* Passage." *The Chaucer Review* 37 (2003): 365–84.

Oxford English Dictionary. Edited by John Simpson and Edmund Weiner. 2nd edition. Oxford: Clarendon Press, 1989.

The Pastime of Pleasure. Edited by William Edward Mead. EETS 173. London: EETS, 1927.

Plummer, John. "'Beth fructuous and that litel space': The Engendering of Harry Bailly." In *New Readings of Chaucer's Poetry*, edited by Robert G. Benson and Susan J. Ridyard, 107–18. Cambridge: D. S. Brewer, 2003.
The Promptorium Parvulorum: The First English–Latin Dictionary. Edited by A. L. Mayhew. EETS 102. London: EETS, 1908.
Puar, Jasbir K. *Terrorist Assemblages: Homonationalism in Queer Times*. Durham: Duke University Press, 2007.
Pugh, Tison. *Chaucer's (Anti-)Eroticisms and the Queer Middle Ages*. Columbus: Ohio State University Press, 2014.
Pugh, Tison. "Queering Harry Bailly: Gendered Carnival, Social Ideologies, and Masculinity Under Duress in the *Canterbury Tales*." *The Chaucer Review* 41 (2006): 39–69.
The Riverside Chaucer. 3rd edition. Edited by Larry D. Benson. Boston: Houghton Mifflin Company, 1987.
Robertson, Kellie. "Common Language and Common Profit." In *The Postcolonial Middle Ages*, edited by Jeffrey Jerome Cohen, 209–28. Basingstoke: Macmillan, 2000.
Rollo, David. *Kiss My Relics: Hermaphroditic Fictions of the Middle Ages*. Chicago: University of Chicago Press, 2011.
Rowland, Beryl. "Bishop Bradwardine, the Artificial Memory, and the *House of Fame*." In *Chaucer at Albany*, edited by Rossell Hope Robbins, 41–62. New York: Burt Franklin, 1975.
Spivak, Gayatri Chakravorty. "Scattered Speculations on the Question of Value." In *In Other Worlds: Essays in Cultural Politics*, 154–75. New York: Routledge, 1988.
Stevens, Martin. "The Structure of *Beowulf*: From Gold-Hoard to Word-Hoard." *Modern Language Quarterly* 39 (1978): 219–38.
Stockton, Will. "Cynicism and the Anal Erotics of Chaucer's Pardoner." *Exemplaria* 20 (2008): 143–64.
Sturges, Robert S. *Chaucer's Pardoner and Gender Theory: Bodies of Discourse*. New York: St. Martin's Press, 2000.
Takada, Yasunari. "*Commune Profit* and Libidinal Dissemination in Chaucer." In *The Body and the Soul in Medieval Literature*, edited by Piero Boitani and Anna Torti, 107–21. Cambridge: D. S. Brewer, 1999.
Wesling, Meg. "Queer Value." *GLQ* 18.1 (2011): 107–25.
Whitney, Elspeth. "What's Wrong with the Pardoner? Complexion Theory, the Phlegmatic Man, and Effeminacy." *The Chaucer Review* 45 (2011): 357–89.
Zarins, Kim. "Intersex and the Pardoner's Body." *Accessus: A Journal of Premodern Literature and New Media* 4 (2018): 1–63.

Haylie Swenson
Chapter 8
Resisting Sex and Species in the *Squire's Tale*

The *Squire's Tale* is an odd duck, or, maybe, an odd falcon. Lesley Kordecki describes it semi-ironically as "an obscure narrative, an anomaly, unfinished, a lesser tale, concerned with the unimportant (a bird), and curtailed before the important (a human story of heroism and incest) can take place."[1] And it *is* a weird tale, a queer tale, a horse-of-a-different-color kind of tale, which has two parts – famously disjointed in both tone and content – each clearly defined by two very different miraculous animals: a brass horse in the first, seemingly masculine, realm, and a talking falcon in the second, feminine, space.

Of course, animal bodies figure heavily in many Middle English romances, and the fourteenth-century romance *Octavian* provides a clear example of what these bodies frequently signify for human identity. Wrongly accused of adultery, the empress of Rome is driven by her husband and mother-in-law into the forest with her twin boys. The wilderness is "full thyke of wylde bestes" and a series of unfortunate events ensues, by the end of which one of the boys has been abducted by a lion, the other by an ape.[2] Although the boy abducted by the lion is the tale's titular hero, the bulk of the narrative's drive is given to his brother. After being rescued by a knight and captured by outlaws, the baby is sold to a Parisian merchant named Clement, who names the child Florent. However, as Jeffrey Cohen notes in his book *Medieval Identity Machines*, "Clement's repeated attempts to indoctrinate Florent into a mercantile identity fail as the boy proves incapable of assigning anything but absolute values to the animals that for his father are the negotiable commodities of the marketplace."[3]

Sent with the family's oxen to pay for his apprenticeship to a butcher, Florent's trajectory is arrested by the "seemly syghte" of a squire selling a falcon,

---

[1] Lesley Kordecki, *Ecofeminist Subjectivities: Chaucer's Talking Birds* (New York: Palgrave Macmillan, 2011), 79.
[2] *Octavian*. In *Four Middle English Romances: Sir Isumbras, Octavian, Sir Eglamour or Artois, Sir Tryamour*, edited by Harriet Hudson (*TEAMS Catalogue*, 2006, https://d.lib.rochester.edu/teams/text/hudson-octavian), line 293.
[3] Jeffrey J. Cohen, *Medieval Identity Machines* (Minneapolis: University of Minnesota Press, 2003), 66.

which Florent promptly trades both oxen to buy.[4] When he discovers the trade, Clement beats Florent severely, betraying an inability to appreciate the intrinsic beauty of the hawk that shocks the boy. Florent chastises his father:

> "Would ye stoned now and beholde
> How feyre he can hys fedurs folde,
> And how lovely they lye,
> Ye wolde pray God with all your mode
> That ye had solde half your gode,
> Soche anodur to bye."[5]

Soon after, Florent is sent back to town with "fowrty pownde," but once again he is deterred from his errand by an animal body. This time, it is a horse, "stronge yn eche were," with a coat as "whyte as any mylke" and a beautiful bridle and harness.[6] As Cohen tells it, when asked the price, the horse's owner

> declares the value of the warhorse to be precisely "thyrty pownde, / eche peny hole and sownde" [730–31], a statement of exaggerated firmness that betrays the expectation of a counteroffer. Whereas Clement immediately bargained down the asking price of the infant Florent from forty pounds to twenty, Florent announces that thirty pounds is too mean a sum for so noble an animal and insists upon giving the man his full forty pounds.[7]

As Cohen goes on to explain, "Forty pounds, by no coincidence, was also repeatedly declared to be the statutory threshold of English knighthood, so that Florent's seemingly impulsive purchase actually enfolds and attenuates the economic, the social, the aristocratic, the animal, and the chivalric."[8] Through his aesthetic appreciation and acquisition of these courtly animals, Florent is able to narrow the gap between his adopted father's middle-class identity and his inevitable return to a chivalric nobility defined in part by its engagement with animal life. Coming into his young life at a pivotal moment, the horse and falcon help usher Florent away from his father's practical and mercantile identity, teaching him instead how to be a different kind of man.

This privileging of warhorse and falcon as uniquely able to signify chivalric masculinity is also evident in the two parts of the *Squire's Tale*, and this, perhaps, is unsurprising. Like *Octavian*, the *Squire's Tale* is a romance, a genre in which, as Susan Crane notes, "a powerful animal's devotion reflects well on the

---

4 *Octavian*, line 654.
5 *Octavian*, lines 694–99.
6 *Octavian*, lines 720, 721.
7 Cohen, *Medieval Identity Machines*, 67.
8 Cohen, *Medieval Identity Machines*, 67.

hero, and the hero's responding devotion also reflects well on him."[9] But, if romance privileges the relationship between man and animal to some extent, it also sets restrictions upon that relationship. For, as Cohen notes, even as Florent's desire for the falcon and the hawk opens up spaces of possibility,

> a second, circumscriptive circuit activates simultaneously, attempting what Deleuze and Guattari would call a reterritorialization, striving to articulate into socially useful form this dangerous and potentially nonhuman flux of identity. The second movement works through equivalence: a warhorse, an aristocratic boy, and a knight are all given the same absolute value (forty pounds), because it is necessary that they all in the end become the same predictable, discernable, deployable thing.[10]

In spite of its ability to imagine alternate possibilities, Cohen argues, chivalry is nevertheless an "apparatus of normalization." But chivalry, like all normalizing mechanisms, "always ultimately falters," and this is evident in the *Squire's Tale*.[11] Like Florent's desires, the *Tale*'s two parts are also dominated by a warhorse and a falcon, but these animals work very differently in the *Squire's Tale* than in *Octavian*. In their uncanny abilities to elude categories, or what Chaucer might call "kynde," the *Tale*'s brass steed and talking falcon resist being reduced to "deployable thing[s]." Instead, they offer opportunities for transformation, creating spaces of possibility for nonnormative sexualities and a reimagining of human relationships with other marvelous bodies. In the sensually evocative first part of the text, a mysterious rider arrives at Genghis Khan's fabulous court. The rider bears four fantastic gifts: a mechanical brass horse that can carry its rider anywhere he wishes within the space of a day; a sword that can both cut any armor and heal any wound it creates; a mirror that identifies both friend and foe; and a ring that grants its bearer the ability to speak to and understand birds. These gifts are all treated as marvels; however, the brass steed dominates the first part of the narrative. But it will not dominate the first part of this essay. Rather, in an attempt to further destabilize the disconnect between masculine horse and feminine bird, I will take these animals out of order, first turning to the falcon's half of the tale before circling back to the strange brass horse. The narrative attempts to fix both the brass horse and talking bird in place. But both creatures ultimately resist this reduction, in the process creating space for both interspecies and intrasexual relationships of care outside of the gendered human norms of chivalric romance.

---

9 Susan Crane, "For the Birds," *Studies in the Age of Chaucer* 29 (2007): 21–41 at 24.
10 Cohen, *Medieval Identity Machines*, 67.
11 Cohen, *Medieval Identity Machines*, 71.

"Hir Hauke Kepyng"

Mutely receiving her gifts and joining the knight for a dance, the host's daughter, Canacee, barely registers in the *prima pars* of the *Squire's Tale*. As the *pars segunda* begins, however, the story shifts, following Canacee as she goes early to bed to take joy with her "queynte ring":

> For swich a joye she in hir herte took
> Bothe of hir queynte ryng and hire mirour,
> That twenty tyme she changed hir colour;
> And in hire sleep, right for impressioun
> Of hire mirour, she hadde a visioun.[12] (V, ll. 368-72)

This description of Canacee in bed transitions the reader from the serious, mechanical space of the first part of the story to the dream-like, organic space of the second; the tale switches from robots to rings, from horses to falcons.

For Kordecki, the falcon has a "very different" effect on the text from the brass horse; the horse is "a symbol of manipulated animality" and serves to emphasize the text's reliance on "masculine subjectivity."[13] By contrast, the falcon "breaks into the set vision, draws out the heroine instead of the hero, and moves the narrative into far more exotic and dangerous sensibilities."[14] Consequently, the obscene (possibly masturbatory?) pun on Canacee's "queynte ring" is important, establishing from the get-go the significance of both biological and cultural sex to Canacee's connection to the falcon. That is, it's important that Canacee's ability to talk to the falcon be tied to both her ring and her *ring*; it matters that her tale is grounded in the genre-specific requirements for cisgendered heterosexuality, and it matters because of the way Canacee and her falcon will slyly exceed those limitations. Canacee's relationship with the hawk, I argue, triangulates hetero- and homonormative desires, alongside species difference, toward a queer intersubjectivity that includes – indeed, depends on – animals. This alternative to bounded human selfhood, furthermore, reflects backward to expand the possibilities of both parts of the tale.

Birdlike, Canacee arises early the morning after the party in order "to pleye and walke on foote" with her magical ring (V, ll. 390–91). And it isn't long before she's able to try it out, as very soon she spies a peregrine falcon crying in a tree:

---

[12] All citations from Chaucer are taken from *The Riverside Chaucer*, ed. Larry D. Benson, 3rd edition (Boston: Houghton Mifflin, 1987).
[13] Kordecki, *Ecofeminist Subjectivities*, 79.
[14] Kordecki, *Ecofeminist Subjectivities*, 287.

Chapter 8 Resisting Sex and Species in the *Squire's Tale* — 185

> Amydde a tree, for drye as whit as chalk,
> As Canacee was pleyyng in hir walk,
> Ther sat a facoun over hire heed ful hye,
> That with a pitous voys so gan to crye
> That all the wode resouned of hire cry. (V, ll. 409–13)

But this is no ordinary falcon. From the beginning, the falcon is presented in terms both avian and human. As Crane argues,

> In *The Squire's Tale*, Chaucer draws on the genre of romance as a way into thinking about the cultural place of falcons. He presents the peregrine falcon of this tale as richly symbolic, but also as a living bird, raising the issue of species difference and the question of how to respond to this difference – what Chaucer would call difference of "kynde."[15]

When Canacee first spies her, the falcon is performing violence upon herself that evokes the frantic movements of a bird stuck in a cage: "Ybeten hadde she hirself so pitously/ With both hire wynges til the rede blood/ Ran endelong the tree ther-as she stood" (V, ll. 414–16). As Kordecki points out, "Birds, of course, do self-mutilate in moments of distress by tearing out their feathers. The cause is often related to encaging them, but molting in the wild can also become a bloody experience. The story works common happenings of actual creatures into the fabric of romance."[16] This first description of the bird is thus unmistakably avian; but then, of course, life for people with vaginas is also, often, a "bloody experience."

The particularly avian nature of this violence is further undercut by the distinction the narrator immediately draws between the falcon and other creatures:

> And evere in oon she cryde alwey and shrighte,
> And with hir beek she hirselven so she prighte
> That ther nes tygre, ne noon so crueel beest
> That dwelleth outher in wode or in forest,
> That nolde han wept, if that he wepe koude,
> For sorwe of hire, she shrighte alwey so loude. (V, ll. 417–22)

The falcon's cries are so hideous, the narrator suggests, that even otherwise insensible beasts would be moved by her to weep if they could. The falcon is already indicating how complicated species division will be in this tale. Although the violence that she does to herself is described in unmistakably avian (and therefore animal) terms, the falcon is simultaneously positioned as the most sensitive of creatures, sensitive enough that she is even able to engender sensitivity in other

---

15 Crane, "For the Birds," 23.
16 Kordecki, *Ecofeminist Subjectivities*, 95.

creatures. As Crane has noted, such sensitivity and exceptionality can be understood as directly related to the falcon's position as a courtly animal, which means it is therefore necessarily already noble. This kind of "totemic thought explains lineal and social distinctions among humans by reference to species distinctions. The evident difference between sparrows and falcons is recruited to make the difference between peasants and princes look natural."[17] The falcon, by being falcon, is thus also very much a human symbol, more inherently sensitive than other creatures and able to elevate them to a more symbolic plane.

This nebulous place of the falcon between the human and animal realms is further emphasized by the narrator's description of her:

> For ther nas nevere yet no man on lyve,
> If that I koude a faucon wel discryve,
> That herde of swich another of fairnesses,
> As wel of plumage as of gentillesse
> Of shap, of al that might yrekened be. (V, ll. 423–27)

This use of the trope of *occupatio* – "If that I *koude* a faucon wel discryve" – echoes the Squire's first description of Canacee, "for to telle yow al hir beautee,/ It lyth nat in my tongue,/ n'yn my konnyng" (V, ll. 34–36). Indeed, the falcon merits a longer description than Canacee, which is also in keeping with the more eloquent, less hesitant articulation of the second part of the tale. In thus framing both Canacee and the falcon in similarly hyperbolic terms, the *Tale* situates them both within their genre. However, this fixation within genre is not necessarily only a limiting thing, for, as Crane explains, "Closer to romance's sensibilities than official science and theology were pervasive lay convictions about animals' similarities to humans."[18]

The falcon's slippage between human and bird only intensifies as the narrative goes on, to the point that some critics have even suggested that the bird must actually be a transformed human princess, the "true" story of whom is lost in the aborted third part.[19] While I want to resist the impulse to make the falcon's story overtly human,[20] I agree that she is by no means entirely avian. We see this even before the bird's first speech, which we are told she speaks

---

17 Crane, "For the Birds," 28.
18 Crane, "For the Birds," 25.
19 Crane, "For the Birds," 26.
20 Susan Crane's dismissal of this point is, I think, particularly eloquent, and deserves to be quoted in full: "This view is neither sustainable nor refutable, given the tale's irresolution; but whether the formel is or is not *also* a human hardly makes her 'kynde' less problematic. Indeed, it redoubles the species question, by taking her to be not only different from Canacee as bird from woman, but divided within herself as woman from bird. Most evidently, she's not

in her "haukes ledene" (V, l. 478). That word *ledene* is important for, as the *Middle English Dictionary* notes, it means not only language and birdsong but also the undifferentiated cry of an animal.[21] In the tale that follows, the falcon vacillates between describing herself and her tercelet lover in terms both avian and human. She describes her childhood in deeply romantic terms: she is "fostred in a roche of marbul gray," and does not know adversity until she meets the tercelet that becomes her lover (V, ll. 500, 503). She describes herself as a "womman" (V, l. 559) and relates a conversation with the tercelet that is deeply human, not only in its adherence to romance narrative but also in her multiple allusions to figures of speech and classical sources. Lest the reader could forget that she is a bird, however, this is immediately undercut by her pointed acknowledgement that once her conversation with the tercelet is over, "forth he fleeth" (V, l. 605).

It is worth pausing for a moment on the tercelet here. For he, too, is described in romantic and often anthropomorphizing terms by the falcon. Not only does she use markedly human terms to articulate his body – he falls "on his knees with so devout humblesse," she takes "hym by the hond" (V, ll. 544, 596), – but she also attributes literariness to him:

> Whan it cam hym to purpos for to reste,
> I trowe he hadde thilke text in mynde,
> That "alle thyng, repeirynge to his kynde,
> Gladeth hymself;" thus seyn men, as I gesse. (V, ll. 606–9)

In her vividly descriptive reading of this passage, Kordecki describes how "the tercelet's 'text' conjures a convoluted image of a speechless creature who perches with a little bird-size volume at his side."[22] That "speechless" is crucial; unlike the female falcon, and in spite of the human qualities attributed to him, the tercelet's birdiness is preserved by his lack of speech. This avian quality of the tercelet, as well as the humanistic qualities of the falcon, is perhaps most evident in her poetic injunction of the cage:

> Men loveth of proper kynde newefangelnesse,
> As briddes doon that men in cages fede.

---

simply human within, and animal without, since her heart belongs to a tercel, a male falcon, along with her feathers. The question of animal difference could only be dismissed by declaring every bird in the tale to be no more and no less than human" ("For the Birds," 26).

21 "Ledene," *Middle English Dictionary*. The Regents of The University of Michigan, 2001. https://quod.lib.umich.edu/m/middle-english-dictionary/dictionary/MED24958.
22 Kordecki, *Ecofeminist Subjectivities*, 97.

> For though thy nyght and day take of hem hede,
> And strawe hir cage faire and soft as silk,
> And yeve hem sugre, hony, breed and milk,
> Yet right anon as that his dore is uppe
> He with his feet wol spurn adoun his cuppe,
> And to the wode he wole and wormes ete. (V, ll. 610–17)

By unselfconsciously comparing her tercelet lover to a bird, it is almost as though the falcon forgets that she, herself, is a bird. Indeed, as Susan Crane has noted, this exemplum is the pinnacle of the falcon's species disorientations: "she is the example for other creatures as the whipped dog is an example of taming lions; her lover is a tiger but one with knees to fall on in fake humility; he is a snake hidden under flowers who longs to eat worms like a captured songbird."[23] These "queasily shifting descriptions" continue the work of category dissolution that began with the brass steed in the *Tale*'s first part.[24] By the end of her long speech the falcon's unique "kynde" seems nearly impossible to determine. And this, of course, is in some ways the point: the falcon's vacillation between human and bird is part of the joke, perhaps even more so than Chaucer – and certainly more so than the Squire – intends. Canacee and the falcon, human woman and womanly bird, are both the same and other in the text's romantic frame, and this is important for how we read the queer space of the mews.

Once the falcon has finished her tale, Canacee bears her safely home "in hir lappe,/ and softely in plastres gan hire wrappe,/ Ther as she with hire beek hadde hurt hirselve" (V, ll. 635–37). Over the course of a full day, Canacee gathers herbs to heal the falcon and busily prepares a home for her within her own room:

> Fro day to nyght
> She dooth hire bisynesse and al hire myght,
> And by hire beddes heed she made a mewe
> And covered it with veluettes blewe,
> In signe of trouthe that is in wommen sene.
> And al withoute, the mewe is peynted grene,
> In which were peynted alle thise false fowles,
> As ben thise tidyves, tercelettes, and owles;
> Right for despit were peynted hem bisyde,
> Pyes, on hem for to crie and chyde. (V, ll. 641–50)

---

23 Crane, "For the Birds," 33.
24 Crane, "For the Birds," 33.

Critics differ on how they understand this strange domestic space. Many scholars see the falcon's home as a reductive form of pet-keeping; as Kordecki notes, "the velvet cage is still a cage, positioned a mere twenty lines after the caged bird gloss, a reminder that the falcon loses."[25] Crane imagines a different future for the falcon and Canacee, and much of this difference is based on Crane's careful reading of the difference between Canacee's "mewes" and the cage of the exemplum:

> The cage had a "dore" (V.615), but this structure called a mews may not have one, if it resembles a conventional mews with many openings or open sides to imitate the breezy nesting conditions of hawks in the wild. This unclarity around whether Canacee's "mewe" has a door evokes Derrida's conundrum that hospitality requires and repudiates a door. . . . Calling Canacee's little structure a "mews" elides the uncomfortable question of the door, as if to imagine that the falcon can be taken in without reservation.[26]

For Crane, the space that Canacee creates in her bedchamber is not a cage but an open mews, "a wonderfully complex attempt at hosting without taking hostage."[27]

In her bedroom, Canacee creates a categorically and sexually nonnormative, purely feminine space, nonreproductive (although not necessarily asexual). Midas Dekker argues that in spite of the taboos against recognizing them as such, our relationships with animals – and especially pets – have a strong erotic component.[28] The groundwork for this is laid at the very beginning of the falcon's tale, and not only with those puns on Canacee's ring.

As Kordecki points out, "the falcon does not tell her tale until she is comforted in the lap of Canacee, a sexualized iconography akin to the union of the virgin and the unicorn."[29] Just as importantly, by cradling the falcon in "hir lappe," Canacee makes that lap unavailable for other users, cultivating intimacy between a conspecific in sympathy and desire, if not, technically, in biological species. In this way, Canacee and the hawk emphasize sameness over difference, a distant echo of the opening up of the self advocated by a spate of queer critics. Kuzner offers a particularly useful distillation of these proposals:

> In place of the self's structural hardening would be its accession to susceptibility, and in place of the language that constitutes subject positions – that does the work, for good or

---

25 Kordecki, *Ecofeminist Subjectivities*, 97.
26 Crane, "For the Birds," 39.
27 Crane, "For the Birds," 38.
28 See Midas Dekker, *Dearest Pet: On Bestiality*, trans. Paul Vincent (New York: Verso, 1994).
29 Kordecki, *Ecofeminist Subjectivities*, 87.

ill, of interpellation – would be language that disorients and decontextualizes us, speech that is our undoing. We would, similarly, no longer seek to protect or cordon off our bodies from others.[30]

In the human, animal, multilingual, feminine space of the mews, important elements of structural hardening and difference – species difference, heterosexuality – have melted away, replaced by an open-ended attempt at intimacy, care, and coming together.

Significantly, this openness persists in spite of the Squire's attempt to move on, to leave the queer for the sake of the chivalric romance. For although the Squire promises a heteronormative (or, at least, mostly heteronormative – heteronormatish), "properly" romantic conclusion to his tale, he is interrupted by the Franklin before he can tell it. This allows the feminine space created by Canacee and the falcon to linger on. The Franklin's interruption serves to shut down the possibility of incest, but leaves open a different kind of nonnormative sexuality. And through this interruption, the Squire's transitional line proves unintentionally prophetic: "Thus lete I Canacee hir hauk kepyng" (V, l. 651). In spite of the Squire's desire to move on to "aventures and . . . batailles" (V, l. 659), Canacee and her hawk are, ultimately, left alone in their mews, the last vivid image of the text.

"Bitwixe us two"

Here, I'll also leave the mews in order to return to the brass horse. Keeping Canacee in mind, it becomes more evident that the first part of the *Squire's Tale* displays the same kind of boundary-erasing triangulation of sex, species, and gender as the second. Just as Canacee and the falcon bond over a third party (the tercelet) in a pleasurable mash-up of species and desire, the brass horse draws the knight and Cambyuskan into a surprisingly intimate, even erotic, exchange of masculine knowledge.

The first thing the reader is told about the mysterious knight regards his proximity to the horse: "In at the halle dore al sodeynly/ Ther cam a knyght upon a steede of bras" (V, ll. 80–82). This should not be surprising; as Cohen notes, "Because of its corporeal adaptability and consequent long history of having been bred for a proliferation of specialized functions, all the people of

---

[30] James Kuzner, "Unbuilding the City: *Coriolanus* and the Birth of Republican Rome," *Shakespeare Quarterly* 58.2 (2007): 174–99 at 184. Kuzner is particularly referencing Agamben, Bersani, Butler, and Nancy.

medieval Europe, regardless of social class, had a close relationship to the horse. Yet the animal functioned as an especially revered body for knights."[31] The brass horse merits the longest initial description of any of the gifts. Indeed, according to Scott Lightsey's count, it dominates the entirety of the *Tale*'s first part, ultimately taking up over a third of those 346 lines.[32]

Part of this fascination, surely, comes from the horse's ability to symbolize man's dominion over the animal: "The horse, a symbol of manipulated animality, in its silent servility remains a standard detail in masculine magic and masculine subjectivity."[33] Karl Steel similarly argues that "love for horses, like that for any animal, finally gives way to human self-love."[34]

It is certainly possible to read this subjugation in the "Squire's Tale," especially considering the tale's subtle, but significant, martial context, which is evident in the way the Squire begins: "At Sarray, in the land of Tartarye,/ There dwelte a king that werreyed Russye,/ Thurgh which ther dyde many a doughty man" (V, ll. 9–11). There are other signs of war, too; the horse is part of a martial arsenal, other pieces of which include the mirror, the sword, and the mysterious knight himself. This, along with the particular attention to the loss of "many a doughty man," suggests an under-recognized attention in the tale to the costs of war. The brass horse is intended to reduce those costs:

> This steede of bras, that esily and weel
> Kan in the space of o day natureel –
> This is to seyn, in foure and twenty houres –
> Wher-so yow lyst, in droghte or elles shoures,
> Beren youre body into every place
> To which youre herte wilneth for to pace,
> Withouten wem of yow, thurgh foul or fair,
> Or, if yow lyst to fleen as hye in the air
> As dooth an egle whan hym list to soore,
> This same steede shal bere yow evere moore,
> Withouten harm, til ye be ther yow leste,
> Though that ye slepen on his bak or reste,
> And turne ayeyn with writhyng of a pyn. (V, ll. 115–27)

---

31 Cohen, *Medieval Identity Machines*, 46.
32 Scott Lightsey, *Manmade Marvels in Medieval Culture and Literature* (New York: Palgrave Macmillan, 2007), 75.
33 Kordecki, *Ecofeminist Subjectivities*, 79.
34 Karl Steel, *How To Make A Human: Animals and Violence in the Middle Ages* (Columbus: Ohio State University Press, 2011), 224.

The horse's supernatural abilities make it the perfect body of war. Unlike a horse of flesh and blood, the brass horse is tireless and seemingly invincible – a shield made animal. It is a perfect object. Like Canacee and her falcon, then, the horse initially reads as a prop, particularly crafted to fit a romantic story. But, also like the falcon and Canacee, the magically transportive horse is *too* well crafted: en route to the tale's intended end, it swerves, evading the Squire's narrative control. Indeed, it takes the narrative itself with it.

This sense of narrative instability is first evident in this same passage. Cohen argues that "the horse's intimacy to the human involves more than the utilitarian functions of labor and transportation," and that is especially true of *this* horse.[35] The brass horse offers almost unthinkable pleasures to its rider, pleasures in excess of its role as a weapon and military tool. The steed not only has the ability to translate its rider from one terrestrial space to another, but it can literally take its rider to an entirely different plane. The rider's desire combines with the horse's ability to precipitate new becomings, in this case, a becoming-eagle. In this ability to engender marvelous transformations, the horse-as-steed reconfigures and decomposes the understood limits of the human body.

Perhaps because of this excess, the horse exerts a gravitational pull on the story, frequently disrupting the narrative. For instance, once the knight has described all his gifts, the Squire attempts to turn his narrative energy back to the party. Canacee is given her ring, the sword and the mirror are "born anon into the heighe tour," and the horse is ridden to the courtyard where he stands, "stille as any stoon" (V, ll. 176, 171). But the Squire's attempts to return to the party are fruitless, as the reader's attention is drawn back immediately to the horse in the courtyard, around which a crowd quickly develops:

> Greet was the prees that swarmeth to and fro
> To gauren on this hors that stondeth so
> For it so heigh was, and so brood and long,
> So wel proporcioned for to been strong,
> Right as it were a stede of Lumbardye;
> Therwith so horsly, and so quyk of ye,
> As it a gentle Poilleys courser were.
> For certes, fro his tayl unto his ere
> Nature ne art ne koude hym nat amende
> In no degree, as al the people wende. (V, ll. 189–98)

The repetition of the word "so" aurally signifies the "broken record" affect of this passage, as the horse's beauty has transfixed the Squire just as firmly as it

---

35 Cohen, *Medieval Identity Machines*, 46.

transfixes the courtiers.[36] This is also evident in an important pronoun shift within the passage: the horse begins as an "it" and ends as a "he." The pleasure and wonder of the horse have made it that much more alive. Like the bird, its, or rather *his*, status is constantly shifting.

Critics have argued that the knight's description of the mechanisms controlling this mechanical animal undercut its magic somewhat. For example, Lightsey argues that the "late fourteenth century presents a fascinating cultural tipping point when marvels manufactured by men . . . were explicitly used for political and ideological purposes, participating in the establishment of a courtly culture whose politics of display was enhanced by manmade marvels."[37] These marvels (the greatest of which were "the elaborate clockworks and animated creatures or *automata*, mechanical imitations of life") were, according to Lightsey, creatures for the court, "employed for the purpose of enhancing political capital or religious awe."[38]

This use of marvels as political tools could be seen as normalizing; indeed, Kordecki explicitly contrasts the feminine, magical space of the tale's second part with the "patriarchal indication of progress" that she reads as the result of the first part.[39] Similarly, Lightsey suggests that the mechanical quality of the brass horse makes it less marvelous, for "once the cause is understood, the marvel ceases to be marvelous in the traditional sense."[40] I disagree.

Although the knight explains the horse's "governaunce," explaining how to make it work is a different thing from explaining how it works. The latter knowledge remains a secret, as the knight's frequent deferrals make clear:

> Sire, ther is namoore to seyne,
> But, whan you list to ryden anywhere,
> Ye mooten trille a pyn, stant in his ere,
> Which I shall yow telle bitwixt us two . . .
> Or, if yow liste bidde hym thennes goon,
> Trille this pyn, and he wol vanysshe anoon . . .
> And come agayn, be it by day or nyght,
> Whan that yow list to clepen hym ageyn
> In swich a gyse as I shal to yow seyn
> Bitwixe yow and me, and that ful soone. (V, ll. 314–17, 327–33)

---

36 I am grateful to Jonathan Hsy for drawing my attention to this aural repetition.
37 Lightsey, *Manmade Marvels*, 10.
38 Lightsey, *Manmade Marvels*, 10.
39 Kordecki, *Ecofeminist Subjectivities*, 79.
40 Lightsey, *Manmade Marvels*, 80.

The effect of this secrecy is to make the horse more mysterious, not less. Although the knight explains that the horse is made to work through a complex system of pins in its ear, the reader is excluded from a full understanding – or even a clear representation – of this mechanism. Moreover, the knight's explanation of the usage of the horse seems insufficient: "This hors anoon bigan to trippe and daunce,/ Whan that this knyght leyde hand upon his reyne" (V, ll. 312–13). If the knight's simple action of laying a hand upon the horse's rein (as opposed to twirling a complicated series of pins) can cause him to "trippe and daunce," it would seem that the brass steed retains at least some of its secrets. The closest we get to a full vision of the working of this marvelous creature is at the very end of the *prima pars*, when the Squire notes only that "The hors vanysshed, I noot in what manere/ Out of hir sighte; ye gete namoore of me" (V, ll. 342–43). Even after the knight's long description of the workings of the horse, the Squire – and, by extension, the reader – can only express wonder at the manmade marvel. This is significant, as the knight's reticence to share the workings of the horse with the general assembly clears the ground for the queer potential of horse, knight, and king.

In "Chevalerie," Cohen writes extensively about the knight–horse relationship and the "possible bodies" that are engendered through it. This relationship was an intimate one by necessity, "for it is not as if the horse is a passive vehicle and the knight its all-controlling driver."[41] Rather, all horses are objects of desire and privileged knowledge, complex creatures requiring intimate and embodied understanding and technique passed between men.

This sense of animal-mediated intimacy is especially emphasized in the *Squire's Tale*, as the knight frequently promises to let the king in on the brass horse's secrets at another time, presumably when they can be alone. Unlike in the second half of the tale, however, we never get to see the fulfillment of this promised intimate exchange of secrets. The king and knight never build their stable, as it were. On the other hand, their conversation points to the very real intimacies of coming to know and learning to manage flesh-and-blood horses, intimacies of which Chaucer and his readers would have been well aware. In this way, the queerly interspecies, homoerotic possibilities of the text radiate outward beyond its magical and romantic bounds.

A question posed by Cohen has helped to animate this project. He asks: "Why should the queer stop at the boundaries of the human? Why can't it, in the Middle Ages, include the horses, hawks, greyhounds that are integral to

---

41 Cohen, *Medieval Identity Machines*, 49.

knightly and aristocratic identity?"[42] In this essay, I have argued that not only *should* medieval queerness engage with nonhuman species, but also that it is, in many ways, *dependent* on nonhuman animals. In their ability to engender different relationalities than those foregrounded by chivalric romance, the brass steed and the talking falcon reconfigure the human, opening up spaces of possibility for homoerotic and heterospecies relationships of care. In their uncanny abilities to resist compartmentalization, the tale's nonhuman creatures facilitate nonnormative sexualities and a reimagining of human relationships with other marvelous bodies.

Bibliography

Chaucer, Geoffrey. *The Riverside Chaucer*. 3rd edition. Edited by Larry D. Benson. Boston: Houghton Mifflin, 1987.
Cohen, Jeffrey J. *Medieval Identity Machines*. Minneapolis: University of Minnesota Press, 2003.
Crane, Susan. "For the Birds." *Studies in the Age of Chaucer* 29 (2007): 21–41.
Dekker, Midas. *Dearest Pet: On Bestiality*. Translated by Paul Vincent. New York: Verso, 1994.
Kordecki, Lesley. *Ecofeminist Subjectivities: Chaucer's Talking Birds*. New York: Palgrave Macmillan, 2011.
Kuzner, James. "Unbuilding the City: *Coriolanus* and the Birth of Republican Rome." *Shakespeare Quarterly* 58.2 (2007): 174–99.
"Ledene." *Middle English Dictionary*. The Regents of The University of Michigan, 2001, https://quod.lib.umich.edu/m/middle-english-dictionary/dictionary/MED24958.
Lightsey, Scott. *Manmade Marvels in Medieval Culture and Literature*. New York: Palgrave Macmillan, 2007.
Octavian. In *Four Middle English Romances: Sir Isumbras, Octavian, Sir Eglamour or Artois, Sir Tryamour*. Edited by Harriet Hudson. TEAMS Catalogue, 2006, https://d.lib.rochester.edu/teams/text/hudson-octavian
Steel, Karl. *How To Make A Human: Animals and Violence in the Middle Ages*. Columbus: Ohio State University Press, 2011.

---

[42] Cohen, *Medieval Identity Machines*, 71.

Epilogue: Opening Up Queerness

Michelle M. Sauer

Chapter 9
Queer Time and Lesbian Temporality in Medieval Women's Encounters with the Side Wound

> Rock of Ages, cleft for me,
> let me hide myself in thee;
> let the water and the blood,
> from thy wounded side which flowed,
> be of sin the double cure;
> save from wrath and make me pure.[1]
>
> Lord, hide my soul securely,
> Deep in Thy wounded side,
> From every danger shield me
> And to Thy glory guide[2]

The above two hymns from the eighteenth century both hail from the Protestant tradition – the first is Methodist while the second is Lutheran. Each, in turn, plays off the pre-Reformation interpretation of Christ's side wound as, among other things, shelter from the storm, that is, safety from the troubles of earthly existence. Though not overtly eroticized, in these hymns the side wound evokes images of birth and the vagina by mention of protection, emergence, blood, and water, implying rebirth when reemerging from the shelter and nurturing love when sheltered within it. In fact, despite the very Protestant origins of these works, they strongly recall medieval, Pre-Reformation, texts. In one such work, the late medieval *Stimulus Amoris*, for example, the author determines that he will enter into Christ's side wound and dwell there, progressively moving backward from Passion to Nativity. He drinks from Christ's side, imbibing blood and

---

[1] "Rock of Ages," Augustus M. Toplady, 1776. Toplady supposedly wrote this while he sheltered himself during a storm amidst the rocks of Cheddar Gorge in England, and the experience called to mind the metaphorical storm in his soul.
[2] "Hymn 210.4," Valerius Herberger.

Note: My thanks to the editors for careful reading as well as to the various audiences who have heard pieces of this project over several years, beginning with a conference paper at Kalamazoo in 2010.

fluids, feeling along the edges of the wound, always reaching deeper into Christ's intestines, eventually entering and living inside, awaiting someday the advent of "childbirth," when Jesus expels him, only to restart the process.[3] The speaker of the *Stimulus* clearly desires both refuge and nurturing, and craves creating a home within Christ's very body, living off the fluids provided and crafting a "home-like" space.

The later, Protestant, devotion to the side wound stretched across denominations and countries, being, perhaps, most explicit within the Moravian traditions in the eastern United States just prior to and immediately after the Revolutionary War. As Peter Vogt notes, "references to the side wound can be found in a number of areas within the life of Moravian communities. Most prominent is the area of congregational singing. Moravian hymnody, especially from the 1740s, is full of allusions to the side wound."[4] This is all likely part of the pietist movement, but also points to a resurgence of a rich religious material culture, one that had been suppressed in Protestant sects since the Reformation. The Moravians in particular seized upon this trend. Numerous prayer cards bearing images of the side wound proliferated, and many of these little cards also contain striking water colors depicting the side wound in the form of female genitalia, and/or showing daily activities – eating, sleeping, going for a walk, and so on – *inside* the "womb-like" wound.[5] In writing, the wounds were described in sensual terms, including "worthy, beloved, miraculous, powerful, secret, clear, sparkling, holy, purple, juicy, close, long-suffering, dainty, warm, soft, hot, and eternal," and the Litany of the Wounds assumed a central place in devotions. The followers were described generally as "little bees – ones who crawl inside the Side Hole."[6] The images, as representations of the side wound itself, were to be revered by touching, stroking, and kissing, accompanied by short ecstatic expressions, such as: "Deep inside! Deep inside! Deep inside the little side!" (Tief nein! Tief nein! Tief nein ins Seitlein!). The side wound was a site of birth and rebirth, a safety net,

---

[3] See A. C. Peltier, *Sancti Bonaventurae: Opera Omnia* (Paris: Ludovicus Vives, 1868),, xii, pp. 631–703. Several others discuss the *Stimulus*. See Flora Lewis, "The Wound in Christ's Side and the Instruments of the Passion: Gendered Experience and the Response," in *Women and the Book*, ed. Lesley Smith and Jane Taylor (Toronto: University of Toronto Press, 1997), 204–29; Sara Beckwith, *Christ's Body: Identity, Culture, and Society in Late Medieval Writings* (New York: Routledge, 1993), esp. 58–60.

[4] Peter Vogt, "'Honor to the Side': The Adoration of the Side Wound of Jesus in Eighteenth-Century Moravian Piety," *Journal of Moravian History* 7 (2009): 83–106 at 86.

[5] Aaron Spencer Fogleman, *Jesus Is Female: Moravians and Radical Religion in Early America* (Philadelphia: University of Pennsylvania Press, 2008), 80.

[6] Peter Williams, *Popular Religion in America: Symbolic Change and the Modernization Process in Historical Perspective* (Champaign: University of Illinois Press, 1989), 73.

and a shelter upon death. Both domestic and sacred, both spiritual and sexual, the period 1743–1749 saw an especially fervent devotion to the wound itself, not just the entirety of Jesus's sacred body.[7] And although they may not have explicitly noted the connection to earlier works, it seems likely that the originators might have had contact with the *Stimulus* or other such works – the *Stimulus* itself was very widespread. Its original thirteenth-century text was expanded in the fourteenth century, and was a common and popular addition (in whole and in part) to private devotional materials and books of hours.

I start this essay with these observations about eighteenth-century Protestant revivalism of a medieval devotion as a tangible way of demonstrating queer temporality. In her book *Time Binds: Queer Temporalities, Queer Histories*, Elizabeth Freeman weaves together affect studies, critical historiography, and politics to nuance our understanding of queer time, an alternate formation of time with the power to disrupt. She suggests that interesting things happen when we "rub up against the past."[8] For Freeman, queer time works on bodies; indeed, she is most interested in what happens when bodies meet across time, corporeal entanglements across past and present, non-sequential interactions that articulate queerness. Religious texts, with their recurrent themes, their devoted followers who reclaim the past, repeat rituals, and revisit practices, are particularly fertile ground for such queer explorations. And, in examining the touch of, to, and with Christ's body, as well as the handling of (historical) material objects, we can articulate more clearly a queer encounter. Thus, these eighteenth-century versions of devotion to Christ's side wound demonstrate a part of the queer continuum that lives on in our interpretations of medieval texts as well as in the continued fascination with artists and congregants alike with the side wound. Further, to use Heather Love's phrase, medieval people, especially women, often engaged in "feel[ing] backward" – a nonnormative way of remembering that differs from traditional memory in its preoccupation with loss and failure and in its concern with mobilizing that loss and failure for strategic purposes.[9] In short, feeling backward allows a subject to transform her abject marginalization into opportunity. Building on these notions of queer time, I am seeking the intersection of a feminized Christ, and more especially the lesbian past and present within the

---

7 See especially Vogt's "'Honor to the Side,'" but also Craig D. Atwood, "Little Side Holes: Moravian Devotional Cards of the Mid-Eighteenth Century," *Journal of Moravian History* 6 (2009): 61–75.

8 Elizabeth Freeman, *Time Binds: Queer Temporalities, Queer Histories* (Durham: Duke University Press, 2010), xii.

9 See Heather Love, *Feeling Backward: Loss and the Politics of Queer History* (Cambridge: Harvard University Press, 2007).

literature and architecture of anchoritism and the literature of mysticism. By remembering such, I hope to contribute to the growing awareness of a lesbian premodern in particular, with a broader sense of a queer sense of time and space otherwise.

The cult of the Side Wound was widespread throughout the early Church, but was superseded by devotion to the Sacred Heart in the thirteenth century. Nonetheless, both styles of devotion remained popular throughout the Middle Ages, and continue forward today. The biblical passage supporting devotion to the side wound is John 19:33–34, "But when they came to Jesus and found that he was already dead, they did not break his legs. Instead, one of the soldiers pierced Jesus's side with a spear, bringing a sudden flow of blood and water." In the Vulgate, these verses use the word "aperuit," or "opened," rather than any variant of pierced, struck, stabbed, or even wounded. In this way, the foundation for later exegetical readings of the side wound as the gate of life was laid. These early devotions were also more particular in locating the wound in Christ's side, not necessarily in his heart. Only from the twelfth century forward was the text understood to mean that Christ's heart was pierced. As George Hardin Brown notes, "What had been considered a wound that opened the interior of Christ's body so that fountains of sacramental grace welled up from it became a wound in his heart so that that organ as a source of life and love poured forth its vital power on man and woman."[10]

After the eleventh century, Christ's heart gradually became the focus of union between Savior and devotee. At the same time, the "long-standing devotion to the wounds was clearly shifting to the concrete and the visual, and visions, images, and bodies all demonstrate this desire to *see* Christ's wounds."[11] Gradually, the appearance of Christ as wounded (and often suffering) became more prominent in art and literature than Christ with an untouched body. Many guided meditations led believers through the Passion. And mystics, whose visions usually centered on meeting Christ or Mary in some capacity, reported a wounded body of God. Furthermore, St. Francis of Assisi (d. 1226) received his stigmata during an extended meditation ushered in by an increase in devotions specifically to the Five Wounds.[12] Moreover, Rosalynn Voaden has

---

10 George Hardin Brown, "From the Wound in Christ's Side to the Wound in His Heart: Progression from Male Exegesis to Female Mysticism," in *Poetry, Place, and Gender: Studies in Medieval Culture in Honor of Helen Damico*, ed. Catherine E. Karkov (Kalamazoo: Medieval Institute Publications, 2009), 253.
11 Lewis, "The Wound in Christ's Side," 209.
12 Francis strove to keep his wounds secret during his own lifetime, a desire that was neither truly successful nor unsuccessful. One attempt to penetrate his defenses, for instance, occurred

shown that the "discourse of the Sacred Heart . . . employs images drawn from biological *female* characteristics – blood, flowing, opening, and enclosure."[13] Thus, devotion to the Sacred Heart also became an especially female devotion. In fact, the shift in emphasis from side wound to Sacred Heart is often attributed to the nuns of Helfta, particularly Gertrude the Great (January 6, 1256–ca. 1302) and Mechtilde (ca. 1240–1298). Both experienced visions involving the wound. In Gertrude's, she lay her head near the opening, symbolized by a golden tube, and could hear Christ's heartbeat. This demonstrates the connection between holy heart and holy wound, a connection built upon by Mechtilde and countless others afterher, and while not all followers were female, the imagery remained so.

The wounded Christ is an especially important part of anchoritic literature, as I have argued elsewhere. Christ's wounds allow, among other things, for mimetic overlapping, for bodily identification, and for purification of the anchoress who seeks pure contemplative merger with her spouse.[14] St. Augustine himself says contemplation of the Savior only truly happens through the "imagination" of the crucifed Jesus in one's own heart.[15] There his porous, wounded body became one with the body of the faithful, blood mingling with blood. This becomes a dominant theme in mystic literature. Frank Graziano writes,

> In this . . . image, many of mysticism's predominant themes converge. The wound in Christ's side is a refuge; a nuptial bedchamber; a womb from which one is reborn into eternal life; a breast that nourishes, infuses the soul with grace, and provides erotic pleasure; a pair of lips that kisses; a flower; a warehouse that stores mystical paraphernalia . . . a well of living waters; a showering fountain of blood that washes away sin; an attribute of the New Adam; and a symbol of Christ's final contribution to a vicarious sacrifice by quotas.[16]

---

when a young friar glimpsed Francis while he was changing robes, and then walked over and touched his side wound, measuring it. However, the side wound was the most controversial point of Francis's holy gift. See Rosalind B. Brooke, *The Image of St. Francis: Responses to Sainthood in the Thirteenth Century* (Cambridge: Cambridge University Press, 2006), esp. 166. Still, his hagiographers included rather lurid descriptions of it, including emphasizing that the wound dripped blood and seeped fluids.

13 Rosalynn Voaden, "All Girls Together: Community, Gender, and Vision at Helfta," in *Medieval Women in their Communities*, ed. Diane Watt (Cardiff: University of Wales Press, 1997), 74.
14 See, for example, Michelle M. Sauer, "'Þe blod þ[at] bohte': The *Wooing* Group Christ as Pierced, Pricked, and Penetrated Body," in *'May your wounds heal the wounds of my soul': The Milieu and Context of the Wohunge Group*, ed. Susannah Mary Chewning (Cardiff: University of Wales Press, 2009), 123–47.
15 Augustine, *De sancta virginitate*, PL 40 (1887), 428 (I:53).
16 Frank Graziano, *The Wounds of Love: The Mystical Marriage of Rose of Lima* (Oxford: Oxford University Press, 2004), 205. Graziano suggests the term "quotas" for the cultural

Here the multifaceted aspect of the wounded Christ becomes apparent. The side wound is a refuge, a hiding place, and a chamber. It is a suggestive bower – a place of mystical union. It is a divine womb – a place of spiritual rebirth. And, overall, the side wound is depicted in three main ways: it is eroticized, paternalized, or glorified – and sometimes as a combination of these. Catherine of Siena, for example, writes to nuns at San Gaggio and Monte San Savino that she "long[s] to see you hidden and enclosed in the side of Christ Crucified."[17] Here, the side wound offers both the protection of the convent and the nurturing of the soul within such an enclosure. While Catherine's perspective here is primarily salvific, other writers focus on the sensual and the erotic. For instance, a particularly vivid representation of the late medieval anchorite seeking refuge in Christ's side wound is highly suggestive and intensely feminized. Taken from a late fourteenth-century redaction of Aelred's *Rule for a Recluse*, the image is simultaneously comforting, disturbing, and sexualized:

> Crepe into that blessed syde where that blood and water cam forthe, and hyde the ther as a culuer in the stoon, wel likynge the dropes of his blood, til that thy lippes be maad like to a reed scarlet hood.[18]

Here, the wound in Christ's side is described in two distinct ways – as a place of protection and as a place of carnal passion. The protective stone shelter recalls the anchorhold itself, a small stone structure attached to the side of a church that shelters the precious anchoress inside, while still assuring her ready access to her spouse and savior.[19] Similarly, dovecotes were small hive-like structures that housed doves kept for meat and messages, protecting them from the elements and predators.[20] Here, the anchoress is compared to a dove living in stone, but this is a bird who revels in the blood dripping from Christ's

---

process of constructing a saint from multiple narratives, each with its own agenda and conditions. For a fuller explanation of this terminology, see *The Wounds of Love*, 35–36.

17 Letter 62, in *The Letters of Catherine of Siena*, trans. Suzanne Noffke, vol. 1 (Tempe: Arizona Center for Medieval and Renaissance Studies, 2000), 196–97.

18 See *Aelred of Rievaulx's de Institutione Inclusarum: Two English Versions*, ed. John Ayto and Alexandra Barratt, EETS o.s. 287 (Oxford: Oxford University Press, 1984), 22. Based on MS Bodley 423.

19 Tertullian referred to the Church as *columbae domus*, "the house of the dove."

20 Dovecotes were built by wealthy people to supply themselves and their households with a luxurious food, the tender meat of young pigeons, although sometimes doves were also kept as messenger birds. As dovecotes were always associated with a luxurious way of life they came to symbolize high social status – or high social aspirations. In domestication the pigeon-keeper "searched" the dovecote for "squabs," the young birds which were almost fully developed, and wrung their necks. For more information on dovecotes, see John McCann, "An

side, who eagerly laps it up, enjoying every drop, like the author of the *Stimulus* who feeds from blood and fluids at Christ's side. Altar imagery around Western Europe includes doves drinking from the chalice, sharing grapes, and/or pecking at eucharistic bread, demonstrating their continual feeding from the body of Christ.[21] And the comparison of the anchoress to a dove furthers the erotic oral play. According to medieval bestiaries, doves were especially known for sitting in their nests and kissing.[22] The dove-like anchoress therefore anticipates and fulfills her role by kissing and nibbling on the wound. Further eroticizing the scene, besides the fervent licking and sucking, are references to lips. While it is clear that lips in one sense refer to the facial apparatus used to consume the blood, the vaginal shape of Christ's wounds suggests that another set of lips should also be called to mind. Further, that the lips are referred to as a "reed scarlet hood" is distinctly reminiscent of clitoral imagery. If the anchoress is not only hiding within the wound but also drawing from it, licking, kissing, and sucking it, she is also embracing the vaginal opening with her mouth. In short, this scene is generally one of queer divine cunnilingus, with the female anchoress engaging in pleasurable caressing and kissing.

This passionate sucking of blood will be echoed two centuries later in *A Talkyng of the Loue of Gode*, a fifteenth-century text for monks adapted from *The Wooing of Our Lord*, a thirteenth-century anchoritic text written for women (and perhaps by a woman), as well as *An Exceedingly Good Orison to God Almighty*, another thirteenth-century anchoritic text, as well as parts of St. Anselm's *Liber Meditatio et Orationum* and some work of unknown origin, perhaps even of original generation. Although not directly lesbian-like as presented in *A Talkyng*, it is still eroticized and still queer – both in the ecstasy a male reader finds in sucking Christ and in the gender displacement crafted by the adaptation of female-oriented texts for a male audience without wholesale changes. The reader thus performs as female even while embodying male. In this treatise, the speaker directly references sucking from Christ's side:

> Þer wol I cluppen & cussen . . . þer wole I souken of þi syde þat openeþ a ȝeyn me so wyde wiþ outen eny fluttying, þer wol I a bide.

Historical Enquiry into the Design and Use of Dovecotes," *Transactions of the Ancient Monuments Society* 35 (1991): 89–160.

21 See, for example, the eleventh-century Tournai Marble baptismal font in Winchester Cathedral, http://www.winchester-cathedral.org.uk/gallery/tournai-marble-font/.

22 See Isidore of Seville, *Etymologies*, ed. W. J. Lewis, J. A. Beach, and Oliver Berghof (Cambridge: Cambridge University Press, 2006), Book 12, 7:61–62 and Bartholomaeus Anglicus, *De proprietatibus rerum*, ed. M. C. Seymour (Oxford: Clarendon Press, 1975), Book 12.

There I will embrace and kiss you . . . There I, without wavering, will suck from your side, which opens towards me so wide, and there I will stay.[23]

Christ's wound actively invites kissing, caressing, and sucking. In fact, the verb used, "souken," usually means to suck from a breast or udder, to draw milk, or to receive nourishment. However, the third definition includes drawing liquid into the mouth, to drink the blood of Jesus, and to draw in honey or nectar.[24] The blood of Christ is both nourishing and connected to the female breast. Earlier in *A Talkyng*, the speaker calls Jesus his "honey-bird" (dove) and his "nectar," saying, "sweeter are you than honey or milk in the mouth, than mead, meeth, or piment[25] prepared with sweet spices, or any delicious liquor that may be found anywhere."[26] No wonder that later on, the speaker in ecstasy cries,

> My song is the delight of love without a note. I leap upon him swiftly as a greyhound on a deer, quite beside myself, and with a loving manner wrap in my arms the base[27] of the cross. I suck the blood from his feet; that sucking is extremely sweet. I kiss and I embrace, but occasionally stop, as would a man who is mad with love and sick from the pains of love. . . . I embrace and I kiss as if I were mad. I wallow and I suck, I know not how long, and when I am done in, yet still do I lust. Then do I feel that blood in my imagination as if it were bodily warm on my lips, and the flesh of his feet, in front and in behind, so soft, and so sweet to kiss and to embrace.[28]

At first this scene reads like male–male erotic content since the monk embraces and sucks Jesus, another male-bodied individual – and certainly a queer moment no matter what. However, the speaker in *A Talkyng* can be read as a "cross-dressed soul."[29] The text is primarily a compilation of other texts written for (and perhaps by) women, and throughout the treatise the pronoun usage mostly remains female. Thus, although it would have been read by monks for use by men in a monastery, they end up having to identify with the female pronouns and undertake female actions, experiencing a sort of trans-moment. In

---

[23] *A Talkyng of the Loue of God. Edited from MS Vernon (Bodleian 3938) and collated with MS Simeon (Brit. Mus. Add. 22283)*, ed. Sr. Dr. Salvina Westra (Leiden: Martinus Nijhoff, 1950), p. 69 (ll. 5–8). My translation.
[24] See *Middle English Dictionary*, entry for "souken," https://quod.lib.umich.edu/m/middle-english-dictionary/dictionary/MED41787/track?counter=7&search_id=290760.
[25] Various spiced wines with honey.
[26] *A Talkyng*, 27/14–19.
[27] Literally the "start."
[28] *A Talkyng*, 61. My translation.
[29] See Michelle M. Sauer, "Cross Dressing Souls: Same Sex Desire and the Mystic Tradition in *A Talkyng of the Loue of God*," in *Intersections of Sexuality and Religion in the Middle Ages: The Word Made Flesh*, ed. Susannah Mary Chewning (Farnham: Ashgate, 2005), 153–76.

this way, the wallowing and sucking here can also be read as a queer "lesbian" moment, another instance of divine cunnilingus.

In *Speculum of the Other Woman*, Luce Irigaray uses premodern Christian mystical and devotional traditions to establish what she sees as the beginnings of a feminine imaginary. Amy Hollywood notes, "entry into Christ's wound, in that tradition as in Irigaray's text, marks the shattering of vision into affect, an experience of wounding laceration that is simultaneously the site of an ineffable ecstatic *jouissance*."[30] Irigaray herself goes on to describe Christ's wound as a "glorious slit" into which the mystic enters, wherein she is covered in "hot and purifying blood." It is a place where ecstasy reigns, where "she [the mystic] curls up in her nest, where she rests as if she had found her home."[31] This description, although clearly related to the medieval narratives of mystics, anchoresses, and saints, as discussed later, also recalls the Moravian prayer cards and tapestries of the mid-1700s with their homely and cozy illustrations of bedrooms and kitchens set up within the space of the side wound, providing "nests" for faithful followers. Irigaray further says: "to know myself I scarcely need a 'soul,' I have only to gaze upon the gaping space in your loving body." She then writes that she recognizes herself in "the lips of that slit . . . by touching myself there (almost) directly." Contemplating the nails and spear piercing the body of Jesus, she observes: "if the Word was made flesh in this way, and to this extent, it can only have been to make me [become] God in my *jouissance*."[32]

The correlation between Christ's side wound and the vagina suggested by Irigaray becomes most apparent in devotional images produced in the later Middle Ages. Clearly related to the tradition of meditation on Christ's Passion, visual representations of Christ's side wound are startling, not only in their vulvic/vaginal resonances, but also in their visual intensity. Take, for instance, depictions of this side wound as a place of birth. From the earliest centuries, Christ's open side and the mystery of blood and water were meditated upon, and the Church was beheld issuing forth from the side of Jesus – the New Adam – as Eve came forth from the side of Adam. Although we have no written words about Eve's emergence, the gospels report that when the side of Jesus was pierced at the crucifixion, both blood and water flowed forth. This echoes the water and the blood that issue with the birth of a child. And, as Flora Lewis

---
[30] Amy Hollywood, "That Glorious Slit: Irigaray and the Medieval Devotion to Christ's Side Wound," in *Luce Irigaray and Premodern Culture*, ed. Theresa Krier and Elizabeth D. Harvey (New York: Routledge, 2004), 106.
[31] Quoted in Hollywood, "That Glorious Slit," 105. See also Luce Irigaray, *Speculum of the Other Woman* (Ithaca: Cornell University Press, 1985).
[32] Quoted in Hollywood, "That Glorious Slit," 105.

notes, "the wound was a place of parturition for the individual soul, and in the later thirteenth and fourteenth centuries there was an emphasis, most importantly in Julian of Norwich, on the anguish of Christ giving birth to the world in his Crucifixion."[33] This is both a feminization of Christ and a reminder that the side wound itself simultaneously protects and nourishes.

The maternalization of Christ also results in the connection between the side wound and the female breast, making his blood homologous with breast milk in its nurturing and salvific nature. For instance, in "The Intercession of Christ and the Virgin" attributed to Lorenzo Monaco (Piero di Giovanni), ca. 1370–1425, Florence, both Christ and the Virgin Mary ask for the favor of God the Father through virtue of their breast – in Christ's case, via his side wound, and in Mary's via her dripping breast. As the Metropolitan Museum of Art description notes, "Pointing to the wound in his side, Christ says, 'My Father, let those be saved for whom you wished me to suffer the Passion.' The Virgin, holding one of her breasts, pleads, 'Dearest son, because of the milk that I gave you, have mercy on them.'"[34] The words given to each divine figure substantiate what the viewer instantly notes – Jesus's side wound and Mary's breast are equivalent. Medieval medical discourse underlines the polysemy of the wound and its blood. Breast milk was thought to be created from surplus menses not released during childbirth. Thus, the association of blood with Christ's side wound ties the wound both to the vagina and to the breast, thereby enabling the threefold association of wound, vagina, and breast. In turn, this allows for eroticization and maternalization simultaneously.

Regardless of the result, the side wound functions to feminize Christ, although it is constructed as an active portal rather than a passive one. Instructed in religious literature to taste, touch, suck, kiss, and enter into Christ's side wound, those who held and saw these images seem to have made them the object of intense affective response, both imaginatively and physically. Jill Bennett has suggested that this process is similar to Roland Barthes's idea of the *punctum*, the shock that characterizes our affective response to image, the "sting, speck, cut, little hole . . . that accident which pricks me."[35] These words are all ones written in connection to the side wound across time, a queering of the

---

[33] Lewis, "The Wound in Christ's Side," 215.
[34] See https://www.metmuseum.org/art/collection/search/470328. As the catalogue also notes, "The drama of the bold devotional image, with a geometric composition typical of Florentine painting of the later fourteenth century, was heightened by its original placement inside the entrance of the cathedral, where it faced the length of the vast interior."
[35] Jill Bennett, "Stigmata and Sense Memory: St. Francis and the Affective Image," *Art History* 24.1 (2001): 1–16 at 10.

action that binds lovers of the side wound together. Moreover, some manuscripts take this idea of *punctum* quite literally, and show the wound solely as a slit in the parchment, one now so often touched, handled, kissed, and stroked as to render the manuscript itself fragile and opaque. David S. Areford notes an example of a woodcut with a large black wedge shape in the middle of a blood-red heart, a replication of Christ's heart as pierced by Longinus's spear. An actual slit has been made in the paper itself so that devoted followers can insert their finger into the wound – a wound that bleeds red ink onto another page as if seeping blood – penetrating Christ's side and heart, and plumbing the depths of interior mysteries just as Doubting Thomas did in the Bible.[36] These images and physical remnants suggest a homoerotic relationship between the female reader and a feminized representation of Christ's wound, dependent upon hapacity, or the quality of touching.

Medieval readers saw, touched, smelled, and tasted their books while reading their content aloud – and sensory engagements such as this must have created a performance of the manuscript that heightened devotional experience and empowered individuals to curate their own rituals and religious experiences. What type of connection was forged between reader and text via the act of touching? Visuality and materiality are flexible concepts. Like other performative functions, they can slide along a single scale of analysis. So, the visual/visibility becomes visuality when it refers to the whole complex of the production, perception, and cultural locations of the story. The material/medial becomes materiality when it refers to the means of production and materials used and their typical proliferations. Caroline Walker Bynum explains that "medieval materials were pregnant with significance," highlighting these sophisticated belief patterns.[37] Books and, more significantly, images, were powerful not just because they gave an individual control of their religious learning but also because their materiality enabled an individual haptic experience of faith.

In *Getting Medieval: Sexualities and Communities, Pre- and Post-Modern*, Carolyn Dinshaw carefully considers how the queering of history can create communities across time, or, maybe more precisely, suggests that queer desire leads to "affective connection" and the "touch across time."[38] These affective

---

36 David S. Areford, "Multiplying the Sacred: The Fifteenth Century Woodcut as Reproduction, Surrogate, Simulation," in *The Woodcut in Fifteenth-Century Europe*, ed. Peter Parshall (New Haven: Yale University Press, 2009), 141–47.
37 Caroline Walker Bynum, *Christian Materiality: An Essay on Religion in Late Medieval Europe* (London: Zone Books, 2011), 58.
38 Carolyn Dinshaw, *Getting Medieval: Sexualities and Communities, Pre- and Post-Modern* (Durham: Duke University Press, 1999), 21.

connections create a queer history of identification, even across different texts and different times. Together, these touches create a community and a connectedness. Markedly, the haptic ideology of the medieval era, seen by many to underpin almost all interactions, integrates well with this queer historiography. If one thing came into contact with another, the two would absorb the other's qualities. Because vellum had once been living as an animal skin, it was believed to contain a residual memory of that life; a power that was believed to have been instilled by God. Because of this, Bynum notes, "it was so extraordinarily difficult for people in the later Middle Ages to see any matter as truly dead."[39] The process of creating vellum was viewed as having a certain power. A person could take a raw animal skin and transform it into a material that could mediate with the divine and provide a manifestation for miracles. Thomas Aquinas (*Article* 8) explains that God has placed within material objects the potential for divinity, and that it was through a process of refinement that they were able to become divine, making vellum a highly significant material. Thus, vellum contained its own power, activated by the reader's touch.

The book was therefore seen as alive to many medieval users, and by extension any likeness that was placed on its surfaces. To a certain extent, then, touching an image of Christ was akin to touching a proxy of his body. Books and other portable images such as talismans, tokens, birth girdles, and personal plates enabled people to experience divine interactions on their own. Repeated touching (or kissing, or stroking) allowed access to the divine link on an intimate level. Kathryn Rudy has made a study of the effects of haptic interactions using a densitometer. Some of the habits and rituals have become recorded in a cumulative build-up of grease absorbed by the vellum; a fluctuation in build-up between pages has also been noted. To some extent this is because dirt and grease stick to the flesh side of the vellum much more easily than to the hair side, but we can also infer that people interacted with different pages for different lengths of time.[40] This is representative of a non-linear approach to books, in which people could pick and choose what to interact with depending on their spiritual needs. Memory, taste, interplay between static object and active performance – all of these were part of medieval interaction. Christianity was a culture of talismanic and touch relic acquisition which existed alongside standard Church practices, and indeed enhanced them. Manuscripts could create similar literal protection

---

39 Bynum, *Christian Materiality*, 112.
40 Kathryn M. Rudy, "Kissing Images, Unfurling Rolls, Measuring Wounds, Sewing Badges and Carrying Talismans: Considering Some Harley Manuscripts through the Physical Rituals they Reveal," *Electronic British Library Journal*, http://www.bl.uk/eblj/2011articles/article5.html, 2011.

through talismans and charms. Medieval haptic beliefs meant that the material qualities of a manuscript could be used to curate a devotional performance. And the non-linear, personal interaction implies a queer understanding of the manuscript process. Non-linear narratives, sequences that combine past and present, and glimpses of the (multifaceted) past both inform the present and shape the future, but also re-shape the past. These types of encounters bring queerness to the performance, both of reading and of reading later. Viewers/readers/the audience engage with speakers whose past is combined with their present in all sorts of new and unexpected ways. This is a sort of Deleuzian notion of time, which can free us to live, continually opening up possibilities of becoming by providing chance after chance of combining our past and our present. Victoria Hesford suggests that "the queer desire for history [can be] understood as a practice of producing loving attachments to what has often remained marginal or discarded in the writing of history."[41] What is supposedly past has queer potential in its ability to disrupt the present tense – queerness here is about, in Elizabeth Freeman's words, "mining the present for signs of undetonated energy from past revolutions."[42] Contemporary subjects might examine the lesbian feminist past in ways that disrupt the coherence of the queer present in their articulation of a temporal connection outside of anachronisms, opening up interpretive possibilities. The disruption of chrononormativity challenges a linear understanding of temporality, and most especially the institutionalized organization of time, which often involves a staged progression of a heteronormative patterned life. Temporal upheaval, then, involves traces of the past intersecting with the present, so that each female mystic can be seen as embodying queer temporality, living a life unscripted by heteronormativity.

More specifically, however, let me turn again to the side wound and the blood of Christ. Many images were subject to devout interactions, but one that enveloped all sorts of hapticity was the side wound. One remarkable example of this haptic connection is BL MS Egerton 1821. It is English, dating to around 1490, and unique in part of its appearance. It begins with three pages, each painted black, on which large drops of red blood trickle down. The third page has been thoroughly worn. It has been suggested that the black was worn away from kissing,[43] and while kissing may have been employed, it seems that rubbing

---

[41] Victoria Hesford, *Feeling Women's Liberation* (Durham: Duke University Press, 2013), 13.
[42] Freeman, *Time Binds*, xvi.
[43] See John Lowden's Keynote address at the conference "Treasures Known and Unknown," held at the British Library Conference Centre, July 2–3, 2007, https://www.bl.uk/catalogues/illuminated manuscripts/TourKnownA.asp, for manuscript images see: "kissing images": http://www.bl.uk/catalogues/illuminatedmanuscripts/TourKnownC.asp.

would have been more appropriate here. There is no formal image to kiss, merely the somewhat abstract representation of suffering and redemption through the blood of Christ. One part of the page even shows more trauma than the other portions, leading me to think that scratching may even have been employed. There is, interestingly enough, consistency in the arrangement of the drops of blood. Folio 1r also shows some evidence of having been rubbed. It has a pattern of 3 large drops with small points in between across the page (5 rows × 3 drops = 15 large drops; 15 small points). Folio 1v mixes it up, though, with a pattern of 3–2–3–2–3 large drops (5 rows × 3(3 drops) + 2(2 drops) = 13 large drops; 12 small points). It appears as though folio 2r and v follow folio 1v's pattern. The points and the squiggles on top of the large drop definitely make it feel like the blood is trickling, not statically represented. To the touch, the black-painted portions feel smooth. The red drops feel glossy. The worn portions feel rougher and more complex. Of course, the manuscript is now 525 years old, but when new all that black would have left traces on the hands of the devoted – divine residue, if you will.

The next page, folio 2v, has an image of the nursing Madonna. Nursing is, as I mentioned earlier, commonly connected with Christ's side wound. This image seems to be fairly intact, with no signs of devotional osculation or other rubbing. Folio 3 contains only 3 lines of written text in red and black. The vellum feels completely different. It is soft, smooth, and supple – creamy, almost. This goes on for several folios, when, abruptly, the pages turn blood red, and thick gouts of blood pour down them from innumerable wounds. This continues for 10 pages. John Lowden has counted 540 wounds on the "bloodiest page" and speculates that they were together intended to represent the 5400 wounds medieval devotional texts suggest were inflicted upon Christ's body.[44] (Private revelation to St. Bridget of Sweden indicated that all the wounds Our Lord suffered added up to 5,480.) They are very precise. The curved main wound bears either three drops (the two on the outside being longer with the middle one being short), or one long drop, with points interspersed. They feel like Braille.

On folio 8v, there is an opening cut into the blood-red pages, and a woodcut of a Man of Sorrows surrounded by twenty small compartments with instruments of the Passion inserted. It carries an indulgence: "To all them that devoutly say five Pater nosters, five Aves, and a Creed afore such a figure are granted 32,755 years of pardon." The indulgence has since been defaced. The

---

[44] John Lowden, "Treasures Known and Unknown in the British Library: Kissing Images (A Book for Devotion: BL MS Egerton 1821)" <http://www.bl.uk/catalogues/illuminatedmanuscripts/TourKnownC.asp>. All other manuscript comments are based on personal observation by the author unless otherwise noted.

woodcut is obviously a later insertion but has carefully been painted to match the bloody background, and interaction is anticipated through the indulgence. Facing this is a larger woodcut of the *arma Christi*. This manuscript clearly aimed to incorporate numerous rituals into one volume, providing a haptic connection directly with Christ. The text is a reflection on blood and suffering as well as redemption. The text that follows these initial images is written primarily in red so as to recall the blood, and the litany of saints includes several more unusual inclusions, such as Elizabeth of Spalbeek, Mary of Oignies, and Brigitta of Sweden, known for devotion to the wounds of Christ, and Mary Salome and Mary Cleophas who witnessed the crucifixion.

The insertion of the woodcut demonstrates what Rudy calls a cautious rule for devotional books: "owners who treated their manuscript prayer books as objects of physical devotion often both *added* and *subtracted* material. They added small prints, curtains, pilgrims' badges, extra prayers, and notes about the family; they subtracted paint and ink in the course of using, kissing, and rubbing."[45] Another example Areford highlights is found in a fifteenth-century woodcut, originally from Germany. Areford completed an extensive study of this woodcut. Here the mandorla-shaped wound stands in for all of Christ's body, and the inscription explains: "This is the length and width of Christ's wound which was pierced in his side on the Cross," going on to offer an indulgence to whoever kisses this wound. As a result, the center of this image is worn thin from physical handling.[46]

The Christian Middle Ages offer rich resources for thinking about sex, sexuality, and divinity in ways that radically destabilize traditional distinctions and hierarchies. In all of these images, Christ is both masculine and feminine – the rock, the cross, the erect, but also bleeding, oozing, and suckling. Female saints in amorous ecstasy put their lips to the lips of a man-woman's wound that is likened both to a breast and a vagina. These common scenes come from a variety of sources, from both male and female authors, but directed to women. For example, St. Bonaventure's *De Perfectione vitae ad Sorores*, written specifically for female religious, encourages nuns not simply to visualize the wounded and suffering Christ, but rather to touch him and to enter his body:

> Draw near, O handmaid, with loving steps to Jesus wounded for you, to Jesus nailed to the gibbet of the Cross. Gaze with the blessed Apostle St. Thomas, not merely on the print of the nails in Christ's hands; be not satisfied with putting your fingers in the holes made by

---

45 Rudy, "Kissing Images," 4.
46 For more on MS Egerton 1821, see Nancy Thebaut, "Bleeding Pages, Bleeding Bodies: A Gendered Reading of British Library MS Egerton 1821," *Medieval Feminist Forum* 45.2 (2009): 175–200.

> the nails in his hands; neither let it be sufficient to put your hand into the wound in his side; but enter entirely by the door in his side and go straight up to the very heart of Jesus.[47]

Bonaventure expects the nuns to penetrate Christ, to delve within him, to merge with his body, to remain in his side. Although Christ's body is male, the mimetic experience for the Franciscan nuns is distinctly feminine – they are women merging with a feminized Christ, at once penetrating and consuming. Similarly, Raymond of Capua, confessor to Catherine of Siena, records one of her experiences as follows:

> Christ put his right hand on her neck and drew her towards the wound on his side, saying "Drink from my side, and by that draught your soul shall become enraptured with such delight that your very body, which for my sake you have denied, shall be inundated with overflowing goodness." Drawn close in this way to the outlet of the Fountain of her Life, she fastened her lips upon that sacred wound, and still more eagerly the mouth of her soul.[48]

In Catherine's repeated descriptions of climbing Christ's body from foot to side to mouth, the body is a female body. Catherine understood union with Christ not as an erotic fusing with a male figure, but rather as a sinking into another female body. And in each of these instances, the female saint may have been aided by images such as these. Clearly the connection to vaginal imagery is evident. And while Bonaventure privileges entrance into the wound and merging with Christ over the initial touches, Catherine insists on the physical connection; touching, kissing, sucking, and mouthing are all vital parts of her experience. Merging Catherine's direct mystical interaction with the haptic devotions found in prayer books and woodcuts, Margareta Ebner, a Dominican nun who lived from 1291–1351 in southern Germany, recalls:

> Wherever I went I had a cross with me. In addition, I possessed a little book in which there was a picture of the five holy wounds. I shoved it secretly against my bosom, open to that place, and wherever I went I pressed it to my heart with great joy and with measureless grace. When I wanted to sleep, I took the picture of the Crucified Lord in the little book and laid it under my face, my lips against the wound in his side. In a dream, as I stood before the image, my Lord Jesus Christ bent down from the cross and let me kiss His open heart and gave me to drink of the blood flowing from His heart.[49]

---

47 Bonaventura, *Opera Omnia (10 vols in-folio)* (Ad Claras Aquas [Quaracchi]: Ex Typographia Collegii S. Bonaventurae. 1882± 1902), vol. 8, p. 120; *Holiness of Life, Being St. Bonaventure's Treatise De Perfectione Vitae ad Sorores*, trans. L. Costello (Herder: St. Louis, 1928), pp. 63–64. Cited in Bennett, "Stigmata and Sense Memory," 10–11.
48 Quoted in Hollywood, "That Glorious Slit," 182.
49 Margaret Ebner, *Major Works*, ed. and trans. Leonard P. Hindsley (New York: Paulist Press, 1993), 96.

Ebner is carrying the *arma Christi* with her. Combining fragmented body parts (hands, feet, head) with graphic figures such as the heart or a representation thereof was popular during the Middle Ages, especially in books of hours. These images functioned as devotional aids and foci for meditation on the five wounds, and many promised indulgences, particularly for kissing the side wound. These *armi Christi* also served as protection against misfortune, as amulets of sorts. Ebner's possession of such an object, then, would not have been unusual; the extreme and repeated caressing may have been. The manner in which she holds the image – "secretly" clasped to her bosom – is somewhat erotic, and certainly "secret" implies special and perhaps queer. And she does not simply kiss the image to gain an indulgence or focus her prayers; instead, she sleeps with her lips positioned directly on the vaginal wound so as to encourage erotic dreams in which she tongues and mouths the heart of Christ while blood streams around and in her.

These mystics, as well as the unnamed anchoresses, can be seen as queer figures who, rather than exclusively reveling in heteroerotic pleasure, slip into a sexual identity category that Eve Sedgwick identifies as the masturbator or "onanist,"[50] an identity suggested, for instance, by the sexually charged language that characterizes the pleasure they feel while stroking pictures of the side wound or kissing devotional images. That these feelings of pleasure are enhanced by the feminized Christ suggests a same-sex dimension to the self-pleasuring attributes of the actions. Furthermore, this erotic identity informs the women's employment of time and space throughout their devotions. While praying and reading – while giving themselves pleasure – mystics often had involuntary body memories that allowed them to reflect on and embody past and present simultaneously. To use Heather Love's phrase, the mystics "feel backward" – a nonnormative way of remembering that differs from traditional memory in its preoccupation with loss and failure and in its concern with mobilizing that loss and failure for strategic purposes. In short, feeling backward allows the female mystic subject to transform her abject marginalization into opportunity. Love writes, "Rather than disavowing the history of marginalization and abjection, I suggest that we embrace it, exploring the ways it continues to structure queer experience in the present. . . . [P]aying attention to what was difficult in the past may tell us how far we have come, but that is not all it will tell us; it also makes visible the damage that we live with in the present."[51]

---

50 Eve Kosofsky Sedgwick, "Jane Austen and the Masturbating Girl," *Critical Inquiry* 17.4 (1991): 818–37 at 825.
51 Love, *Feeling Backward*, 29.

Centuries prior to Love's theorization, the mystics use their indulgences in sensuality to reassert their own agency and ignite passion between a feminized Christ and their own female bodies.

The mystics "feel backward" during their moments of deep prayer, a practice that can be likened to a masturbatory self-indulgence that troubles heteronormative expectations of an individual's relationship to conventions of time and space. Articulating this relationship between masturbation and time and space, Sedgwick writes,

> [T]here are senses in which autoeroticism seems almost uniquely – or, at least, distinctively – to challenge the historicizing impulse.... Because it escapes both the narrative of reproduction and (when practiced solo) even the creation of any interpersonal trace, it seems to have an affinity with amnesia, repetition or the repetition-compulsion, and ahistorical or history-rupturing rhetorics of sublimity.[52]

In other words, because masturbation is non-procreative and therefore works outside of heterosexual reproduction, and because it involves and affects no other person and therefore is an untraceable act (we can never be sure when or where it happens), it resists being historicized. Like the involuntary body memories that the mystics have while contemplating and praying, masturbation has an "affinity with amnesia" and "repetition-compulsion": these are acts of solitary and self-indulgent experience, and, as such, exist outside of historical recordability.

Since the mystics' erotic identities cannot be severed from their body memories and therefore from their uses of time and space, it is not surprising that they dwell within what J. Halberstam refers to as "queer time and space." Halberstam defines queer time as "a term for those specific models of temporality that emerge ... once one leaves the temporal frames of bourgeois reproduction and family, longevity, risk/safety, and inheritance."[53] He argues that queer subjects "use space and time in ways that challenge conventional logics of development, maturity, adulthood, and responsibility."[54] In other words, the pleasure derived from mystical contemplation and prayer and traveling back and forth between past and present not only challenges the normative sexual practices of the medieval sensibility, but also poses a threat to heteronormative temporality and spatiality – particularly notions of time and space that are intimately connected to sex between a man and a woman, and, therefore, structured around reproduction

---

[52] Sedgwick, "Masturbating Girl," 820.
[53] J. Halberstam, *In a Queer Time & Place: Transgender Bodies, Subcultural Lives* (New York: New York University Press, 2005), 6.
[54] Halberstam, *Queer Time & Place*, 13.

and family. The mystics are then doubly queered, both because they experience same-sex desire, although it is shrouded by a veneer of heterosexuality, and because they give pleasure to themselves and refuse to relegate their mind and body to the present moment and the physical reality of the isolated convent or anchorhold.

This reverberation of queer time, disjointed travels throughout time and space, leaves us with after-images of Christ's vaginal wound – a trope that continues today – being licked, sucked, and tongued by female saints. The idea of queer time, coupled with explorations of queer space and homospatiality, engage the possibility of same-sex desire in such an encounter, which increases our understanding of the polyvalent, ambiguously gendered, intersexed Christ that dominated late medieval Incarnational theology. The simultaneous sexualization and feminization of Christ produces a multitude of queer possibilities – if he is gendered male, it is easier to think of him as aggressively sexual, especially in penetrative actions, but if he is gendered female, passive sexuality, including cunnilingus, becomes an uncomfortable subject. Undoubtedly, the material body of Christ provides a wide array of queer possibilities to be explored.

Bibliography

Aelred of Rievaulx's de Institutione Inclusarum: Two English Versions. Edited by John Ayto and Alexandra Barratt. EETS o.s. 287. Oxford: Oxford University Press, 1984.

Areford, David S. "Multiplying the Sacred: The Fifteenth Century Woodcut as Reproduction, Surrogate, Simulation." In *The Woodcut in Fifteenth-Century Europe*, edited by Peter Parshall, 119–53. New Haven: Yale University Press, 2009.

Atwood, Craig D. "Little Side Holes: Moravian Devotional Cards of the Mid-Eighteenth Century." *Journal of Moravian History* 6 (2009): 61–75.

Bartholomaeus Anglicus, *De proprietatibus rerum*. Edited by M. C. Seymour. Oxford: Clarendon Press, 1975.

Beckwith, Sara. *Christ's Body: Identity, Culture, and Society in Late Medieval Writings*. New York: Routledge.

Bennett, Jill. "Stigmata and Sense Memory: St Francis and the Affective Image." *Art History* 24.1 (2001): 1–16.

Bonaventura. *Opera Omnia (10 vols in-folio)*. Ad Claras Aquas [Quaracchi]: Ex Typographia Collegii S. Bonaventurae. 1882 ± 1902.

Brooke, Rosalind B. *The Image of St. Francis: Responses to Sainthood in the Thirteenth Century*. Cambridge: Cambridge University Press, 2006.

Brown, George Hardin. "From the Wound in Christ's Side to the Wound in His Heart: Progression from Male Exegesis to Female Mysticism." In *Poetry, Place, and Gender: Studies in Medieval Culture in Honor of Helen Damico*, edited by Catherine E. Karkov, 252–74. Kalamazoo: Medieval Institute Publications, 2009.

Bynum, Caroline Walker. *Christian Materiality: An Essay on Religion in Late Medieval Europe.* London: Zone Books, 2011.

Dinshaw, Carolyn. *Getting Medieval: Sexualities and Communities, Pre- and Post-Modern.* Durham: Duke University Press, 1999.

Ebner, Margaret. *Major Works.* Edited and translated by Leonard P. Hindsley. New York: Paulist Press, 1993.

Fogleman, Aaron Spencer. *Jesus Is Female: Moravians and Radical Religion in Early America.* Philadelphia: University of Pennsylvania Press, 2008.

Freeman, Elizabeth. *Time Binds: Queer Temporalities, Queer Histories.* Durham: Duke University Press, 2010.

Graziano, Frank. *The Wounds of Love: The Mystical Marriage of Rose of Lima.* Oxford: Oxford University Press, 2004.

Halberstam, Jack [Judith]. *In a Queer Time and Place: Transgender Bodies, Subcultural Lives.* New York: New York University Press, 2005.

Hesford, Victoria. *Feeling Women's Liberation.* Durham: Duke University Press, 2013.

Hollywood, Amy. "That Glorious Slit: Irigaray and the Medieval Devotion to Christ's Side Wound." In *Luce Irigaray and Premodern Culture*, edited by Theresa Krier and Elizabeth D. Harvey, 105–25. New York: Routledge, 2004.

Irigaray, Luce. *Speculum of the Other Woman.* Ithaca: Cornell University Press, 1985.

Isidore of Seville. *Etymologies.* Edited by W. J. Lewis, J. A. Beach, and Oliver Berghof. Cambridge: Cambridge University Press, 2006.

The Letters of Catherine of Siena, Letter 62. Translated by Suzanne Noffke, vol. 1. Tempe: Arizona Center for Medieval and Renaissance Studies, 2000.

Lewis, Flora. "The Wound in Christ's Side and the Instruments of the Passion: Gendered Experience and the Response." In *Women and the Book*, edited by Lesley Smith and Jane Taylor, 204–29. Toronto: University of Toronto Press, 1997.

Love, Heather. *Feeling Backward: Loss and the Politics of Queer History.* Cambridge: Harvard University Press, 2007.

Lowden, John. "Treasures Known and Unknown in the British Library: Kissing Images (A Book for Devotion: BL MS Egerton 1821)" <http://www.bl.uk/catalogues/illuminatedmanuscripts/TourKnownC.asp>.

McCann, John. "An Historical Enquiry into the Design and Use of Dovecotes." *Transactions of the Ancient Monuments Society* 35 (1991): 89–160.

Middle English Dictionary. https://quod.lib.umich.edu/m/middle-english-dictionary/dictionary.

Peltier, A. C. *Sancti Bonaventurae: Opera Omnia.* Paris: Ludovicus Vives, 1868.

Rudy, Kathryn M. "Kissing Images, Unfurling Rolls, Measuring Wounds, Sewing Badges and Carrying Talismans: Considering Some Harley Manuscripts through the Physical Rituals they Reveal." *Electronic British Library Journal.* http://www.bl.uk/eblj/2011articles/article5.html.

Sauer, Michelle M. "Cross Dressing Souls: Same Sex Desire and the Mystic Tradition in *A Talkyng of the Loue of God.*" In *Intersections of Sexuality and Religion in the Middle Ages: The Word Made Flesh*, edited by Susannah Mary Chewning, 153–76. Farnham: Ashgate, 2005.

Sauer, Michelle M. "'Þe blod þ[at] bohte': The *Wooing* Group Christ as Pierced, Pricked, and Penetrated Body." In *'May your wounds heal the wounds of my soul': The Milieu and*

    Context of the Wohunge Group, edited by Susannah Mary Chewning, 123–47. Cardiff: University of Wales Press, 2009.

Sedgwick, Eve Kosofsky. "Jane Austen and the Masturbating Girl." *Critical Inquiry* 17.4 (1991): 818–37.

A Talkyng of the Loue of God. Edited from MS Vernon (Bodleian 3938) and collated with MS Simeon (Brit. Mus. Add. 22283). Edited by Sr. Dr. Salvina Westra. Leiden: Martinus Nijhoff, 1950.

Thebaut, Nancy. "Bleeding Pages, Bleeding Bodies: A Gendered Reading of British Library MS Egerton 1821." *Medieval Feminist Forum* 45.2 (2009): 175–200.

Voaden, Rosalynn. "All Girls Together: Community, Gender, and Vision at Helfta." In *Medieval Women in their Communities*, edited by Diane Watt, 72–91. Cardiff: University of Wales Press, 1997.

Vogt, Peter. "'Honor to the Side': The Adoration of the Side Wound of Jesus in Eighteenth-Century Moravian Piety." *Journal of Moravian History* 7 (2009): 83–106.

Williams, Peter. *Popular Religion in America: Symbolic Change and the Modernization Process in Historical Perspective*. Champaign: University of Illinois Press, 1989.

Notes on Contributors

Margaret Cotter-Lynch is Professor of English and Director of the Honors Program at Southeastern Oklahoma State University. A scholar of medieval hagiography and gender studies, she received her BA in Comparative Literature and Classical Studies from Brown University, and her MA and Ph.D. in Comparative Literature from the University of Michigan, Ann Arbor. She is the author of *St. Perpetua Across the Middle Ages: Mother, Gladiator, Saint* (2016) and co-editor, with Brad Herzog, of *Reading Memory and Identity in the Texts of Medieval European Holy Women* (2012). She is currently working on a monograph comparing versions of the *Life of St. Mary of Egypt* in Latin, Old and Middle English, and Old French, with particular attention to the varying ways in which Mary's gender is represented. Her research has received grant funding from the South Central Modern Language Association, the Newberry Library, and the National Humanities Center, as well as the faculty research fund at Southeastern Oklahoma State University. In 2019, she was awarded the Oklahoma Medal of Excellence for best professor at a regional university or community college in the state. In addition to Southeastern, she has also taught at the University of Texas at Dallas, Southern Methodist University, and the University of Lausanne, Switzerland. She currently lives in McKinney, Texas, with her spouse and two daughters.

Joseph Derosier is Visiting Assistant Professor and Lead of the French Program in the Department of Modern Languages at Beloit College. He completed his Ph.D. in 2016 at Northwestern University. His research focuses on medieval French romance and hermeneutics, and on the intersections of medieval race, gender, nation, territory, and biopolitics. He recently published an article entitled "The Forest and the Heath: Defining the Human in Medieval Romance" (*Literature Compass*, Special Cluster: *Critical Race and the Middle Ages*, fall 2019), exploring the racial and biopolitical stakes of romance. He has forthcoming work on the ethics of romance.

Micah James Goodrich is a Ph.D. Candidate in the English Department, Medieval Studies Program at the University of Connecticut. He studies early and late Middle English literature, gender, sexuality, and embodiment, labor and (re)production, and queer/trans ecologies. Micah has published in the *Yearbook of Langland Studies*, has a forthcoming essay in *Early Middle English*, and a chapter on the biopolitics of debility and transgender embodiment in medieval texts forthcoming in *Trans Before Trans: The Many Genders of the Past*. Alongside Mary Rambaran-Olm and M. Breann Leake, Micah is co-editing a special tenth anniversary issue of *Postmedieval* on race and revolution in medieval studies.

Michael Johnson specializes in the Latin and French Middle Ages with a focus on sexuality and theories of language. He has published on medieval grammar and sexuality, the excremental lady figure in Occitan lyric, and queer French and Francophone comics, among other things.

Maud Burnett McInerney is the Laurie Ann Levine Professor of Comparative Literature at Haverford College. She is the author of *Eloquent Virgins from Thecla to Joan of Arc* (2003) and articles on topics ranging from the fifteenth-century Burgundian prose romance *La Belle Hélène de Constantinople* to Arthurian horses and the knights that love them. She is presently finishing a monograph on Benoît de Sainte-Maure's *Roman de Troie*.

https://doi.org/10.1515/9781501513701-011

Notes on Contributors

Will Rogers is currently an Assistant Professor in the English Department at the University of Louisiana Monroe and is working on two different book-length projects: the first is on trauma and narration in Chaucer's *Canterbury Tales* and the second focuses on queerness and medievalism in the 1980s cartoon *He-Man and the Masters of the Universe*. His book project, *Writing Old Age and Impairments in Late Medieval England*, a study of old age, impairments, and prosthesis, understood both poetically and rhetorically, is forthcoming in 2020 from Arc Humanities Press. He has published on medieval and early modern literature, with essays that focus on impairments in John Gower's work, Julian of Norwich and first-year writing, and Richard Maidstone and the Carmelites. He is the co-editor of the book series, *New Queer Medievalism* (MIP).

Christopher Michael Roman is Professor of English at Kent State University, where he specializes in queer theory and medieval studies with a secondary interest in comic books and graphic novels, as well as the emergent field of sound studies. He offers a variety of undergraduate and graduate courses, including medieval literature, Chaucer, J. R. R. Tolkien, the graphic novel, medieval mysticism, and gender, sexuality, and queer studies as they intersect with the Middle Ages. His first book, *Domestic Mysticism in Julian of Norwich and Margery Kempe* (2005) interrogates queer family formation in medieval mystical texts. His new book, *Queering Richard Rolle* (2017), investigates the queer identity of the medieval hermit, Richard Rolle. His other articles, lectures, and presentations work with medieval beasts, the acoustics of medieval dreams, the ecology of J. R. R. Tolkien's Middle Earth, the ethics of *Game of Thrones*, and the queer poetics of the poet, Alice Notley, as well as other subjects. He is the recipient of a Beinecke Rare Book and Manuscript Library Visiting Research Fellowship, and an Erika and Kenneth Riley Fellowship at the Huntington Library in California for work on a new edition of Richard Rolle's Middle English works to be published by the Medieval English Text Series (METS) in 2020. He is the co-editor of the book series, *New Queer Medievalism* (MIP). He also serves as the associate editor of *The Chaucer Review*.

Michelle M. Sauer is Professor of English and Gender Studies at the University of North Dakota, where she teaches a wide range of medieval language and literature as well as linguistics. She earned degrees from Purdue University (BA, 1993), Loyola University Chicago (MA, 1995), and Washington State University (Ph.D., 2000). Sauer specializes in Middle English language and literature, especially women's devotional literature and monastic texts, and publishes regularly on anchoritism, mysticism, asceticism, hagiography, queer/gender theory, spatial theory, monasticism, and Church history. Her publications include the books *Celebrating St Albert & His Rule: Rules, Devotion, Orthodoxy, & Dissent* (2018, with Kevin Alban), *Gender in Medieval Culture* (2015), *The Lesbian Premodern* (2011, with Diane Watt and Noreen Giffney), *How to Write about Chaucer* (2009), and *The Companion to Pre-1600 British Poetry* (2008), as well as articles appearing in journals such as *Gender & History* and *Journal of the History of Sexuality*. Her article "Representing the Negative: Positing the Lesbian Void & Medieval English Anchoritism" (2004) was awarded the first LGBT-Religious Archives Network Award for best scholarly article on LGBTQIA+ Religious History. Current projects include *Companion to Sexuality in the Medieval West* (ARC Humanities), a searchable database of the works of St. Birgitta, a digital map of English anchorholds, and several other works, most focusing on the intersections of gender and space or sexuality and religious expression in medieval Christian devotional and theological texts.

Lynn Shutters teaches in the English Department at Colorado State University. Her research interests include feminist approaches to medieval literature, late medieval narratives of marital affection, and the medieval reception of classical antiquity. These interests come together in her current book project *Chaucer's Pagan Women*, in which she demonstrates continuities between Chaucer's early–mid career interest in classical antiquity and his later engagement with marital love and wifehood in the *Canterbury Tales*. Her recent work includes co-editing the *Companion to New Critical Thinking on Chaucer*, forthcoming with Arc Humanities Press, and the article "The Host, the *Man of Law's Tale*, and the Fantasy of the Foreign Wife," forthcoming in a special issue of the *Chaucer Review*. She is also interested in medievalism, particularly in popular romance, and is writing an article on erotic desire, female agency, and consent in Chaucer's *Wife of Bath's Prologue* and *Tale*, and *Fifty Shades of Grey*.

Haylie Swenson received her Ph.D. from George Washington University and is the Program Assistant for Scholarly Programs at the Folger Library in Washington, D.C.

Index

Adler, Alfred 125
Aelius Donatus 20
Aimon de Varennes 66–7
Ahmed, Sara 40, 50, 51, 53, 57, 104, 120, 123, 155
Akbari, Suzanne Conklin 72, 74
Alan of Lille 6, 11–15, 18–9, 21–2, 25, 29, 34, 35, 41–2, 48, 50, 61, 66, 68, 71, 72, 74, 76–80, 102
Alexandre de Villedieu 13, 15, 29–34
Alford, John 13
Alighieri, Dante 11, 14, 16, 19, 28
Altercatio Ganimedis et Helene 6, 16–19, 40, 42, 46–57
Aspegren, Kerstin 134

Baker, Juliet 110
Bakhtin, M.M. 7, 107
Baldwin, James 62
Barber, Richard 110
Bardzell, Jeffrey 34
Barker-Benfield, Bruce C. 110
Baswell, Christopher 116
Baudrillard, Jean 163
Beechy, Tiffany 163
Benjamin, Walter 64–5, 76
Benson, C. David 159
Bennett, Judith M. 83
Benoît de Saint-Maure 107, 115, 120–6
Berlant, Lauren 77
Bersani, Leo 61–3, 79–80, 165–166, 190
Bibla sacra iuxta vulgatem versionem 161
Blud, Victoria 135, 138, 142, 145–7
Boswell, John 4–5, 14–18, 42–9, 56–7
Burger, Glenn 85, 89–90, 104
Burgwinkle, William 50, 83, 88, 111–5
Burrus, Virginia 136
Bychowski, M.W. 131, 146–8

Calabrese, Michael A. 157
Cadden, Joan 50
Catherine of Siena 204, 214
Catullus 114
Cestaro, Gary P. 11, 14

Chaganti, Seeta 170
Chaucer, Geoffrey 156–176, 181–194
Chrétien de Troyes 65–66
Cobb, L. Stephanie 134, 145
Coon, Lynda 136
Cotter-Lynch, Margaret 132, 145
Crane, Susan 182–3, 185–6, 188–9

Dares Phrygius 121–2
Davis, Brian McGrath 135
Dembowski, Peter F. 132, 149
D'Emilio, John 165
Derrida, Jacques 26, 189
Desmond, Marilynn 18, 47
Dictionnaire du Moyen Français 98
Dinshaw, Carolyn 1, 5, 108, 120, 153, 157, 209
Dumitrescu, Irina 144

Ealy, Nicholas 68–9, 73
Edelman, Lee 80, 120, 165
Epstein, Robert 163
An Exceedingly Good Orison to God Almighty 205
The Exeter Book 171

Feiss, Hugh 132
Ferruolo, Stephen C. 21
Foucault, Michel 45, 63, 78–9
Fowler, Don 114, 116–7
Freeman, Elizabeth 2, 7, 40, 52–4, 57, 86–7, 94, 97, 101, 104, 201, 211
Fresne, Dolores Warwick 176
Freud, Sigmund 68, 76–7, 81

Ganymede and Helen (see *Altercatio Ganimedis et Helene*)
Gaunt, Simon 111–3
Gautier de Coinci 11, 14, 18–9
Geoffrey of Monmouth 99–101
Geoffroy de la Tour Landry 83–89
Gertrude the Great 203
Godlove, Shannon 98–100
Green, Richard Firth 159
Grigsby, John L. 94, 96

Gudmarsdottir, Sigridur 135
Gutt, Blake 131, 135
Guynn, Noah D. 111

Hafner, Susane 111
Haidu, Peter 74–5
Halberstam, J. (see Halberstam, Jack)
Halberstam, Jack 6, 39, 44–45, 108–11, 116, 120, 126, 134–135, 148, 165, 216
Harley, Marta Powell 65
Hennessey, Rosemary 154
Heron, Onnaca 143–145
Hicks, Eric 65
Hocquenghem, Guy 77
Holsinger, Bruce 17
Hult, David F 64, 74–5

Ingham, Patricia Clare 100, 158
Irigaray, Luce 207
Isidore of Seville 18, 20, 205

Jagose, Annamarie 3
Johansson, Warren 55
John of Salisbury 13, 15, 18, 22, 25–6, 28–30, 36
Jones, Michael 99
Jordan, Mark 14, 18, 34, 83, 87, 91

Keller, Catherine 134–5, 147
Kim, Dorothy 148
King, Katherine Callen 123
Klaeber's Beowulf 171
Kolve, V.A. 42–3, 52, 55
Kordecki, Lesley 181, 184–5, 187, 189, 191, 193
Krueger, Roberta L. 84–5
Kruger, Stephen F. 41, 159
Kuefler, Matthew 43, 56
Kushner, Tony 41, 45–7, 57

Lankewish, Vincent A. 111
Lees, Clare 116, 131, 138–9, 143, 145–8
Legros, Huguette 115
Lehman, Paul 32
Lenzen, Rolf 18, 42
Lightsey, Scott 191, 193

Lochrie, Karma 5, 84, 92
Lombardi, Elena 15, 77
Love, Heather 40, 41, 44–5, 57, 201, 215–6
Lowerre, Sandra 146

Machado, Ana Maria 132, 136, 146
Magennis, Hugh 132–3, 137–44, 149
Makowski, John F. 113
Malo, Robyn 153
Mann, Jill 160
Marie de France 30, 117–9
McAlpine, Monica 159
McInerney, Maud Burnett 117
McNamara, Jo Ann 116, 134, 145
Meban, David 113
Mechtilde 203
Medieval Latin Poems of Male Love and Friendship (see Stehling, Thomas)
Miller, Patricia Clark 136
Miller, Robert P. 159
Mills, Robert 84, 96, 148
Montgomery, Benilde 41, 47
Morton, Jonathan 74, 77
Moser, Thomas C. 12
Muñoz, Jose Esteban 3, 77, 165

Newman, Barbara 42, 48, 134, 145
Norris, Robin 136
North, J.D. 52

Octavian 181–3
Ormod, Mark W. 164
Osborn, Marijane 176
Overing, Gillian R. 138
Ovid 18, 33, 47, 63–5, 67, 69, 71, 73–6, 93, 114
Ovide moralisé 18, 67

Queers Read This 1

Paetow, Louis John 22
Parry, Adam 115
Pastime of Pleasure 171
Pepin, Ronald E. 132
Percy, William A. 55
Petrus Helias 15, 26, 28–9, 31

Plummer, John 172
Povinelli, Elizabeth A. 104
Priscian 11, 16, 26, 30
Promptorium Parvulorum 158
Puar, Jasbir K. 104, 165
Pugh, Tison 5, 61, 148, 168, 173, 174
Pyrame et Thisbé, Narcisse, Philomena 67

Raskolnikov, Masha 40, 75
Rauer, Christine 144
Robertson, Kellie 164
Rollo, David 153
Roman de la Rose 6, 12, 18, 61–5, 68–81
Rottenberg, Catherine 104
Rowland, Beryl 171
Ruys, Juanita Feros 110

Salih, Sarah 92
Salisbury, Joyce E. 134
Sauer, Michelle M. 203, 206
Schulenburg, Jane Tibbetts 134
Sedgwick, Eve K. 4, 112, 215–6
Sex Auctores 13, 30–1
Sophronios 132
Spivak, Gayatri Chakravorty 154
Srinivasan, Amia 104
Staley, Lynn 88
Steel, Karl 191

Stehling, Thomas 17, 42, 153
Stevens, Martin 172
Stimulus Amoris 199–201, 205
Stock, Brian 13
Stockton, Will 156, 160, 171, 175
Strohm, Paul 74
Stryker, Susan 148
Sturges, Robert 153–4, 157, 160, 167

Takada, Yasunari 164
A Talkyng of the Loue of Gode 205–6

Valentine, David 148
Vance, Eugene 16
Vergil 113–4, 116–7, 119

Ward, Benedicta 136
Warner, Michael 104
Watchtower 110
Watt, Diane 131, 139, 143, 145–8, 203
Wesling, Meg 154–5
Whitney, Elspeth 159
Wojnarowicz, David 79
The Wooing of Our Lord 205

Zarins, Kim 159
Ziolkowski, Jan 11, 14, 21–2, 25, 72

www.ingramcontent.com/pod-product-compliance
Lightning Source LLC
Chambersburg PA
CBHW070802230426
43665CB00017B/2458